From Mother to Caregiver

Mothering children with lifelong care
needs across the life course

Edited by Genevieve Currie
and Kinga Pozniak

From Mother to Caregiver
Mothering children with lifelong care needs across the life course
Edited by Genevieve Currie and Kinga Pozniak

Copyright © 2024 Demeter Press

Individual copyright to their work is retained by the authors. All rights reserved. No part of this book may be reproduced or transmitted in any form by any means without permission in writing from the publisher.

Demeter Press
PO Box 197
Coe Hill, Ontario
Canada
K0L 1P0
Tel: 289-383-0134
Email: info@demeterpress.org
Website: www.demeterpress.org

Demeter Press logo based on the sculpture "Demeter" by Maria-Luise Bodirsky
www.keramik-atelier.bodirsky.de

Printed and Bound in Canada

Cover image: Watercolour by Layers, 2021
Cover design and typesetting: Michelle Pirovich
Proof reading: Jena Woodhouse

Library and Archives Canada Cataloguing in Publication
Title: From mother to caregiver : mothering children with lifelong care needs across the life course / edited by Genevieve Currie and Kinga Pozniak.
Names: Currie, Genevieve, editor. | Pozniak, Kinga, editor
Description: Includes bibliographical references.
Identifiers: Canadiana 20250203081 | ISBN 9781772585414 (softcover)
Subjects: LCSH: Mothers of children with disabilities. | LCSH: Caregivers. | LCSH: Motherhood.
Classification: LCC HQ759.913.F76 2025 | DDC 649/.151—dc23

 The publisher gratefully acknowledges the support of the Government of Canada

We dedicate this collection of work to all those caregivers caring for children and adult children with lifelong care needs.

Acknowledgments

We thank all caregivers who have shared their stories of being caregivers for children and adult children with lifelong care needs in research projects over the years.

Genevieve Currie would like to thank all her mentors, researchers, and family members who have supported her work in understanding the experience of being a caregiver to a child with lifelong care needs. She especially thanks her son Callum for teaching her how to use her voice and words to increase support for caregivers and families caring for children with medical complexity.

Kinga Pozniak would like to thank her amazing colleagues at CanChild Centre for Childhood-Onset Disability Research for their mentorship and support. She also wants to thank her children, Jamie and Jack, for teaching her what truly matters in life.

Contents

Introduction
Kinga Pozniak and Genevieve Currie
11

Section I
History and Theoretical Background on Mothering, Caregiving, and Carework
17

1.
Mothering and Carework
Genevieve Currie
19

2.
From Seeker to Crusader:
How Complex Care Motherhood Shifted My Identity
Donna Thomson
33

Section II
Mothering and Carework of Children with Disabilities and Lifelong Care Needs: Strengths, Dilemmas, and Challenges
45

3.
Poetic Narratives of Mothers Who Have
a Child Living with Rarity
Genevieve Currie and Joanna Szabo
47

4.
Mothering Disabled Children
Gretchen Good
77

5.
Homeschooling, Cancer, and Letting Go:
A Parenting Journey
Anne Borden King
97

Section III
Intersectionality-Intersections
105

6.
Navigating the Intersections:
The Complexities of Black Mother Caregivers of
Division I Student-Athletes with Chronic Illnesses
Yvette C. Latunde
107

7.
When Carework and Paid Work Intersect:
Challenges and Learnings of Lifelong Caregiving
in Mothers' Professional Trajectories
Ana Carolina Rodriguez
131

Section IV
Caregiving Children with Disabilities
beyond Mothering
149

8.
Siblings of Children with Medical Complexity
Hanae Davis, Samantha Bellefeuille, and Linda Nguyen
151

9.
My Life as a Lifelong Sibling Caregiver:
An Exploration of Choice and Complex Feelings
Mary Sword
165

Section V
Mothering and Caregiving with Adult Children with Disabilities
175

10.
"It Is What It Is": Mothers Caring for Adult Children with an Intellectual and Developmental Disability in Rural Ontario during the COVID-19 Pandemic
Anna Przednowek, Sharon Desormeau, and Sarah Ederer
177

11.
Mothering in a Sandwich Generation
Joy Seguin
195

Section VI
Reimagining and Restorying Narratives and Care Models for Children with Lifelong Care Needs
205

12.
Children with Medical Complexity: An Integrated Village Approach to Support Mothers and Their Families
Anneliese de Groot, Yvonne Zurynski, Karen Hutchinson, Jeffrey Fletcher, Amy Hickman, and Raghu Lingam
207

13.
Raising Rural: Rethinking Raising and Caring for Children with Medical Complexity Living in Rural Communities
Ngoc Huynh
229

Afterword
Fierce Advocacy, Fierce Love
Eva Feder Kittay
255

Notes on Contributors
259

Introduction

Kinga Pozniak and Genevieve Currie

"Once a mother, always a mother."
"Mothering never ends."
"A mother's job is never done."

Although these statements ring true for all mothers, they hit home differently for mothers whose children have lifelong care needs due to medical conditions. The lives of these mothers and their children do not fit into mainstream societal narratives of how life is supposed to unfold.

So where can we find the stories of mothers who are, or will be, providing care to their adult children throughout their lives? When we solicited contributions for this volume, we were overwhelmed by the submissions we received. This response highlighted the degree to which these individuals and their stories are often invisible. We were disappointed we could not include them all because of space limitations, and we hope those mothers whose contributions did not make it into this volume will nonetheless see their experiences reflected through someone else's words.

This is a collection written by mothers (and other caregivers), about mothering and caregiving, and for mothers and caregivers. The submissions straddle the continuum between personal accounts and research, often blurring the line between them by using autoethnographic approaches. Some are research-based pieces written by academics, many of them inspired by personal experiences with caregiving. Others are personal accounts written by non-academic mothers. They tell those stories that lie outside the box. The collection includes stories of how disabling societal structures hamper the lives of individuals with medical needs and their families, including lack of adequate financial support (e.g., needed therapies, equipment, and housing), lack of inclusive and supportive schools, excessive bureaucracy and red tape, and lack of adequate caregiving supports (e.g., workplace laws and policies that enable caregivers to work). All of these gaps point to ableist and patriarchal societal structures that do not value the lives of people who do not contribute to society through paid employment (whether due to illness and disability or because they perform unpaid carework) and that assign carework little or no value, since it is work that is traditionally performed by women in the private sphere. As Borden King in chapter five eloquently puts it, "The day-to-day life with disabled children can be challenging but not because of the children."

These unhelpful and often downright harmful societal structures lead mothers to fear for their children's futures: what will happen to their children when they are gone? Thus, the mothers continue to speak, write, and advocate to make support systems more humane so that when they let go of their children, they can lead safe, happy and meaningful lives.

At the same time, the accounts in this collection also capture the joy and reward of caregiving and the beauty that can come from living a life "outside of the box". They ground us and remind us of what is truly important in life.

The first section, "History and Theoretical Background on Mothering, Caregiving and Carework," lays the groundwork for the issues that weave throughout the collection. In chapter one, "Mothering and Carework," Genevieve Currie provides a historical and theoretical background on mothering and carework. In chapter two, "From Seeker to Crusader: How Complex Care Motherhood Shifted My Identity," Donna Thomson describes the evolution of the lives of mothers as they become advocates, storytellers, and researchers of their own experiences.

The submissions in section two, "Mothering and Carework of Children with Disabilities and Lifelong Care Needs: Strengths, Dilemmas, and Challenges," explore the challenges and joys of mothering a child with lifelong care needs. In chapter three, "Poetic Narratives of Mothers Who Have a Child Living with Rarity," Genevieve Currie and Joanna Szabo generate and interpret "poetic clusters" from the narratives of mothers

INTRODUCTION

raising children who live with rare conditions. These poetic clusters vividly illustrate the mothers' experiences with trying to live their lives and raise their children in a world that neither accepts nor supports families like theirs. Next, in chapter four, "Mothering Disabled Children," Gretchen Good uses an autoethnographic approach to describe both the structural challenges and the joys of raising disabled children as a disabled mother. In chapter five, "Homeschooling, Cancer, and Letting Go: A Parenting Journey," Anne Borden King examines the lack of inclusive education. She describes her family's journey with opting out and then back into the education system against her trajectory of reinventing herself professionally and working through her health issues.

Though mothering always intersects with other identities and social locations, the contributions in section three, "Intersectionality-Intersections," explicitly seek to bring those intersections to the forefront. In chapter six, "Navigating the Intersections: The Complexities of Black Mother Caregivers of Division I Student-Athletes with Chronic Illnesses," Yvonne C. Latunde uses an autoethnographic approach to shed light on how racism and sexism shape the experiences of a Black mother caring for a Black daughter who lives with a chronic illness. In chapter seven, "When Carework and Paid Work Intersect: Challenges and Learnings of Lifelong Caregiving in Mothers' Professional Trajectories," Ana Carolina Rodriguez explores the myriad ways in which gendered caregiving responsibilities impinge on mothers' career trajectories and professional identities, eventually leading mothers to burn out and either step back, step down, or step out of the paid workforce altogether—decisions that carry consequences for their financial and emotional well-being.

Although this volume focusses on the lives and experiences of mothers, section four, "Caregiving Children with Disabilities beyond Mothering," shows that caregiving is not exclusively the domain of mothers. Chapter eight, "Siblings of Children with Medical Complexity," weaves together the personal narratives of Hanae Davis and Samantha Bellefeuille through Linda Nguyen's research perspective. They argue it is not always easy to spot a caregiver, and those caregivers are siblings sometimes. Siblings of individuals with complex medication conditions often want to be involved as caregivers and recognized for the unique insights and contributions they bring to the relationship. In chapter nine, "My Life as a Lifelong Sibling Caregiver: An Exploration of Choice and Complex Feelings," Mary Sword unpacks some of the complex emotions that come with being born into caregiving for a sibling and choosing to remain that caregiver after reaching adulthood.

Section five, "Mothering and Caregiving with Adult Children with Disabilities," focusses explicitly on caring for one's adult children. Chapter ten, "'It Is What It Is': Mothers Caring for Adult Children with an Intellectual and Developmental Disability in Rural Ontario during the COVID-19 Pandemic," by Anna Przednowek, Sharon Desormeau and Sarah Ederer, explores how disabled people's challenges in receiving adequate services and support are exacerbated for those who live in rural areas. Such extra challenges include a lack of trained staff, higher cost of services, a lack of public transit, and a lack of reliable internet. In chapter eleven, "Mothering in a Sandwich Generation," Joy Seguin details the challenges of juggling work and caregiving, especially the obstacles to obtaining appropriate care for her adult son who lives in a residential home. Her account is a stark reminder that caregivers who speak up and advocate for better care for their loved ones are often dismissed, and their loved ones are often penalized for their efforts.

The chapters in this collection provide numerous examples of solutions needed to address the systemic ableism and sexism (along with all the other "isms") that perpetuate untenable living conditions for disabled individuals and their caregivers and families. The contributions in section six, "Reimagining and Restorying Narratives and Care Models for Children with Lifelong Care Needs," present specific strategies. In chapter twelve, "Children with Medical Complexity: An Integrated Village Approach to Support Mothers and their Families," Anneliese de Groot and colleagues expand on the idea that "it takes a village to raise a child" to describe a model of care composed of various cross-sectoral, interdisciplinary services designed together with families to offer comprehensive support for the entire family. In chapter thirteen, "Raising Rural: Rethinking Raising and Caring for Children with Medical Complexity Living in Rural Communities," Ngoc Huynh outlines the key factors required to support raising children with complex care needs. These include excellent community-based care (including primary care), comprehensive support systems (including educational, recreation, and home-based support, such as respite, adequate housing and mental health), and appropriate financial support.

Taken together, the accounts in this volume capture many of the themes related to caregiving for children with disabilities throughout the lifecourse. Yet the collection still has gaps that should be explored in future work. For example, most contributions hail from Canada, with one each from the United States, Australia, New Zealand and Brazil. We would have loved to include examples of caregiving from other parts of the world, as we think they might provide alternate possibilities of how to think about and do carework. We also wish we had received more contributions explicitly exploring intersections between caregiving and identities, such as race, ethnicity, religion, indigeneity, and LGBTQ2+ status. Notwithstanding these gaps, we hope this collection gives voice to some of the narratives of lifelong caregiving for children and adults with medical complexity. It serves as a starting point for needed discussions on how we can change the world so that disabled individuals and their caregivers can live their lives as fully as possible.

Section I

History and Theoretical Background on Mothering, Caregiving, and Carework

1.

Mothering and Carework

Genevieve Currie

Introduction

Historically, the art of caring for others has long been the responsibility and work of mothers. Mothering has been a gender-based role with practical, physical, and emotional dimensions and women are socialized to fulfill this role across cultures, races, and social conditions (Cowdery and Knudson Martin 339). Mothers are socially responsible for preserving and fostering the lives of their children and families, sometimes under extreme social pressure and expectations (Green 199). I use the word "mother" deliberately, recognizing the gendered nature of the word used to describe the caregiving of children. I understand the construct "mother" can include anyone who describes themselves in this way (Friedman et al. 48). It is, however, beyond the scope of this chapter to provide a breadth of feminist literature on these concepts. They are introduced as important concepts to consider, which intersect with a larger understanding of caring for a child with disabilities across the life course.

Mothering responsibilities extend to creating and sustaining personal relationships and networks, communal obligations, improving the quality of life for the family, and the physical and emotional work of care and connection within the family and community (Arendell 1192, 1194; O'Reilly). These responsibilities that traditionally take precedence over all other forms of work for women have been defined as carework (England 384). Carework is further distinguished by Amy Armenia (470) as meeting the physical, emotional, and social work of others and should not be devalued or depreciated based on payment (or lack of), location of where care takes place or the relationship between caregiver and the person who is cared for.

Regarding caring for and providing caregiving to children with complex health and social needs, this carework is also the responsibility of mothers and women (Douglas et al. 44). The social expectation in most cultures is that mothers should be able to care for their children regardless of the medical, social, economic, or physical circumstances (Knudson Martin and Silverstein 156; Runswick-Cole and Ryan 1129). This caregiving is undervalued, unremunerated, and underestimated but essential in preventing institutional care, healthcare costs and expenditures, and keeping children healthy and alive (McKeever 202–3; Singer et al. 98, 104–5). These experiences of mothering and carework, structured from women's daily lives, have been largely unknown, hidden, or silenced and not considered important knowledge (Aptheker 34; Douglas 51). The constructs of mothering and motherhood will be explored from historical, cultural, and social perspectives.

Mothering and Motherhood

Adrienne Rich was one of the first feminist writers who legitimized mothers' perceptions, experiences, and memories of being mothers. She saw mothering as an important way of knowing. Sara Ruddick was also a feminist scholar who analyzed the experience of mothering and moved beyond a focus on the mother's identity. Mothering was something that could be practised and required intent and thinking. Consequently, mothers committed to mothering provided "preservation, growth and social acceptance" for their children (Ruddick 17). These ideals required mothers to practise "preservative love, nurturance and training" (17). Mothering has been expanded within feminist literature in the last few decades to include the realities and influence of the intersections of economic, class, gender, sexuality, geography, and cultural, racial, and ethnic dimensions (Arendell 1198–1201; Elliott and Bowen 510; Green 199; hooks 133–35; O'Reilly 23–25; Runswick-Cole and Goodley 236).

Motherhood (or the state of being a mother) is also a social construct with many public and moral expectations and regulations. Motherhood has developed and adapted to serve larger social, cultural, economic, and political purposes often determined by others with power and influence in society (O'Reilly 2; Rich 13-15, 42). Historically, motherhood has been referred to as an institution in feminist literature because it is structured by these political and patriarchal foundations (Rich 13). Motherhood is considered a key component within a woman's identity and is influenced by the values and expectations of the dominant culture (Arendell 1195; Green 198). Therefore, women who are not mothers are judged harshly by others in society as missing a significant purpose and meaning in their lives (Aptheker 133; O'Reilly 23-25; Warner). Traditionally, motherhood conceptualizations portray white mothers in heterosexual marriages within a nuclear family unit and do not include diversity in skin colour, sexual orientation, class, or marriage (Arendell 1193; Breton; Green 199).

Mothering, Caring, and Caregiving

Care is a key aspect of mothering. The caring process was defined by Berenice Fisher and Joan C. Tronto (40): caring about (emotional support), caring for (responsibility for), caregiving (the act of providing care), and care receiving. The caring process is considered a significant practice for humans to survive and thrive and is an interdependent relational and physical process between human beings (Barnes and Brannelly 3; Noddings; Robinson; Tronto 142). Mothers, who are often primary caregivers, care for and provide caregiving to their children physically and emotionally as they grow and develop (Cowdery and Knudson Martin 342; Tarlow 56; Tronto 140; Waerness 188). Caring for a child requires responsibility, accountability, and judgment when choosing actions and making decisions for the child's overall health and development. Caregiving is the hands-on physical work of providing care. Both caring for and caregiving require time, resources (e.g., physical, emotional, economic, and social), knowledge, skills, and critical reasoning. If any of these elements are missing, the acts of caring can become problematic and overwhelming.

The caring process within families is considered a gold standard for care. As Barbara Tarlow explains, "Caring as experienced in the family has come to act as the metaphor and standard for all forms of caring" (56). These practices of caring for and caregiving in the home are generally personal, private, and individual. However, if care is not provided adequately to family members, carers are judged within the public and moral spheres of life because care practices are situated socially, institutionally, and politically within society (Tronto 140). Hence, scholars classify care as a political concept, as the provision of care and those who are care recipients are influenced by access to power structures, economic, and social resources, as well as gender, ethnic, racial, and cultural dimensions and societal expectations (McKeever 202-03; Robinson; Tronto). The literature references inequities surrounding who provides care, has access to care, and receives care (Armenia 472; Robinson; Tronto). Other scholars in this book will further explore these issues.

Feminist scholars in the last thirty years have provided more realistic realities of mothering and caring for children, including joy, excitement, growth, transformation, love and attachment, entangled with tension, exhaustion, isolation, loss of self, powerlessness, anxiety, financial stress, and overwhelming responsibility (Lamott; McCullough 110; Oberman and Josselson 345-48; Rose; Ross 399; Tronto). There is also recognition of the intersection and entanglement with other forms of care, such as provisioning, earning, and breadwinning (Doucet; Ruddick). Recently, some scholars have asserted mothering is independent of gender and biology, and all genders can provide mothering (Doucet; Douglas; Green et al.; Runswick-Cole and Ryan 1133).

Good Mother and Good Mothering

References to the historical, social, and cultural constructs of motherhood include ideologies contributing to social stories of the good mother (Douglas and Michaels; Green 198; Rich 42; Smith et al. 512; Thurer; Wearing). Stories of good mothers laud women devoted to their children (Bassin et al. 2; Chodorow; Green 198; Hays, 15). Good mothers are responsible for the health of their children (Fierheller 213-14) and campaign, advocate, and fight for services and medical care for their children as warrior mothers and superheroes against structural inequities (Runswick-Cole and Ryan 1132; Sousa 231). This includes assuming a curative role to find interventions to change the course of their child's diagnosis (Sousa 221). In addition, mothers are considered responsible for the actions and demeanour of their children, regardless of physical and medical manifestations (Blum 7; Caplan 593; Green et al. 272; Ryan and Runswick-Cole 205; Smith et al. 512). These norms inherent in the good mother ideology remain unattainable and unreachable. They provide unrealistic social expectations of mothering, contributing to feelings of incompetence and inadequacy when these expectations are not reached (Knudson Martin and Silverstein 156). Despite these contributions to the literature and understanding of mothering, the good mothering ideology remains the most popular conceptualization of mothering in popular culture.

Importantly for this chapter, the complexities of the good mother and good mothering serve to create and sustain constructs of parenting and, therefore, expectations and norms for parenting behaviours.

Good Mothering and Children with Complexity

The social construct of good mothering does not always provide insight into the experience of caring for children who require intensive intervention and management. Complex, struggling, or overwhelming parenting experiences are rarely coherent within good mothering constructs, leading to misunderstanding and judgment (Currie et al., "Mothering" 8; Currie et al., "Unable" 743). Mothers caring for children with chronic conditions requiring regular care can rarely change the medical and behavioural outcomes for their children. For example, in the context of parenting a child who displays behaviours considered challenging, these behavioural ideals can be unreachable, and expectations of them can be unreasonable. Mothers are placed in a conflicted position by keeping their children healthy and alive with lifelong dependency on others. Children who display behavioural challenges also contradict good mothering practices of social acceptability and good mothers having good children. In most cases, no amount of socialization and behaviour management will change the behavioural issues for children, resulting in a lack of acceptance and tolerance in many social situations (Currie et al., "Unable" 744). Mothers may feel marginalized if their nonneurotypical children display emotional and behavioural outbursts within social and community arenas (Blum; Currie et al., "Mothering" 746; Galpin et al. 576; Robertson 11–12; Williams and Murray 330). Therefore, there is a need to consider the intersections and complexities of the constructs of mother, mothering, and care to understand better the experience of caring for children with lifelong care needs.

Mothers caring for children with complex needs experience additional challenges within the social constructs of good mothering. Mothering a child with chronic care needs disrupts normative views of mothering. Normative views of mothering include good mothering and having good children, who become independent and self-sufficient (Currie et al., "Mothering" 750). Blaming mothers has only partially shifted from mothers being directly responsible for causing their children's neurological disability (e.g., autism and ADHD) to a focus on mothers as relentless warriors, navigating structural inequities, and interceding to manage their children's differences and disabilities (Blum; Douglas; Singh 1196). Mothers must advocate for medical care and a diagnosis to legitimize their children's medical and behavioural concerns. However, with the label of a specific medical pathology, children become situated within society as less-than neurotypical children and are often pushed to the margins of society (Runswick-Cole and Goodley 236). Mothers and their children learn to navigate the world as the other, with this exclusion being true for both mothers and their children (Blum; Williams and Murray 325). As a result, mothers often feel excluded and socially isolated (Currie and Szabo; Runswick-Cole and Goodley 236–37). Hence, Patty Douglas et al. argue that normative expectations for mothers and their children must be reconstructed to reduce stigmatization and alienation for families and become inclusive of mothering with differences (46–47).

Social norms for mothering put pressure on mothers of children with lifelong care needs to intensively intervene with every available means of therapy in their children's lives, including applied behavioural analysis, physiotherapy, speech, and occupational therapy. These extraordinary measures attempt to reform or rehabilitate children to a normative state so they can assimilate into society (Chamak 768; Douglas and Klar 205–06; Lowe et al., 206–07). "Intensive mothering" (Hays 15) involves mothers assuming a myriad of roles, such as nurturer, translator, advocate, teacher, medical coordinator, nurse, physiotherapist, pharmacist, behavioural analyst, and disability lawyer, while trying to meet their children's complex care needs (Blum; Douglas and Klar 210; Sousa 235).

Steeves also states that children with disabilities are given prescriptive narratives and predetermined scripts. She described children being given predetermined identities instead of their identities developing over time. Mothers of children with disabilities are prepositioned in storied roles with such identities as nurturers, warriors, healers, and rehabilitators. Mothers are not considered good mothers if they are not fulfilling these roles.

Recently, mothers have rejected the binary definitions of their children as nonnormal-normal, disabled-abled, and health-impaired in favour of defining disability through a wider spectrum of understanding (Rosenbaum et al. 2). This poststructural lens problematizes the conception of normal and has mothers questioning the restrictive parameters within the definition of normality (Blum; Currie et al., "Mothering" 751; Ryan and Runswick-Cole 50). Furthermore, variation in brain function has been questioned as a "difference rather than a deficit" with the uptake of the concept of neurodiversity (Kapp et al. 67). Neurodiversity has reframed autism and ADHD, as examples, along a spectrum of difference rather than labelling a child with these conditions as not normal. Parents, however, can be caught in the tension between proponents of the medical model and the social disability model. They cannot discount the ongoing realities of care required for their children yet are criticized for not embracing a broader adaptive view of disability (Kapp et al. 67; Thomas 463).

In addition, there is also a small but growing body of literature examining the intersections of social, political, and economic structural inequities and caring for children with chronic health issues. There are moral, social, political, and cultural pressures and expectations that mothers, as primary caregivers of their children with disabilities, will take care of their children's medical care, functional limitations, and behavioural challenges (Curran and Runswick-Cole 18; Hogan; Runswick-Cole and Goodley 236; Scott 691). Mothers, then, struggle to coordinate and navigate medical, social, and educational resources through fragmented systems (Kuo, "Care" 225). Care supports are hard to find, expensive to implement, and require hours of dedicated therapy with the child (Macvarish et al. 796–97; Woodgate et al. 1917). These conditions often prevent mothers from seeking employment as they must provide and coordinate extensive medical, educational, and social care for their children (Krantz et al. 26; Thomas 461). Furthermore, mothers can miss a significant amount of work when juggling appointments and medical care for their children, thus only managing part-time employment (Krantz et al. 26). For mothers who do try and work outside of the home, it can be difficult to find adequate and appropriate caregiving support (Runswick-Cole and Goodley 235). In addition, mothers are valorized for not working outside the home and providing caregiving to their children (O'Reilly 66). Overall, forgoing careers while being caregivers contributes to a lower social and economic standing (Foster 3, 6; Krantz et al. 28).

Mothers must also advocate strongly to access required support for their children in health, education, and government disability systems (Currie and Szabo 101; Runswick-Cole and Ryan 1130; Thomas 459). Scholars show this requires a certain privilege and political savviness to navigate structural restraints and advocate for resources, thus advantaging some parents over others (Thomas 461). This lack of equity in service provision is situated in systems with resource restrictions and limited access. Overall, these pressures and socially constructed barriers shape and reinforce systemic social, political, and economic inequities for mothers and families caring for children with disabilities.

In summary, scholars suggest there are numerous complexities and tensions associated with mothering and caring for children with medical complexity and lifelong care needs. Therefore, mothers are caught in a bind. On the one hand, mothers are expected to be self-sacrificing, emotionally compassionate, resourceful, nurturing, hyperresponsive and hyperresponsible, and social advocates and activists (Blum 7; Brock et al. 3; Ryan and Runswick-Cole 204–05; Williams and Murphy 332). On the other hand, they must provide structured basic care, which can contradict the acceptance of neurological and physical differences. Somewhere amid these tensions in mothering practices and identities lie stories of experience that can provide compelling insights into parenting a child with lifelong care needs. There is a need to understand the everyday tensions, physical, emotional and social complexities, and lifelong accountability and responsibilities for mothers as lifelong caregivers. These experiences can offer insight into how to support and build capacities for mothers' profound courage, creativity, persistence, and strengths in meeting these care responsibilities. These experiences can also provide insight and build capacity to create equitable care arrangements and care models in communities, organizations, governments, and other systems that intersect with the care of children and the lifelong care needs for mothers and families.

Works Cited

Aptheker, Bettina. *Tapestries of Life: Women's Work, Women's Consciousness, and the Meaning of Daily Experience*. University of Massachusetts Press, 1989.

Arendell, Terry. "Conceiving and Investigating Motherhood: The Decade's Scholarship." *Journal of Marriage and Family*, vol. 62, no. 4, 2000, pp. 1192–1207.

Armenia, Amy. "Caring as work: Research and theory." *Handbook of the Sociology of Gender*. Edited by B. Risman, C. Froyum, and W. Scarborough, Springers, 2018, pp. 469–78.

Barnes, Marian, and Tula Brannelly. "Introduction: The Critical Significance for Care." *Ethics of Care: Critical Advances in International Perspective*. Edited by M. Barnes and T. Brannelly. Policy Press, 2015, pp. 3–20.

Bassin, Donna, et al. "Introduction." *Representations of Motherhood*. Edited by Donna Bassin, et al. Yale University Press, 1984, pp. 1–25.

Blum, Linda M. *Raising Generation Rx: Mothering Kids with Invisible Disabilities in an Age of Inequality*. New York University Press, 2015.

Breton, Pat. "Deserving Children and 'Risky Mothers': Situating Public Policy and Maternal/Child Welfare in the Canadian Context." *Mothering in the Age of Neoliberalism*. Edited by Melinda Vandenbeld Giles. Demeter Press, 2014, pp. 315–26.

Brock, Sophia, et al. "The Experiences of Mothers with Children with Disabilities." *Afin Disability Press*, vol. 68, 2015, pp. 1–12, https://ddd.uab.cat/pub/afin/afinENG/afin_a2015m1n68iENG.pdf. Accessed 28 Mar. 2025.

Caplan, Paula J. "Don't Blame Mother: Then and Now." *Maternal Theory: Essential Readings*. Edited by Andrea O'Reilly. Demeter Press, 2007, pp. 592–600.

Chamak, Brigitte. "Autism and Social Movements: French Parents' Associations and International Autistic Individuals' Organizations." *Medecine Sciences*, vol. 24, no. 8–9, 2008, pp. 768–70.

Chodorow, Nancy J. *The Reproduction of Mothering: Psychoanalysis and the Sociology of Gender*. University of California Press, 2023.

Cowdery, Randi S., and Carmen Knudson Martin. "The Construction of Motherhood: Tasks, Relational Connection, and Gender Equality."

Family Relations, vol. 54, no. 3, 2005, pp. 335–45.

Curran, Tillie, and Katherine Runswick-Cole. "Disabled Children's Childhood Studies: An Emerging Domain of Inquiry." *Disability & Society*, vol. 29, no. 10, 2014, pp. 1617–30.

Currie, Genevieve, et al. "Mothering a child with complexity and rarity: A narrative inquiry exploring Prader-Willi Syndrome." *Qualitative Health Research*, vol. 34, no. 8–9, 2024, pp. 742–55.

Currie, Genevieve, et al. "'Unable to Feed My Hungry Child': Experiences of Mothers Caring for Children With Prader-Willi Syndrome." *Global Qualitative Nursing Research*, vol. 11, 2024, https://pmc.ncbi.nlm.nih.gov/articles/PMC10981224/. Accessed 28 Mar. 2025.

Currie, Genevieve, and Joanna Szabo. "Social Isolation and Exclusion: The Parents' Experience of Caring for Children with Rare Neurodevelopmental Disorders." *International Journal of Qualitative Studies on Health and Well-Being*, vol. 15, no. 1, 2020, https://doi.org/10.1080/17482631.2020.1725362.

Doucet, Andrea. *Do Men Mother?* University of Toronto Press, 2018.

Douglas, Patricia Noelle. *Autism and Mothering: Pursuing the Meaning of Care*. University of Toronto, 2016.

Douglas, Patty, and Estée Klar. "Beyond Disordered Brains and Mother Blame: Critical Issues in Autism and Mothering." *The Routledge Companion to Motherhood*. Edited by Lynn O'Brien Hallstein, Andrea O'Reilly and Melinda Giles. Routledge, 2019, pp. 205–14.

Douglas, Patty, et al. "Mad Mothering: Learning from the Intersections of Madness, Mothering, and Disability." *Journal of Literary & Cultural Disability Studies*, vol. 15, no. 1, 2021, pp. 39–56.

Dow, Dawn Marie. "Integrated Motherhood: Beyond Hegemonic Ideologies of Motherhood." *Journal of Marriage and Family*, vol. 78, no. 1, 2016, pp. 180–96.

Elliott, Sinikka, and Sarah Bowen. "Defending Motherhood: Morality, Responsibility, and Double Binds in Feeding Children." *Journal of Marriage and Family*, vol. 80, no. 2, 2018, pp. 499–520.

England, Paula. "Emerging Theories of Care Work." *Annual Review of Sociology*, vol. 31, no. 1, 2005, pp. 381–99.

Ennis, Linda Rose. *Intensive Mothering: The Cultural Contradictions of Modern Motherhood*. Demeter Press, 2014.

Fierheller, Dianne. "'Good' Mothers, 'Risky' Mothers, and Children's Health." *Journal of the Motherhood Initiative for Research and Community Involvement*, vol. 13, no. 1, Apr. 2022, https://jarm.journals.yorku.ca/index.php/jarm/article/view/40652. Accessed 29 Mar. 2025.

Fisher, Berenice, and Joan C. Tronto. "Toward a Feminist Theory of Caring." *Circles of Care: Work and Identity in Women's Lives*. Edited by Emily Abel and Margaret Nelson. State University of New York Press, 1990, pp. 36–54.

Foster, Carolyn C., et al. "Children with Special Health Care Needs and Forgone Family Employment." *Pediatrics*, vol. 148, no. 3, 2021, doi: 10.1542/peds.2020-035378.

Friedman, May, et al. "'It Feels a Bit Like Drowning': Expectations and Experiences of Motherhood during COVID-19." *Atlantis*, vol. 42, no. 1, 2021, pp. 47–57.

Galpin, James, et al. "'The Dots Just Don't Join Up': Understanding the Support Needs of Families of Children on the Autism Spectrum." *Autism*, vol. 22, no. 5, 2018, pp. 571–84.

Green, Fiona Joy. "Re-conceptualising motherhood: Reaching back to move forward." *Journal of Family Studies*, vol. 21, no. 3, (2015), pp. 196–207.

Green, Sara A., et al. "Struggles and Joys: A Review of Research on the Social Experience of Parenting Disabled Children." *Sociology Looking at Disability: What Did We Know and When Did We Know It?* Edited by A. S. Green and Sharon N. Barnartt. Emerald Publishing, 2017, pp. 261–86.

Hays, Sharon. *The Cultural Contradictions of Motherhood*. Yale University Press, 1996.

Hogan, Denis P. *Family Consequences of Children's Disabilities*. Russell Sage Foundation, 2012.

hooks, bell. "Revolutionary Parenting." *Maternal Theory: Essential Readings*. Edited by Andrea O'Reilly. Demeter Press, 2007, pp. 145–56.

Knudson Martin, Carmen, and Rachelle Silverstein. "Suffering in Silence: A Qualitative Meta Data Analysis of Postpartum Depression." *Journal of Marital and Family Therapy*, vol. 35, no. 2, 2009, pp. 145–58.

Krantz, Chantal, et al. "The Price of Love: Understanding the Financial and Psychosocial Costs of Caring for Children with Medical Complexities." *Healthcare Quarterly*, vol. 26, no. 4, 2024, pp. 24–30.

Kuo, Dennis Z., et al. "Care Coordination for Children with Medical Complexity: Whose Care Is It, Anyway?" *Pediatrics*, vol. 141, Supplement 3, 2018, pp. S224–S232.

Lamott, Anne. *Operating Instructions: A Journal of My Son's First Year*. Anchor, 2011.

Lowe, Pam, et al. "Biologising Parenting: Neuroscience Discourse, English Social and Public Health Policy and Understandings of the Child." *Children, Health and Well Being: Policy Debates and Lived Experience*, vol. 37, 2015, pp. 27–40.

Macvarish, Jan, et al. "The 'First Three Years' Movement and the Infant Brain: A Review of Critiques." *Sociology Compass*, vol. 8, no. 6, 2014, pp. 792–804.

McCullough, Kate. "Of Woman (but Not Man or the Nuclear Family) Born: Motherhood Outside Institutionalized Heterosexuality." *From Motherhood to Mothering: The Legacy of Adrienne Rich's: Of Woman Born*. Edited by Andrea O'Reilly, SUNY Press, 2004, pp. 103–24.

McKeever, Patricia. "The Family: Long Term Care Research and Policy Formulation." *Nursing Inquiry*, vol. 3, no. 4, 1996, pp. 200–06.

Moraga, Cherríe. *Waiting in the Wings: Portrait of a Queer Motherhood*. Haymarket Books, 1997.

Noddings, Nel. *Caring: A Feminine Approach to Ethics and Moral Education*. University of California Press, 1984.

Oberman, Yael, and Ruthellen Josselson. "Matrix of Tensions: A Model of Mothering." *Psychology of Women Quarterly*, vol. 20, no. 3, 1996, pp. 341–59.

O'Reilly, Andrea. "Matricentric Feminism: A Feminism for Mothers." *The Routledge Companion to Motherhood*. Edited by Andrea O'Reilly. Routledge, 2019, pp. 51–60.

Rich, Adrienne. *Of Woman Born: Motherhood as Experience and Institution*. W. W. Norton & Company, 1976.

Robertson, Rachel. "'Misfitting' Mothers: Feminism, Disability and Mothering." *Hecate*, vol. 40, no. 1, 2014, pp. 7–19.

Robinson, Fiona. *The Ethics of Care: A Feminist Approach to Human Security*. Temple University Press, 2011.

Rose, Jacqueline. *Mothers: An Essay on Love and Cruelty*. Farrar, Straus and Giroux, 2018.

Rosenbaum, Peter L., et al. "Perspectives in Childhood-Onset Disabilities: Integrating Twenty-First Century Concepts to expand our horizons." *Disability and Rehabilitation*, 2024, https://www.tandfonline.com/doi/full/10.1080/09638288.2024.2394647#summary-abstract. Accessed 29 Mar. 2025.

Ross, Ellen. "New Thoughts on 'the Oldest Vocation': Mothers and Motherhood in Recent Feminist Scholarship." *Signs*, vol. 20, no. 2, 1995, pp. 397–413.

Ruddick, Sara. *Maternal thinking: Toward a Politics of Peace*. Beacon Press, 1989.

Runswick-Cole, Katherine, and Dan Goodley. "The 'Disability Commons': Re-thinking Mothering through Disability." *The Palgrave Handbook of Disabled Children's Childhood Studies*. Edited by Katherine Runswick-Cole. Palgrave Macmillan, 2018, pp. 231–46.

Runswick-Cole, Katherine, and Sara Ryan. "Liminal Still? Unmothering Disabled Children." *Disability & Society*, vol. 34, no. 7–8, 2019, pp. 1125–39.

Ryan, Sara, and Katherine Runswick Cole. "Repositioning Mothers: Mothers, Disabled Children and Disability Studies." *Disability & Society*, vol. 23, no. 3, 2008, pp. 199–210.

Ryan, Sara, and Katherine Runswick Cole. "From Advocate to Activist? Mapping the Experiences of Mothers of Children on the Autism Spectrum." *Journal of Applied Research in Intellectual Disabilities*, vol. 22, no. 1, 2009, pp. 43–53.

Scott, Ellen K. "'I Feel as if I Am the One Who Is Disabled' The Emotional Impact of Changed Employment Trajectories of Mothers Caring for Children with Disabilities." *Gender & Society*, vol. 24, no. 5, 2010, pp. 672–96.

Singer, George, et al. "Toward a Cross-Disability View of Family Support for Caregiving Families." *Journal of Family Social Work*, vol. 12, no. 2, 2009, pp. 97–118.

Singh, Ilina. "Doing Their Jobs: Mothering with Ritalin in a Culture of Mother-Blame." *Social Science & Medicine*, vol. 59, no. 6, 2004, pp. 1193–1205.

Smith, Jacqueline M., et al. "Mothers' Experiences of Supporting Adolescent Children through Long-Term Treatment for Substance Use Disorder." *Qualitative Health Research*, vol. 28, no. 4, 2018, pp. 511–22.

Steeves, Pam. "Sliding doors—Opening our world." *Equity & excellence in education*, vol. 39, no. 2, 2006, pp. 105–114.

Tarlow, Barbara. "Caring: A Negotiated Process That Varies." *Caregiving: Readings in Knowledge, Practice, Ethics, and Politics*. Edited by Suzanne Gordon, Patricia Benner and Nel Noddings. University of Pennsylvania Press, 1996, pp. 56–82.

Thomas, Gareth M. "Dis-mantling Stigma: Parenting Disabled Children in an Age of 'Neoliberal-ableism.'" *The Sociological Review*, vol. 69, no. 2, 2021, pp. 451–67.

Thurer, Sherry. *Myths of Motherhood: How Culture Reinvents the Good Mother*. Penguin, 1995.

Tronto, Joan. "Care as a Political Concept." *Revisioning the Political: Feminist Reconstructions of Traditional Concepts in Western Political Theory*. Edited by Nancy Hirschmann and Christine Di Stefano. Routledge, 1996 pp. 139–56.

Waerness, Kari. The rationality of caring. *Caregiving: Readings in Knowledge, Practice, Ethics, and Politics*. Edited by Suzanne Gordon, et al. University of Pennsylvania Press, 1996, pp. 231–55.

Warner, Judith. *Perfect Madness: Motherhood in the Age of Anxiety*. Penguin, 2006.

Williams, Joan. *Reshaping the Work-Family Debate: Why Men and Class Matter*. Harvard University Press, 2012.

Williams, Karen J., and Duncan W. Murray. "Negotiating the Normative: The Other Normal for Mothers of Disabled Children." *Journal of Family Studies*, vol. 21, no. 3, 2015, pp. 324–40.

Woodgate, Roberta Lynn, et al. "How Families of Children with Complex Care Needs Participate in Everyday Life." *Social Science & Medicine*, vol. 75, no. 10, 2012, pp. 1912–20.

2.

From Seeker to Crusader: How Complex Care Motherhood Shifted My Identity

Donna Thomson

When parents continue to encounter needs that cannot be met by existing societal resources, they may embark on a prolonged career of seekership. The goal of seekership is normalization, or the establishment of a lifestyle that approximates that of families with only nondisabled children. Seekership results in advocacy and activism or "entrepreneurship" when certain situational contingencies or turning points occur. For most parents, active entrepreneurship ends after they reach what they consider to be normalization, while for some it continues to "crusadership". These are the parents who continue to work for disabled children and adults even when the needs of their own children are met.

Rosalyn Benjamin Darling (150)

Our son Nicholas was born in 1988 with severe cerebral palsy. It was the same year disability scholar Rosalyn Benjamin Darling wrote the above words. When I first read Darling's words, I felt breathless and lightheaded with amazement that someone I'd never met could see my life so clearly. Living a life I could never have imagined did lead to justice-driven seekership, entrepreneurship, and crusadership. But I have been transformed by my motherhood experiences in other ways as well. I finally learned that disability is natural; it cannot be fixed. I learned the power of my love and my will could not relieve my son's suffering. I learned to forgive myself for being an imperfect mother who chose surgical interventions that often ended with unintended, painful outcomes. And I learned my lived experience of motherhood held storylines that could influence future generations of families like mine through engagement in disability research.

The Building Blocks of Seekership

Before Nicholas was born in 1988, I was an actor and director. I worked in a horse-drawn touring theatre company, at the National Arts Centre in Ottawa, Canada, and the Kennedy Centre in Washington, DC. I had been the director of an Ottawa-based program to develop new plays, and I had just begun to explore an interest in how the process of script development could be leveraged to explore social justice issues. But having a baby who is medically complex and requires round-the-clock care derailed all those interests and plans. Nicholas was my firstborn, so when he arrived early, I was naïve enough to believe nothing bad could happen to him or us. The doctor's diagnosis of neurological irritability did not come close to describing Nicholas's high-pitched screams and constant distress. His struggle to suck and swallow were our private challenges I assumed could be overcome by education; I needed to learn more about mothering. "Who knows what makes the little turkeys cry?" asked our paediatrician breezily. When it was clear that Nick was dehydrated, the white-haired emergency room doctor quietly examined him, keeping his eyes averted from mine and asked, "Has anyone spoken to you about your baby's development?" I thought he meant Nick's height and weight. "Oh, they said he'd take a bit longer to catch up because he was born a couple of weeks early," I replied. Months later, I would come to understand that the word "development" was code for disability.

Our Nicholas was far from normal in his development; consequently, I felt desperate to locate signs of belonging—of being within the community of other mothers and children around me, not separate from it. But increasingly, incorporating our baby's medical care into my days and nights kept me isolated from other young parents and from the very world itself. Our family was like a satellite, floating without a tether in space, experiencing a different life from what I knew or ever expected. I answered Nick's cries every twenty minutes at night, and bleary-eyed in the morning, I made the coffee, let the dog out, and administered a tube feed. Hypervigilance became my operating system. Once, while walking Nick in his stroller, he spluttered from the effort to coordinate his breathing in the face of a strong wind and turned blue. *Right*, I thought. *That's one more reason to stay home and not go outside.* I'd already learned sudden noises caused startles so severe that screams of pain ensued. Bright light was another source of neurological distress. Our home became like a tomb: dark and lonely. Still, I struggled to find evidence of my competent mothering. If love was the proof I needed, then no problem. But it soon became apparent that love was not enough. I set the course for a new career as my son's therapist. My mission was to know what professionals knew and to dominate cerebral palsy with the power of my love and my will. I believed I could craft a bright future for Nicholas, one with friends, marriage, employment, and normality. I believed I could control outcomes.

But the checks and balances of complex care mothering came in moments of clarity and humility. It was a sunny summer day as I was doing symmetry exercises with Nicholas's arms and legs when I glanced at his eyes. I realized then his face had changed and filled out. When had I last looked at my son's face? I had been so focused on physical therapy that I had lost sight of my baby as himself. In that instant, I realized my quest for normalization had shifted to seeking a new normal—one *we* defined. I scooped up Nick and held him, letting my tears fall. I vowed to put therapy in its place: a sidebar to our mother-child bond.

Entrepreneurship

In the early months and years of our son's life, I knew I craved some sense of normalcy, but I didn't know where to find it. I fled in tears of humiliation from a neighbourhood mother-baby group and from the grocery store when Nick screamed inconsolably and people stared, frowning, with judgment in their eyes. Our first taste of normal belonging came at church. I wanted Nick to be baptized, and on the appointed day, a children's choir processed us down the aisle, carrying a banner that read "We all belong." Finally, a place of welcome, and there was even a "crying room" behind glass at the back where mothers of raging toddlers could commiserate. But our family's assumptions of inclusion were shattered when our treatment centre therapists and paediatrician diagnosed Nicholas with a profound cognitive impairment and assigned him to a segregated preschool for children who were labelled mentally retarded. I knew our son had cognitive capacity, but his physical limitations made it difficult for him to communicate. As it turned out, the quiet, peaceful playroom with its "sing and swing" gentle rocking helped Nick to acclimate his acutely painful senses to the stimuli of sights and sounds. However, after one year, I realized a turning point had occurred, one requiring advocacy to address the disconnect between community early childhood education and the needs of disabled children. I lobbied successfully for a mainstream preschool placement. I wanted Nicholas to have the benefits of rehabilitation therapy incorporated into his learning in his mainstream school.

Other local parents of disabled children felt the same way, and together, we created The Ottawa Parent Pre-School Advocacy Group. Our first success was brokering the opportunity for treatment centre therapists to visit integrated preschools. That drew the attention of Sharon Hope Irwin, founder and executive director of SpeciaLink, the National Centre for Early Childhood Inclusion. In 1990, Sharon invited me to attend a ground-breaking SpeciaLink conference for inclusion leaders in Sydney, Nova Scotia. I felt a swell of parental pride at being called a leader. I will never forget that conference. The audience consisted of both parent leaders and frontline educators. Together, we gasped at a presenter dressed in army fatigues and a flak jacket who taught us about advocacy strategies based on Sun Tzu's *The Art of War*. Sharon Hope Irwin noticed me in the audience nursing my son's baby sister (she was a mere four months old at her first conference) and then passing her to my tablemate for expert cuddles, Sharon said, "Ahh, you have the touch. You all have the touch! That's why we are here. We're going to educate children of all abilities together, but we're also going to educate Canada!" That day, I began to imagine myself as a seeker, an entrepreneur, and maybe even a future crusader.

As a young mother, choosing therapies or learning environments that felt right for Nicholas was my first foray into the tricky process of lining up my values and gut instincts with the available opportunities. "What's the best we can do with who we are, where we are, with what we have?" became the questions I would use as guideposts for seeing myself as a good enough mother over the years. The shift from seekership to entrepreneurship affected my relationship with Nicholas: My fearful love shifted to include a powerful parental pride that connected me to other families. And certainly, normalization felt much more achievable with the support and friendship of other families in the childhood disability community. But Nicholas's health took a turn for the worse. Soon, he fitted this definition of medical complexity:

> Children with medical complexity (CMC) have been defined as those with complex chronic conditions requiring specialized care, with substantial health care needs, functional limitations, and high health resource utilization. CMC and their families interact with multiple services along the care continuum and often experience substantial gaps in care due to poor care coordination, disjointed services, multiple prolonged and potentially preventable hospitalizations, receiving care from multiple clinicians, higher risk of medication order errors, and extraordinary stress on parents and caregivers. The consequences include social isolation, poor caregiver health, fragmentation between family caregivers and health care professionals, and profound financial and social hardships. (Cohen 1)

This textbook definition of a complicated medical reality barely touches the surface of lived experience. Mothering a child with medical complexity requires a clear mind despite sleep deprivation. It requires mustering a cool exterior while careening from hope to despair. It requires carrying on in the face of existential dread. Most of all, it requires a level of entrepreneurship and advocacy that Darling probably never imagined.

Part of what makes the emotional and physical load of complex care mothering so heavy is that over the early years of Nicholas's life, I felt alone with my husband in undertaking an impossible level of parenting. From one day to the next, we did not know whether our son would live or die. No wonder, then, when in 1998, I learned about Planned Lifetime Advocacy Networks (PLAN), an organization founded by parents to answer the question, "Who will care for and about my child with disabilities after I die?" I decided to bet on Nick's survival, and with another complex care mother, I cofounded Lifetime Networks Ottawa, a PLAN affiliate. The organization's core value is that caring relationships are the key to a good life, as well as safety and security after my husband and I die. The answer lay in a model of personal networks of friends and family who would actively care for and about a person with disabilities for their entire life. This idea resonated deeply with me, and I began to imagine that perhaps our local community held a place of belonging and affection for someone as unique as our son. Like that table of preschool teachers who shared the care of Natalie at the Nova Scotia conference, I began to imagine the possibility that "it takes a village to raise a child" wasn't a hollow adage after all.

The Building Blocks of Crusadership

As Darling says, "crusadership" is what occurs in some parents who continue to work towards justice for children with disabilities and their families even when their children's needs are met. In 2005, our family won a lengthy appeal process with the Ontario government to enable access to a far greater level of paid home support for Nicholas due to parental exhaustion and increasing medical complexity. Nick was seventeen years old when we began to benefit from night nursing and the help of palliative care services at home. Having practical support offered me a new opportunity to reflect on the meaning of my unique experience of motherhood. In 2006, my husband's employer transferred us to the United Kingdom, where our funding support enabled us to hire a live-in caregiver for Nick. This was the moment that crusadership began in my parenting. I was already reflecting on the meaning and value of Nicholas's life, as well as my experience of caring for him. Stepping back from hands-on nursing offered Nicholas his first taste of independence from me, and I took the newfound personal time to explore ideas and opportunities that could help me craft a path to helping other children and families.

The first opportunity arrived in the form of an idea that transformed how I thought about my family's place in society and notions of belonging for families like mine generally. During a casual conversation, a friend suggested I might be interested in the work of a Nobel Prize-winning economist, Amartya Sen. Sen won the prestigious prize in 1998 for his capability approach, an economic theory that dispensed with the usual monetary measures of human flourishing, such as household income or GDP, believing they offered insufficient insight into the interplay between personal choice and happiness. He began to explore poverty through the lens of the choices or freedoms people have within the circumstances of adversity. The key idea of this approach is that social arrangements should expand people's capabilities or their freedom to embrace whatever elements in life they value. Sen values the freedom of people (even the poorest of the world's poor) to choose a life they value and have reason to value (as opposed to goods and services thrust upon them by state or nonprofit actors). According to Sen:

> The approach explored sees individual advantage not merely as opulence or utility, but primarily in terms of the lives people manage to live and the freedom they have to choose the kind of life they have reason to value. The basic idea here is to pay attention to the actual "capabilities" that people end up having. These capabilities depend both on our physical and mental characteristics as well as on social opportunities and influences (and can thus serve as the basis not only of assessment of personal advantage, but also of efficiency and equity of social policies). (Sen, "The Possibility")

At the World Bank Conference on Disability in 2004, Sen elaborated on the capability approach using a disability lens by lamenting the failure of theories of justice to address the issue of disability adequately. In his keynote speech at that conference, Sen explored the relationship of wealth, disability, freedom and justice:

> Wealth or income is not something we value for its own sake. A person with severe disability need not really be judged to be more advantaged than an able-bodied person, even if he or she has a higher level of income or wealth than the thoroughly fit person. We have to examine the overall capability that any person has to lead the kind of life she has reason to want to lead, and this requires that attention be paid to her personal characteristics (and this includes her disabilities, if any) as well as to her income and other resources, since both can influence her actual capabilities. To ground a theory of justice on the informational foundation of opulence and income distribution would be a confusion of ends and means: income and opulence are things that we seek 'for the sake of something else,' as Aristotle put it. (Sen, "Disability and Justice")

Immersing myself in the capability approach literature, I began to wonder how I, as a mother, would have fared if we had been offered the chance to choose goods and services for our family that were truly helpful. What if policymakers trusted families of children with disabilities enough to buy what we needed and what we wanted using public funds? I began to imagine I might have the right to decide what constituted a good life for our family, and I began to think that if we could choose those elements, we could find belonging in our neighbourhood and our country. Live-in nursing for Nick afforded me a release from 24/7 care responsibilities and the time to exercise my crusadership by writing and publishing my first book, *The Four Walls of My Freedom: Lessons I've Learned from a Life of Caregiving*. The book enabled me to consider our family's experience with a disability as part of a profoundly human continuum—one in which love, imperfection, belonging, and community are foundational.

True Crusadership

It was at an Ottawa book launch in 2011 that I first met Henri Rothschild, the then-board chair of Kids Brain Health Network (KBHN) (previously NeuroDevNet), a research organization funded through the Canadian Government Networks of Centres of Excellence (NCE) program. Henri introduced himself and immediately asked me to join the KBHN board, explaining the organization's mission to fund childhood disability research. "We need a parent like you on the board," he said. "But I don't know anything about scientific research," I declared. "No matter, you'll learn!" I sat on the board of KBHN for seven years and learned how private citizens with lived experience of health challenges could influence research, leading to better lives for families like mine. So began my journey to learning how lived experiences of health challenges or disability can influence both the "how" and the "why" of research. Better support for younger families like mine motivated me to become a crusader in the field of family engagement in research.

The Family Engagement in Research (FER) Program at CanChild, McMaster University, was cofounded in 2017 by me, researcher Andrea Cross, and parent partner Connie Putterman. A 2024 paper titled

"Development, implementation, and Scalability of the Family Engagement in Research Course: A Novel Online Course for Family Partners and Researchers in Neurodevelopmental Disability and Child Health" describes the course rationale and inception this way:

> Together, a team of family caregivers and researchers cocreated the Family Engagement in Research (FER) Course, a 10-week online course. The purpose of the FER Course is for researchers and family partners to learn about family engagement principles and how to use them in research. The course covers core areas in family engagement including how to find each other, how families and researchers can work together, and ways to overcome common challenges in research partnerships. The course uses online group sessions, discussion boards, and various resources such as research papers and videos. Through a group project, family partners and researchers collaborate to create a resource on family engagement. Completing the FER Course researchers and family members earn a McMaster University micro-credential and become part of a growing global community of FER Course graduates.
>
> Over six years (2018–2023), the FER Course has trained more than 430 researchers and family partners from 20 countries. The course has strengthened capacity in family engagement and is building a worldwide community of researchers, trainees, self-advocates, and family partners who are dedicated to improving neurodevelopmental disability and child health research through meaningful engagement. (Cross et al.)

Including patients and family members in health and disability research is a major disruption of how research has been traditionally conducted, and it is evidence of crusadership in the parents who participate in it. Academic institutions operate within rigid systems and hierarchies. However, training parents alongside researchers to work in teams so that scientific investigations can be informed by lived and living experiences is a manifestation of crusadership. As one parent learner in the FER course wrote,

> The knowledge and connections I gained through taking the FER Course opened up a whole new world for me. I had already been

sharing our family's experiences with others through online Facebook groups, but to have the opportunity to use our lived experience to inform research was exactly what I was looking for even when I did not know it existed. Taking the FER Course with caregivers, researchers, and others showed me that we can indeed work together, provided a support network, and equipped me with skills and confidence to enter the world of family engagement in research. Today, I am an active patient and public partner on research projects and advisory groups and am actively sharing about partnering in research and connecting others to opportunities. (Cross et al.)

This educational program transforms parents who share my experience of parenting a child with disabilities into seekers, entrepreneurs, and crusaders.

In the fall of 2022, the FER Leadership Academy was launched as an advanced training opportunity for FER course graduates. The FER Leadership Academy is a ten-week online course that includes weekly synchronous sessions, small group mentorship, and an individual project in the form of a FER leadership learning plan. As our team developed the Leadership Academy curriculum, we settled on five core competencies for FER leaders: self-awareness, compassion and empathy, communication, advocacy, and entrepreneurship. Reflecting on my parenting journey, I would assert that these five competencies are the ingredients of crusader-ship.

A question we often ask each other in our FER programs is "Why do you partner in research?" My answer is "I want healthcare experiences to be better and easier for families like mine in the future. And I believe that knowledge is power. We all have the right to the information we need to make informed decisions. It's a matter of fairness and opportunity."

I am proud of my leadership role in evolving programs that can help other families over the years. And I am proud of the person I've become because of my (sometimes very challenging) experiences. Over the years, I have been privileged to transfer my motherhood experience to one of seekership, entrepreneurship, and crusadership. Now, in my seventy-first year, my relationship with Nicholas is an almost normal one of mother and son. I am grateful for a life in which I've had the opportunity to love, care, to learn and use my lived experience to help others.

Works Cited

Cohen, Eyal, et al. "Effectiveness of Structured Care Coordination for Children with Medical Complexity: The Complex Care for Kids Ontario (CCKO) Randomized Clinical Trial." *Jama Pediatrics*, vol. 177, no. 5, 2023, pp. 461–71.

Cross, Andrea, et al. "Development, Implementation, and Scalability of the Family Engagement in Research Course: A Novel Online Course for Family Partners and Researchers in Neurodevelopmental Disability and Child Health." *Research Involvement and Engagement*, vol. 10, no. 80, 2024, https://researchinvolvement.biomedcentral.com/articles/10.1186/s40900-024-00615-w. Accessed 30 Mar. 2025.

Darling, Rosalyn Benjamin. "Parental Entrepreneurship: A Consumerist Response to Professional Dominance." *Journal of Social Issues*, vol. 44, no. 1, 1988, pp. 141–58.

Sen, Amartya. "The Possibility of Social Choice." Nobel Prize, https://www.nobelprize.org/prizes/economic-sciences/1998/sen/lecture/. Accessed 30 Mar. 2025.

Sen, Amartya. "Disability and Justice." Second International Disability Conference, World Bank, 1 Dec. 2004, Washington DC. Keynote address.

Thomson, Donna. *The Four Walls of My Freedom: Lessons I've Learned from a Life of Caregiving.* House of Anansi Press, 2012.

Section II

Mothering and Carework of Children with Disabilities and Lifelong Care Needs: Strengths, Dilemmas, and Challenges

3.

Poetic Narratives of Mothers Who Have a Child Living with Rarity

Genevieve Currie and Joanna Szabo

Introduction

Mothering a child with difference disrupts normative views of mothering. There are moral, social, political, and cultural pressures that mothers, who are often the primary caregivers of their children (Witt et al. 2), experience while managing their children's medical needs and behavioural challenges. Mothers of children with complex and rare differences face unrelenting challenges in meeting the needs of their children and society's expectations of them. These experiences have largely been unvoiced and unknown within the context of mothering and care work (Currie and Szabo, "It Is Like" 97). A larger understanding of these experiences could help families caring for children with rare and complex conditions by providing more understanding of the need for supports and services. This chapter uses the narratives of eleven mothers to better understand the experience of mothering a child with rare and complex conditions in urban and rural communities in Western Canada. Mothers shared their experiences, which the authors have reconstructed as poetic narratives.

Background

One in twelve Canadians has been diagnosed with a rare condition, with children overly affected (Canadian Organization of Rare Disorders). Children with rare conditions often have a lifetime of compounding medical challenges and unmet care needs from multisystem disease involvement (Belzer et al. 2). In addition, many rare conditions cause chronic disabilities in physical, cognitive, social, and behavioural domains (Genetic Rare Diseases Information Center). Insufficient knowledge of rare conditions and lack of funding for medical and social care support have been cited as reasons for the lack of medical and social treatment pathways and support for families (Baumbusch et al. 87; Currie and Szabo, "It Is Like" 97; Glenn 17; Pelenstov et al. 212). Consequently, children with rare conditions are high users of health and social care support (Marshall et al. 1055).

Family members, particularly mothers, exclusively provide care for children with rare and complex conditions (Witt et al. 2). Mothers become expert care providers responsible for the complex day-to-day care of their children and, as a result, experience high caregiver burden and stress (Baumbusch et al. 87; Currie and Szabo, "It Would Be" 1252). Mothers must meet gaps in care with fragmented episodic care models within the healthcare and government support systems; they function as advocates, case managers, and medical experts (Matthews et al. 322; Thomson et al. 171). These relentless and pervasive care needs often affect the physical and mental health of the parent and other family members, yet the interplay and interconnection of the family's and child's health is largely unrecognized and not well understood (Boettcher et al. 8–9; Currie and Szabo 97, "It Is Like" 97; Pelenstov et al. 215; Witt et al. 10–11). Sharing and revealing narratives from mothers is required to dismantle constructs of parenting and mothering a child with a rare disorder (Currie et al., "Mothering" 751). New understandings of these experiences could open the possibilities for alternative and expansive narrative conceptualizations of mothering and rare conditions and influence disparate discourses of normative mothering. These changes could further inspire transformation of current and existing healthcare and social practices (Currie et al., "Unable" 8–9) that are not meeting families' care and social needs. A shift is required from a deficit and impairment model of disease and disability (Rosenbaum and Novak-Pavlic 214) towards supporting mothering and caring of children with complexity and rarity.

Good Mothers

Mothers of children with complex rare neurodevelopmental differences face unrelenting challenges in meeting the needs of their children and society's expectations of them as good mothers (Runswick-Cole and Goodley 276). Mother blame has only partially shifted from mothers being directly responsible for causing their children's rare and complex conditions to a focus on mothers as "relentless warriors" (Sousa 235–36) who must navigate structural inequities and manage their child's differences and capabilities (Frederick et al. 1164). Amy Sousa (235) has grappled with the public performance of mothering children with difference, where the mother takes on the "warrior-hero" identity archetype (235). The cultural expectation of these mothers is to do battle, attain resources, and obtain impossible cures for their children; they are now responsible for fixing their children's disease. A hyperfocus is placed on the expert mother, resulting in strain on the mother, the family, and the larger systems of inevitable inequality (Sousa 235). Trends in the good mother ideology emphasize resilience, adaptation, and transformation with a focus on mothers' ability to psychologically adjust to their caring challenges. The emphasis on family resilience—the ability to cope in adverse circumstances—suggests reliance and burden on the mother in the family unit. Concentrating on adaptive strategies serves to overlook the sociopolitical dimensions of one's experience (Currie et al., "Mothering" 750–51). The good mother ideology limits sociocultural narratives available to these mothers, resulting in their marginalization.

Rare and Complex Conditions

A focus on rare and unusual disease manifestations situates the child and the mother as different and atypical, further excluding them from parenting landscapes (Rabeharisoa et al. 198–199; Robertson 12–13). A focus on impairment with no resolution from the rare disease also dismisses the experiences of families as challenges that cannot be resolved or improved (Rabeharisoa et al. 199) Critical disability studies and feminist scholarship prioritize maternal narratives and rethinking the notion of "misfit." (Robertson 8–11). As such, one's identity is constructed and contested around expectations, assumptions, and negotiations of how mothers care for their child with rare conditions amid the larger discourses of normalcy within healthcare, education, and society. Surveilling a mother of a child with difference is embedded in the understandings and expectations of the mother-child relationship. The ideal mother role is prescriptive and descriptive in perpetuating how modern society functions, where deviation from that norm is problematic (Smith et al. 517). This role, therefore, excludes other mothers, such as lesbian, working-class, single women, women of colour, and immigrants. The oppression and marginalization of mothers of children with rare conditions affirms exclusion where "mother" becomes the "other" within the notion of what is mothering. Groupings of normative mothering, such as in "mother and me" postpartum baby groups, covertly couch the concept of mothering. Normative mothering identifies the mothering relationship as belonging to, or being able to belong to, certain mothering experiences within the catalogue of options. Social exclusion turns into anxiety, social isolation, peer rejection, depression, and restricted access to resources normally available (Currie and Szabo 1257).

Constraints act as antecedents to the experience of social exclusion (Williams and Murray 330). Constraints for mothering and caring for children with rare conditions include barriers to accessing leisure facilities and respite services, as these become exponentially less attainable within the catalogues available to mothers of a child with a rare condition. They also influence participation from intrapersonal (stress, anxiety, and prior experience), interpersonal (family and public), and structural (financial and systemic) constraints (Williams and Murphy 330). The menu of options for participation in everyday activities is not only reduced; these layers of exclusivity serve as additional complexities of participation, where the entrance would result in severe limitations and work effort that would render the effort futile and impossible. Any entry would only serve to highlight not belonging to the main group for which the rules, regulations, and privileges are constructed.

Mothering Disability

Mothers of children with rare conditions and differences in disability studies occupy a liminal position between being not disabled and experiencing forms of disablism (Ryan and Runswick-Cole 199; Sousa). These mothers acquire special competence to care for their children, which is overlooked as a taken-for-granted assumption. By negotiating the governed systems to advocate for her child, the activist mother's value is kept hidden and peripheral (Ryan and Runswick-Cole 201).

Karen J. Williams and Duncan W. Murray have shown how able-bodied/able-minded(ness) act as further constraints, yet mothering a child with a rare condition differs from standardized expectations even within these constraints (325). The deficit paradigms within researching mothering and rarity tend to focus on what the relationship between mother and child is not; that is, concerning the dominant discourse of mothering the normative child (Douglas et al. 45).

Also, trends in disability studies emphasize resilience, adaptation, and transformation with a focus on mothers' ability to psychologically adjust to their caring challenges (Young et al. 640–41). Concentrating on adaptive strategies serves to overlook the sociopolitical dimensions of one's experience. The so-called good mother is linked to limiting sociocultural narratives available to these mothers, resulting in their marginalization (Knight 663). Research and policy focussing on strengths-based approaches to addressing families of children with differences and rare conditions unsurprisingly indicate families are at higher risk of stress, financial disadvantage, and breakdown (Boettcher et al. 2). The emphasis on family resilience—the ability to cope in adverse circumstances—suggests reliance and burden on the individual whose responsibility tends to be expected of the mother (Muir and Strnadova 923–25). In addition, negotiating access to social benefits (e.g., early intervention, ongoing therapies and interventions, and access to education and support) is among the responsibilities left to the mother to access and coordinate (Muthukrishna and Ebrahim 375–77).

Methodology

Hermeneutic inquiry seeks to illuminate and understand taken-for-granted aspects within everyday experience (Moules 3). Understandings and meanings attributed to experience are grounded in cultural, political, historical, and social influences (Polkinghorne) and are generated from individual and social influences (Moules et al. 2).

Poetic narratives illuminate intense experiences through the sensitive use of language and words. George Gadamer suggested poetic narratives integrate the unfamiliar into the familiar and, in doing so, engage our imaginations. According to Gadamer, our existing perspectives can be altered, both enlarged and deepened, through such narratives; our prejudices and biases are highlighted and thus begin to shift. We can more fully understand experiences and the meanings behind them (Davey). Poetic narratives connect intact phrases and dialogue segments from conversations with multiple participants. Expressions can be tied together within a poetic narrative and distill plural and alternative meanings about the experience for reflection and pause (Tasker et al. 6–7).

In particular, narrative expressions combine prose related to human experience and an embodied response between participants, thus creating connection and understanding (Butler-Kisber and Stewart 4; Fitzpatrick and Fitzpatrick 3). Butler-Kisber and Stewart (5) described the use of poetic narratives to highlight significant phrases, nuances, and inter-connections that evolve the tensile emergent rhythms of shared stories. Poetic narrative clusters can be portrayed in ways that maintain accountability to statements from mothers in their own words (Butler-Kisber 233). There is an unfolding understanding from the authors while "engaging in their experience" (Clarke 75) of hearing the narratives of unconventional care and mothering. The following poetic narratives are secondary constructs of the author's primary hermeneutic research study on mothers' experiences of caring for children with complex rare neurodevelopmental differences.

Methods

Mothers were interviewed to provide a greater understanding of the experience of caring for a child with a rare and complex condition. Transcripts from the mothers were reviewed through a secondary analysis of the data to bring forward narratives of those living these experiences. This analysis of the narratives brought forth impressions, diverse understandings and explanations, coherence, and incoherence to generate an increased understanding of mothering and rarity (Moules 3). Poetry narratives or clusters (Butler-Kisber and Stewart 4) were identified and generated as "found poems," or excerpts crafted from the texts of participant datasets. Analysis of the data through clustering looks at the narratives through the affective responses and images evoked (Butler-Kisber and Stewart 4–5) from the words of mothers. Researchers individually and collectively identified these excerpts based on cumulative and iterative understanding of previous analyses (Currie and Szabo; "It Is Like"; "It Would Be"; "Social") to maintain the integrity of the narratives that best represented the contextual narratives of mothers' everyday experiences of caring for children with unique challenges. The formal findings became an iterative reflexive discourse in the shape of a responsive cluster of poems.

The questions below supported the clustering of excerpts, contextualizing a deeper noticing of the everydayness (Bamberg 140) that evoked images or affective responses in the crafting of the found poetry and the resulting discursive reflexivity:

1. What does mothering a child with a rare condition look, sound, and feel like as an embodied experience?
2. Who or what does a mother become concerning her child and related to discourses of disability?
3. How does the act of mothering a child with a rare condition mitigate the expectations, responses, and reactions to the social discourses of that relation?
4. How is the act (and call to act) of mothering a child with a rare condition attending to the subjugation of mothering?

Furthermore, the discursive practice of reflexivity between the researchers was used as a method to engage with the language of participants. We were compelled to attend to the tone of mothering a child with a rare condition and bring that sensory experience to the reader. We asked the following questions:

1. How were we honouring the narratives of mothers in creating these distinct excerpts?
2. How does the poetry continue to resonate with the interviewer's experience in terms of authenticity?
3. Does the excerpt illuminate an image to connect with the designated audience authentically?
4. Does the clustering create awareness to make the experience of mothering a child with rare conditions more meaningful to the reader?
5. Does the poem help the audience get a better view of the everydayness of the participants' experience?
6. What captures the image of mothering a child with rare conditions, assuming one could?

Findings

Five poetic clusters were written by the authors from the collection of the mothers' transcribed experiences. Poetic clusters were used to provide a deeper understanding of the complexity of the mothers' everyday experiences caring for children with rare neurodevelopmental differences. These precious and precarious words are a collection of phrases and experiences from the mothers' narratives. Participants used the words "she" and "her" as pronouns, which we have honoured here. Each poetic cluster is followed by discursive reflexivity and analysis from the researchers in the form of researcher notes as noted in italics.

We didn't name him.
We didn't buy a crib.
Ten pairs of gloves
passing him around.
Then all of a sudden...
he's gone.

It's fifty-fifty.
33 per cent don't continue
33 per cent have lifelong difficulties
33 per cent will be "fine."

First-time mom
I had no clue.
What did I do wrong?
We didn't even know
each other.

On paper,
it looks grim.
With each new test
you put your head
in the sand.
This isn't going away.
They breeze in for a quick chat

in the night
leaving us
holding a sack of flour
sifting through
our fingers.

"I have a child...
with special needs."
There's this
disconnect.

"High risk,"
they say,
but nothing "solid."
A "one-off" mutation.
Rare deletion.
Chromosome mutation.
No name for "it."

They see things
on a spectrum.
"One of a small handful,"
they say.
"At least it's not 'that.'"
But I'm the one dealing with 'this.'

He looked dead.
Tubes and leads
coming out of everywhere.
He went from being
strapped to the bed,
to suddenly projectile vomiting...
"Well, this is exciting,"
she said with a nervous laugh.

Then she asks,
"Did they ever say,
'he looks like
a funny-looking kid?'"

In this poetic cluster, the sharing of statistics by the mother feels distant and impersonal. The numbers do not resonate with what the mother must have been feeling. But the numbers and results will be the most remembered and recounted by the mother of a child with a rare condition in those first important moments. The narrative also speaks to the child with rarity as being part of the puzzle, something to be solved, fixed, cured, not typical. There is a focus on disease and deficit, not a willingness to understand the family's experience. The energy of the words feels frenetic, destabilizing, and somehow distant from the situation. There is a sense that something is not happening as it is supposed to happen, and there is no script for what is unfolding. There is a feeling of tragedy and incongruity between the gravity of the situation and the healthcare provider's response, misplaced humour. This remark is what lingers from that harrowing moment of fear and uncertainty.

My stress was
through the roof.
I wasn't producing milk.
They were always pushing me.
"You must try to breastfeed."
I pushed back,
trusting my mom-instinct.
"I don't think he's ready.
I don't want to do this!"

I said,
"He's really yellow."
My family,
clamouring in the background,
"Why didn't you call?"
We had nothing to say.

"The mother-in-law's a nurse.
She'll know
what to look for."
"You'll be fine at home."
They skipped a lot.
We weren't fine.

My friend said,
"You can say 'no.'"
They did whatever they wanted
to her kid,
while she sat by the bed.
My own pillow.
My own show.
They laugh at me.
I get just enough sleep
to function.

I'm the student
obsessively taking notes.
I need to retain the information,
so it will come out,
make sense,
be useful
for all those
who don't get it.

I have to be
ON
ALL
THE
TIME.
Be aware.
Be present.
Be understanding.
Be everything.

With all of it comes,
a constant crippling grief.
And the guilt.
It punctures my heart.
I'm not a machine.

My whole body
in trauma,
paranoid
flying blind,
with poor, tired eyes
unable to speak.
"You're so lucky,
you haven't gained
any weight!"
"Just give the kid a bottle!"
The experts came.
When they decided,
he was finally readmitted.

Within this poetic cluster there is a sense of endlessness, of constant attention to detail and responsiveness to what is arising and then failing to meet a mark set external to the family's expectations. Like mothering is caught up in this frenetic energy of finding something intangible, inaccessible, and incomprehensible. Mothering becomes an unrelenting responsibility of carework and trying to find answers to questions that have no solution. There is a constant vigilance—holding vigil for the child who has no foreseeable future because the knowledge is somehow out of reach of one's grasp. It is a rollercoaster ride that does not end.

In these excerpts, there is a feeling of interlopers invading intimate spaces with privileges that no one has afforded them. No boundaries are set amid so much happening. No one is positioned to act as a buffer or mediator to others accessing private information when the family is most vulnerable.

The descriptions left us with a feeling of fatigue that doesn't find solace or reprieve. Looks and impressions are deceiving and serve to further distance mothering to the periphery of her own experience as an omniscient observer. This poem claims space and teaches others from one's own experience like informal peer mentorship between mothers.

It's a tough read
cover to cover.
Turn the page and discover
there's more.
Just give us the "big book."
It's here.
Now they're saying,
"'This' isn't it."
He doesn't fit in
one box completely.
Like a jungle gym,
everything is
under construction.

His file is so thick.
When we go
they're all lined up
with their requirements.

Then the resident comes in.
You have to start all over.
"It's in the chart,"
I say.
Cardiology
deals with blood flow.
Neurology
deals with behaviour.
"Who will deal
with the effects of pneumonia
coming in the winter?"

"Just call them all.
Get the MRI done."
I'll walk over
to neurology.

So we don't have to
come back in
two weeks
when it is convenient
for you.
Blank stares.
We also have protocols
that need to be followed.

Some won't even listen to you.
Genetics had no clue.
"We're missing something,"
they said.
They blow off
everything you say.
"There's no road map."

I spend my time
explaining to doctors,
"If you know my kid is coming,
google it.
The textbooks you've read
are probably fifteen years old.
You can't lump him in
in one tiny paragraph
you read somewhere."

This poetic cluster shares the mother's journey of navigating the system as it tries to navigate her. There is something about working the system and how the child is navigated through, but again, for whose benefit? Control is clearly taken away within the healthcare setting. Imagining what it would feel like to have a child's health deteriorating and having to trust in what is happening, when experience has shown, the experts do not know what they are doing (with only questions and no answers).

    There is a sense that "hurry up and wait" is followed by a revolving door of healthcare providers coming through one after the other, not in unison, and always asking the same questions. One could compare what is being relayed to entry to a club filled with restrictions and how difference is being singled out. Any entry would only serve to highlight the "odd one out," as in not belonging to the main group for which the rules and regulations and privileges are crafted. You are being informed that you do not fit where rules were never designed with you in mind. The idea is to make it hard to access the club by being clear that you do not belong, so we do not have to deal with you.

Whatever normal is
I need to know.
I try to lower the bar,
moving slowly
towards his
centre of gravity.

Melt downs
are part of his routine
and also overwhelm him.
He hears things
others don't.
He's like a drunken sailor
walking on
the edge of normal.
He was taking it all in,
but it was sensory overload.
The buzzing hair clipper
and his screaming.
People think he's being funny.
For him,
things get
black and white
when he is at
the end of his rope.

I stand there,
like an embarrassed mother
trying to explain.
"He felt slighted."
"He got mad."
"He wanted to be included."
"He acted out."
I want to stop saying,
"It's going to be fine."

Puberty is starting...
Those volatile emotions
The heightened sensitivity
One moment he's fine.
The next,
he is out of pajamas,
his backpack on.
"What are you doing?"
I ask.
"I'm going to run away!"
It's just the way
his brain works.

We're walking on sunshine,
then she looks at my kid,
and makes a snide comment
destroying that happy place.
They glare
in silence.
He's oblivious.
I'm self-conscious.
I don't owe you an explanation.

He'll hit himself.
Scratch his face.

Scream.
Then he pulls out his feeding tube.
I cringe
with pain.

It was in IKEA.
Lurking eyes finally said,
"Get your kid
under control.
He's disturbing our lunch.
It's not fair to the other kids."

"You know what's not fair?
My kid, having a seizure." I rage,
as my daughter watches on.

Just breathe
and go over.
"If you want to ask questions…"
She just puts her head down.

Kids would point
and say,
"What's happening?"
The parents say,
"Shhhh!"
Or slow their speech
down to his level.
I say,
"It's okay.
You can ask.
We aren't offended."

Instead, they try
to help you parent,

like you haven't got a clue.
Or they just back off
not knowing
what to do.

"Calm down,"
I hear myself say,
so we can move on.
It's just another day.

In this poetic cluster, there is an attempt to mitigate emotions and anticipate how emotions will flux between events, alongside having to take the time and energy to explain what is happening. The mother seems to be seeking someone who will understand, as perhaps she cannot do so herself. Her mothering as an "ambassador" requires her to fulfill a role somewhere in between that of mother and healthcare provider. There is tension here with having to take the time and energy to explain and appease people in this situation or that situation, away from just accepting her child's behaviour as normal, instead of having to walk through "how we do things." When mothering requires mitigating the risks that can occur in the public space, mothering becomes about justifying "otherness" and perpetuating how normal looks, feels, and acts.

Reading these words evokes a feeling of frustration and resignation to external attempts at normalizing situations in public spaces. When one tries to put oneself out there and be social, this is met with resistance, evasiveness, and resignation. Like others are saying, "I'm noticing you are out of place and problematic. I'm not willing to meet you where you are. You don't fit in my boxed IKEA worldview."

You structure your home to
anticipate accidents,
mischief,
and destruction.

I have this kind-hearted loving
sweet kid,

with impulses,
who gets into everything.

She runs the water,
then sits in the tub.
"Hot, hot, hot!"
It's boiling.
She can't get out.
She just sits there.

Next time,
we're in the shower.
My legs and arms
like a straightjacket
around her.
She yells, "Done!"
She bolts out of the shower
and into the backyard.
I find her
squatting naked
eating a big jar of peanut butter
with her bare hands.
I run after her naked
with soap in my eyes,
I've become the
"crazy naked soap lady."

I'm an
isolated,
overwhelmed,
mother bear
with hair trigger reactions.
But those crippling stares,
take years off my life.
Catch an angry eye,

my heart shatters.
One look
the wrong way,
can destroy.

We deserve to do the things
everybody else does.
"F you, world!"
When it is hidden
people only notice
the ugly snapshot.

Everyone is busy,
racing to relax.
She needs time with friends,
but they aren't interested.

Weekends are hard
in memory-filled time.
In that moment,
I pretend
I'm the customer
ordering food in her play kitchen.
I don't want to unload the dishwasher
or make dinner
because then everything
falls apart.

I think of her brain...
all these sockets
and electrical outlets.
Sometimes a strong cord
plugged in,
when she makes a connection.
Other times,

all ripped, frayed, tingly and zappy...
not sorting it all out.

Sometimes she's nonstop chatty
resorting to one repetitive word.
I say, "I beg your pardon?
Speak in sentences.
You're a big girl."
When she's frustrated,
she makes noises and grunts,
or just cries outbursts.
"Go away, Yucky!
You hate me!"

Needing to get at the root
of what is upsetting her.
I set it up to be safe.
I try engaging her in enough
learning opportunities
without the danger.

I hate the locks on all the doors.
But it's inevitable.
Her shaking and squeezing
are not safe for the animals
or anybody.

I am a jerk
saying these things.
She stands out.
She's a lone wolf.
So alone in this world.
In so many ways.
Her desire to connect with people
is heartbreaking.

"She's a real handful
when we have a full class."
"One of a small handful,"
I want to say.
So strong, brave and confident.
Don't let the world
take her spark away.

This mother in the poetic cluster is trying to connect with, keep up with, and convey the uniqueness of her child. This provides a reflection of what it is like for this mother in her understanding of her child's reality and in her being resourceful and following cues and constantly finding that liminal in-between space to support her child to make a connection. This precarious liminality seems to be a hopeful contingency to her success, yet there is also fear and disappointment that the world will not meet her where she is because the only access point is through this vigilance. The mother is also a way into the everydayness, "you communicate with me and hear our story, you get access to our experiences." In this way, the mother acts as a gatekeeper, yet she also holds the key to the complexity of everydayness and how navigating the complex everyday gives insight into the complexity of mothering a neurodivergent child.

The mother in the cluster wants to create fond and cherished memories and hold onto those precious and precarious times when there is play and connection in mothering moments. Thinking about how prescribed routines and social scripts that mothering requires also takes away from being present, playful, and connected.

Discussion

Engaging with mothers' experiences offers insights into their work of nurturing, caring, and contributing to the care of a child with rarity and complexity. Poetic clusters invite a dialogue into the precariousness, fragility, harshness, and invisibility of these everyday moments that manifest and shape mothering rarity. Sharing the challenges of mothers of children with rarity offers a glimpse into the moments that identify but do not define motherhood, as though there were only one way to be a mother. The mothers do not ask for recognition or acknowledgment of their subjectivity. These narratives give voice to the complexities of mothering children with rare conditions, with moments of urgency, uncertainty and uprootedness in these narratives.

Mothering through the lens of rarity is on the fringe, always waiting for more information and the next moment of chaos and uncertainty. Capturing these narrative moments unsettles, unearths and undermines motherhood as belonging or connected to any one script. Mothering may present as a craving to just settle in and know and be.

These moments disrupt the institutionalization of mothering and family and offer a glimpse into navigating systemic structures, and the ensuing feelings of social isolation, resignation and resolve. The image of the ideal mother does not exist for these mothers. They need a place, a voice, and an invitation to be part of and belong to the places they live, including within the healthcare system, where such support would be expected to be less formulaic and more readily available (Currie et al., "Unable" 748). University and college courses that include such unique narratives about rarity and chronicity are critical to influencing change (Picci et al. 521). The nuances of mothering a child with a rare condition need to be brought into healthcare culture and mainstream society so that these mothers do not feel dismissed.

The poetic clusters highlight mothering experiences that need to be attended to. They are part of the everydayness of mothering and caring for a child with medical complexity and rarity across the life course. This caring can be incoherent (Crites 305) as care practices are anything but typical. We hold the tensions between stories that are typical or normalized and disordered. They become (extra)ordinary (Currie et al., "Mothering" 4) in attending to the care needs of the child, but hold a space and place in the mothering landscape for mothering and caring. Our reflections attend to the complicity of healthcare providers, government officials, and researchers in addressing the structures that exist to support equity, diversity, inclusion, and accessibility from the uniqueness of each mother's experience. What does "crazy soap lady" feel like? What is it like to be amid a "jungle gym under construction"? Illuminating these moments showcases glimpses into the everydayness normal for the child and family that exist as divergent from the hegemonic discourses of neurotypical and societal norming of chronicity.

We aim to hold the tensions between the burdens of mothering a child with rarity, the responsibility of caring for a child with rarity, and consider the strengths-based self-care approaches for parents caring for a child with complexity, that push back or trivialize burdens when thinking about recommendations. The focus of what we have learned through the poetic clusters is about listening and sharing power with families in their complexities (Pozniak et al. 7). There needs to be acknowledgement of the weight of the responsibility we have as healthcare providers and researchers when we ask yet another question tempered with assumptions and expectations. We continue to perpetuate what normal and good mothering look like instead of supporting these narratives from mothers caring for children with complexity. We need to shift from only accommodating what is considered typical mothering to including difference and diversity (Rosenbaum and Novak-Pavlic 214).

Mothering a child with rarity may present through advocacy work and seeking access to medical, educational, and, especially, social spaces. When mothering presents as a vessel or conduit for the child living with rarity, this liminality necessarily diminishes the already obscure mothering presence to highlight othering and externally derived parameters for the systematized and institutionalized child via knowing, being, and doing what is prescribed, documented, formed, diagnosed, and accommodated. Engagement with the narratives provokes a reimagining of how we apprehend and expect to receive a rare clinical diagnosis and be managed by healthcare and education systems and institutions.

Engaging with the narratives through critical disability theories of mothering provides insight into the contentious language and contexts shaping the landscape of the poetic clusters. What is deemed socially just, inclusive, and accessible requires a multilayered gaze, attending to assumptions and expectations. This gaze needs to infuse the tensions embedded in subjective identity within discourses and social locations. Theorizing a liminality (of sorts) assists in the excavation and distilling of mothering disability as an approach that dwells in between disparate normative discourses (Lewiecki-Wilson and Cellio). Patricia McKeever and Karen-Lee Miller describe how deinstitutionalization, which began in North America in the 1960s, delegates the responsibility of caring for children with chronic health challenges to mothers. Mothers, as a result of protecting and advocating for their children, have since been pathologized as "over-protective, difficult, unrealistic, or in denial of the extent and impact of their children's disabilities" (McKeever and Miller 1177). The conduct of mothers, according to Bourdieu's theorization of social life, as taken up by McKeever and Miller, represents the tension between their behaviours in sociopolitical contexts and the embodied, private personhood in the valuing of their children. Through this lens, the mothers' subjective experiences of raising their children with disabilities and the extraordinary activities they engage in to do so are lost in the cracks between the hegemonic discourses surrounding motherhood, childhood, and disability. As such, maternal behaviours represent sites of reproduction and resistance. Mothering fluxes and flows between accommodation, resistance, and attending to the stigmatization of a child whose body and behaviours have extended to the actions taken by their mother (McKeever and Miller 1184). Maternal behaviours also reflect the relational environment, which is social, political, and physical. Lived experience reflects the corporeal space constituted by and constituting conceptions and perceptions of spaces (Moss and Dyck), in this case, the act of mothering in multiple social contexts.

Conclusion

Engaging with participants' experiences gives insights into mothers' work of nurturing and caring for children with medical complexity and rarity and offers alternative and expanded understandings (Crites, 298, 302, 305) of mothering and rarity. Poetic narratives invite a dialogue into the precariousness, fragility, harshness, and invisibility of these everyday moments that shape mothering rarity. These narratives provoke a reimagining of how mothers are managed by healthcare and education systems and institutions. The poetic moments from the mothers' voices disrupt the institutionalization of mothering and family and create the chance for reflection and transformation in our assumptions and misunderstandings.

Works Cited

Bamberg, Michael. "Stories: Big or Small: Why Do We Care?" *Narrative Inquiry*, vol. 16, no. 1, 2006, pp. 139–47.

Baumbusch, Jennifer, et al. "Alone in a Crowd? Parents of Children with Rare Diseases' Experiences of Navigating the Healthcare System." *Journal of Genetic Counseling*, vol. 28, no. 1, 2019, pp. 80–90.

Belzer, Leslee T., et al. "Psychosocial Considerations for the Child with

Rare Disease: A Review with Recommendations and Calls to Action." *Children*, vol. 9, no. 7, 2022, pp. 1–25.

Boettcher, Johannes, et al. "Being the Pillar for Children with Rare Diseases—A Systematic Review on Parental Quality of Life." *International Journal of Environmental Research and Public Health*, vol. 18, no. 9, 2021, https://doi.org/10.3390/ijerph18094993

Butler-Kisber, Lynn. *Qualitative Inquiry: Thematic, Narrative, and Arts-Informed Perspectives*. Sage, 2010.

Butler-Kisber, Lynn, and Mary Stewart. "The Use of Poetry Clusters in Poetic Inquiry." *Poetic Inquiry: Vibrant Voices in the Social Sciences*. Edited by Monica Prendergast, Carl Leggo and Pauline Sameshima. Brill, 2009, pp. 3–12.

Canadian Organization of Rare Diseases (CORD). *Canadian Impact of Rare Disease Survey*. CORD, http://www.raredisorders.ca/content/uploads/CORD_2019-Canadian-Impact-of-Rare-Disease_Infographic.pdf. Accessed 2 Apr. 2025.

Clarke, Cindy. "Writing the Borderlands: Poetic Expression and Narrative Inquiry as Methodology Inhabiting the Space between Narrative Inquiry and Poetic Expression." *Landscapes, Edges, and Identity Making*. Edited by Vicki Ross and Elaine Chan. Emerald Publishing, 2019, pp. 53–78.

Crites, Stephen. "The Narrative Quality of Experience." *Journal of the American Academy of Religion*, vol. 39, no. 3, 1971, pp. 291–311.

Currie, Genevieve, and Joanna Szabo. "'It Is Like a Jungle Gym, and Everything Is Under Construction': The Parent's Perspective of Caring for a Child with a Rare Disease." *Child: Care, Health, and Development*, vol. 45, no. 1, 2018, pp. 96–103.

Currie, Genevieve, and Joanna Szabo. "'It Would Be Much Easier If We Were Just Quiet and Disappeared': Parents Silenced in the Experience of Caring for Children with Rare Diseases." *Health Expectations*, vol. 22, no. 6, 2019, pp. 1251–59.

Currie, Genevieve, and Joanna Szabo. "Social Isolation and Exclusion: The Parents' Experience of Caring for Children with Rare Neurodevelopmental Disorders." *International Journal of Qualitative Studies on Health and Well-Being*, vol. 15, no. 1, 2020, pp. 1–10.

Currie, Genevieve, et al. "Mothering a Child with Complexity and Rarity: A Narrative Inquiry Exploring Prader-Willi Syndrome." *Qualitative Health Research*, vol. 34, no. 8–9, 2024, pp. 742–755.

Currie, Genevieve, et al. "'Unable to Feed My Hungry Child': Experiences of Mothers Caring for Children with Prader-Willi Syndrome." *Global Qualitative Nursing Research*, vol. 28, no. 11, 2024, pp. 1–12.

Davey, Nicholas. *Unquiet Understanding: Gadamer's Philosophical Hermeneutics*. State University of New York Press, 2012.

Douglas, Patty, et al. "Mad Mothering: Learning from the Intersections of Madness, Mothering, and Disability." *Journal of Literary & Cultural Disability Studies*, vol. 15, no. 1, 2021, pp. 39–56.

Fitzpatrick, Ester, and Katie Fitzpatrick. "What Poetry Does for Us in Education and Research." *Poetry, Method and Education Research: Doing Critical, Decolonising and Political Inquiry*. Edited by Ester Fitzpatrick and Katie Fitzpatrick. Routledge, 2020, pp. 1–18.

Frederick, Angela, et al. "The Double Edge of Legitimacy: How Women with Disabilities Interpret Good Mothering." *Social Currents*, vol. 6, no. 2, 2019, pp. 163–76.

Gadamer, Hans-Georg. *Truth and Method*. 1960. Continuum, 2004.

Glenn, Adriana D. "Using Online Health Communication to Manage Chronic Sorrow: Mothers of Children with Rare Diseases Speak." *Journal of Pediatric Nursing*, vol. 30, no. 1, 2015, pp. 17–24.

Knight, Kathryn. "The Changing Face of the 'Good Mother': Trends in Research into Families with a child with intellectual disability, and some concerns." *Disability & Society*, vol. 28, no. 5, July 2013, pp. 660–73.

Kuo, Dennis Z., et al. "Associations of Family-Centered Care with Health Care Outcomes for Children with Special Health Care Needs." *Maternal and Child Health Journal*, vol. 15, 2011, pp. 794–805.

Lewiecki-Wilson, Cynthia, and Jen Cellio-Miller, eds. *Disability and Mothering: Liminal Spaces of Embodied Knowledge*. Syracuse University Press, 2011.

Marshall, Deborah A., et al. "Direct Health-Care Costs for Children Diagnosed with Genetic Diseases Are Significantly Higher than for Children with Other Chronic Diseases." *Genetics in Medicine*, vol. 21, no. 5, 2019, pp. 1049–57.

Matthews, Elise J., et al. "Mediating a Fragmented System: Partnership Experiences of Parents of Children with Neurodevelopmental and Neuromuscular Disabilities." *Journal of Developmental and Physical Disabilities*, vol. 33, 2021, pp. 311–30.

McKeever, Patricia, and Karen-Lee Miller. "Mothering Children Who Have Disabilities: A Bourdieusian Interpretation of Maternal Practices." *Social Science & Medicine*, vol. 59, no. 6, 2004, pp. 1177–91.

Moss, Pamela, and Isabel Dyck. *Women, Body, Illness: Space and Identity in the Everyday Lives of Women with Chronic Illness*. Rowman & Littlefield Publishers, 2003.

Moules, Nancy J. "Hermeneutic Inquiry: Paying Heed to History and Hermes, an Ancestral, Substantive, and Methodological Tale." *International Journal of Qualitative Methods*, vol. 1, no. 3, 2002, pp. 1–21.

Moules, Nancy J., et al. "On Applied Hermeneutics and the Work of the World." *Journal of Applied Hermeneutics*, 2011, https://doi.org/10.11575/jah.v0i0.53186

Muir, Kristy, and Iva Strnadová. "Whose Responsibility? Resilience in Families of Children with Developmental Disabilities." *Disability & Society*, vol. 29, no. 6, 2014, pp. 922–37.

Muthukrishna, Nithi, and Hasina Ebrahim. "Motherhood and the Disabled Child in Contexts of Early Education and Care." *Childhood*, vol. 21, no. 3, 2014, pp. 369–84.

Pelentsov, Lemuel J., et al. "The Supportive Care Needs of Parents with a Child with a Rare Disease: A Qualitative Descriptive Study." *Journal of Pediatric Nursing*, vol. 31, no. 3, 2016, e207–e218.

Picci, Rocco L., et al. "Emotional Burden and Coping Strategies of Parents of Children with Rare Diseases." *Journal of Child and Family Studies*, vol. 24, no. 2, 2015, pp. 514–22.

Polkinghorne, Donald E. *Methodology for the Human Sciences: Systems of Inquiry*. Suny Press, 1984.

Pozniak, Kinga, et al. "Building a Culture of Engagement at a Research Centre for Childhood Disability." *Research Involvement and Engagement*, vol. 7, 2021, pp. 1–15.

Rabeharisoa, Vololona, et al. "From 'Politics of Numbers' to 'Politics of Singularisation': Patients' Activism and Engagement in Research on Rare Diseases in France and Portugal." *BioSocieties*, vol. 9, 2014, pp. 194–217.

Robertson, Rachel. "'Misfitting' Mothers: Feminism, Disability, and Mothering." *Hecate*, vol. 40, no. 1, 2014, pp. 7–19.

Rosenbaum, Peter L., and Monika Novak-Pavlic. "Parenting a Child with a Neurodevelopmental Disorder." *Current Developmental Disorders Reports*, vol. 8, no. 4, 2021, pp. 212–18.

Runswick-Cole, Katherine, and Dan Goodley. "The 'Disability Commons': Re-thinking Mothering through Disability." *The Palgrave Handbook of Disabled Children's Childhood Studies*. Edited by Katherine Runswick-Cole, et al. Palgrave Macmillan, 2018, pp. 231–46.

Ryan, Sara, and Katherine Runswick Cole. "Repositioning Mothers: Mothers, Disabled Children and Disability Studies." *Disability & Society*, vol. 23, no. 3, 2008, pp. 199–210.

Smith, Jacqueline M., et al. "Mothers' Experiences of Supporting Adolescent Children through Long-Term Treatment for Substance Use Disorder." *Qualitative Health Research*, vol. 28, no. 4, 2018, pp. 511–22.

Sousa, Amy C. "From Refrigerator Mothers to Warrior Heroes: The Cultural Identity Transformation of Mothers Raising Children with Intellectual Disabilities." *Symbolic Interaction*, vol. 34, no. 2, 2011, pp. 220–43.

Tasker, Diane, et al. "'From the Space Between Us': The Use of Poetics as a Hermeneutic Phenomenological Tool within Qualitative Physiotherapy Research." *Creative Approaches to Research*, vol. 7, no. 2, 2014, pp. 4–18.

Thomson, Joanna, et al. "Financial and Social Hardships in Families of Children with Medical Complexity." *The Journal of Pediatrics*, vol. 172, 2016, pp. 187–93.

Williams, Karen J., and Duncan W. Murray. "Negotiating the Normative: The Other Normal for Mothers of Disabled Children." *Journal of Family Studies*, vol. 21, no. 3, 2015, pp. 324–40.

Witt, Stefanie, et al. "Living with a Rare Disease—Experiences and Needs in Pediatric Patients and Their Parents." *Orphanet Journal of Rare Diseases*, vol. 18, no. 1, 2023, p. 242.

Young, Stephen Young, et al. "Raising a Child with a Disability: A One-Year Qualitative Investigation of Parent Distress and Personal Growth." *Disability & Society*, vol. 35, no. 4, 2020, pp. 629–53.

4.

Mothering Disabled Children

Gretchen Good

Introduction

Mothering disabled children is full of challenges. Parenting children with profound and complex impairments, who will need lifetime support, adds elements of responsibility, planning, work, and worry. I am a mother to children who live with Down syndrome and other complex health and disability support needs. I have undertaken an autoethnographic approach to examine the complexities of my mothering roles and my lived experience as an older, adoptive, and disabled academic mother. The vignettes present personal experiences to illustrate broader, cultural, and social phenomena. Topics for vignettes were derived from a review of autoethnographic studies related to mothering disabled children. An analysis of the vignettes resulted in three identified themes: hoping, coping, and loving. Autoethnography is a research method used widely in the social sciences, education, health and medicine, arts and humanities, communication and media studies, gender and sexuality studies, social work, business and management, and environmental studies. The versatility of autoethnography allows researchers to place personal experience within political, social, and cultural contexts.

Mothering and carework are underresearched areas. The work of mothers, in general, is undervalued, and research informing policymaking that can support mothers, particularly mothers and carers of disabled adults and children, can improve lives. Research is needed to improve social equity and address and advocate for improved resources that could help ameliorate the physical, emotional, and mental health challenges disability can bring to disabled children and adults and their mothers and other caregivers.

This autoethnographic research addresses some of the complex roles and responsibilities of mothers of disabled children and what is required of us when our children have long-term support needs. I tell some of my stories of mothering and managing day-to-day life while planning for the future and address some fears, concerns, and hopes for my children and family. I collate some of the common themes emerging from my stories; the research culminates in recommendations for how to cope, plan, and alleviate worry for other mothers and pleas for change to communities and legal, medical, and political systems, which can play an important part in the future of disabled people. The concluding appendix, though distinct from the affective experiences explored in the vignettes, reflects emotional realities and can demonstrate the complexities of mothering disabled children and can assist other mothers in coping, planning, and feeling hope for the future of their loved ones.

Literature Review

Much literature related to parenting disabled children is about the challenges, frustration, and grief related to raising children with long-term support needs (Johnson). More recently, autoethnographic studies of motherhood and disabled children have captured the mothers' experiences through their voices.

I identified eight autoethnographic articles relating to mothering disabled children published in the past ten years. Some of these are intimate expressions of vulnerability about the "beautifully complex role of motherhood, complicated further by raising a child who has profound (dis)abilities" (Sutton-Browne 228). Elisabeth Lowenstein and Darolyn J. Jones used autoethnography to explore unique work-life tensions experienced as academic mothers of disabled children, which led them to become advocates of reduced stigma and supportive working environments for parents. Dawn C. Zibricky explores the authoritative, male-dominated institutions defining the roles of motherhood and oppressing and marginalizing those at the intersection of motherhood and disability. She writes about negative judgments and misplaced glorification of "special mothers," which can deny the emotional and practical hardships of mothers of disabled children. Susan Comerford used autoethnography to explore her experiences as an adoptive mother of a disabled child, focussing on early childhood school years. Other studies include a collaborative ethnographic study about being advocates as mothers of disabled children (Good et al., "Social Model"), a study of being older mothers of disabled children (Good et al., "Older"), and a study about mothering disabled children during the COVID-19 pandemic (Good et al., "Parenting").

In 2023, Alina Kewanian and colleagues published an autoethnographic study focussing on education, inclusion, and disability from a parent's perspective. These authors used vignettes to highlight the positive aspects of disability and embrace the concept of a "fierce" and empowering parent who assists children through their educational years.

The previously cited articles collectively explore the intersection of motherhood, disability, and advocacy. The stories explore the unique challenges of mothers of disabled children and focus on their emotional struggles and resilience. The social model of disability (Oliver) is often used to focus discussion on changes needed in our environments rather than changes we expect from our children. Mothers' voices are used to advocate for greater inclusion and understanding of disabled people and their families in broader social contexts.

In this chapter, I use storytelling and autoethnographic analysis to explore disability and mothering through the lenses of the social model of disability and motherhood studies to help redefine what motherhood and long-term caregiving for disabled children can mean. I analyzed these eight autoethnographies based on thematic analysis (Braun and Clarke). My method for the autoethnographic study is guided by Anita Gibbs, which I have utilized in multiple studies in recent years (Good et al.). I also draw upon motherhood scholar and theorist Katherine Runswick-Cole, who combines experiences as a mother of a disabled child with broader cultural and social issues, including activism.

Some of the themes emerging from autoethnographic research related to mothering disabled children with a long view to the future include current day-to-day living with disabled children, worries and concerns about the mothers' and children's future, and planning for the future. The vignettes below capture some personal experiences to understand broader cultural and social phenomena and use stories as a primary data source while situating personal experiences within a wider cultural context. Shared here are some of my experiences, including emotions, thoughts, and actions, concerning mothering disabled children who have lifetime support needs. Reflections and subjective descriptive responses to these experiences are included as I critically examine my own experiences and how they are influenced by and contribute to broader social structures, cultural norms, or historical contexts. Cultural contexts are also considered, as I am an immigrant to Aotearoa New Zealand from another culture, and our family has a unique cultural background. Autoethnographic storytelling often examines power dynamics, conflicts, and negotiations within our relationships. The goal of sharing stories and insights is to provide a deep understanding of social issues that can resonate with others who share similar experiences as mothers of disabled children requiring lifetime support due to disability. The following vignettes arise from the topics identified in the literature review: day-to-day living, worries and concerns about the future, and planning for the future.

Author Reflexivity: A Critical Self-Awareness of My Role in Shaping the Narrative and Analysis

Throughout this autoethnography, I use "we" to refer to my husband and me, as our parenting is deeply collaborative. However, the experiences and reflections shared are my own, shaped by our shared journey as a family navigating disability and adoption.

Day-to-Day Living

It is a typical school morning at our house, with our two children who have Down syndrome. L is sixteen, legally blind, hearing impaired, nonspeaking, and has orthopaedic issues and other health complexities. T is thirteen, and besides her Down syndrome, she wears hearing aids and has autism, ADHD, and epilepsy. She cannot be out of sight of an adult at any time. T also has significant sleep disorders, so although she is running around the house at breakfast time, with great exuberance, my husband and I are tired, with severe sleep deprivation.

We are cheerful and persuasive throughout the morning and match the energy L and T start with. I try to let my good cheer and enthusiasm shine through my tiredness. By the time our morning carer arrives at 7:30 a.m., we have all been awake for many hours and have kept T occupied and kept L off devices and screens, as that will prevent him from getting ready for school. T might have unlocked a door and found hidden keys and her way into our car to honk the horn if both of us parents had happened to be distracted for any length of time. Our neighbours do not like these 3:00 a.m. wake-ups! Despite slight feelings of embarrassment, T delights me with her mischief. We have helped L and T with bathroom routines and dressed the children. We have made sure a child feeds our beloved service dog and have breakfast underway.

When our carer arrives, we parents can take turns supervising L and T, getting ourselves showered and dressed and ready for work while we pack lunches and school bags, ensuring charged hearing aids and communication devices, glasses, spare clothes, lunches, and school and home communication books are in school bags. It can be a struggle to persuade L and T to move along and eat, take all medications, brush their hair and teeth, wash their faces, put on their jackets, and get out the door for the van that comes to our home to take them to their high school. The bus driver will theoretically wait up to five minutes, but is not patient, and if our children take more than thirty seconds to get on the van, or have a sudden toileting need, we will receive a complaint. The pressure is sometimes intense and can result in tears from a child or me before the school day begins.

My husband and I breathe a sigh of relief and sometimes take a moment to acknowledge any sweet or funny moments from L or T that morning, as the van drives off and we then scramble to get ourselves off to work. One of us usually must work from home, as most days there is a medical appointment, school meeting, speech therapy session, therapeutic riding session, or dance class that a parent must be there for. Children have been frequently sent home from school with colds, or if they just weren't being cooperative. Work can feel like a reprieve, but I do take pleasure in intentionally prioritizing L and T, and that is satisfying. On office days, before I can settle into work, I text, email, phone, and return communication with several people: after-school carers, if we have one for the day, teachers, therapists, doctors, lawyers, accountants, or the benefits office or any of several agencies we work with on behalf of L and T. Approximately 50 per cent of the time, our contracted carers will cancel, and I must scramble to rearrange work schedules, transportation, etc. After my six-hour morning shift, if all things align, I can get to work and try to accomplish my paid work duties.

This routine captures much of my identity as a mother to disabled children with significant support needs. The pace is sometimes gruelling and requires resilience to function in a society where there is some support but little understanding of our family needs. Despite the difficulty of the routine, we are good at it, can cope with it, and can find joy within it. My identity is very much formed by the caregiving role I fulfil and the other family roles as organizer, choreographer, diplomat, advocate, teacher, and spouse. My academic role fits beautifully into our family life, as I am a disability researcher and lecturer. I conduct and supervise disability-related research, and I teach future disability service providers. As a disabled woman (I am vision impaired and have chronic health conditions), I was a disability academic and advocate long before my children entered our lives. I am an immigrant to Aotearoa New Zealand, and although I have been here for decades, I still can feel isolated from family, friends, support systems, and cultural contexts that I used to understand well. I am continually learning here, in a new country. As an adoptive mom, I can feel the pressure to cope without asking for support. After all, I told the judge and first/birth families that I could handle L's and T's disabilities. I have been repeatedly told by friends and acquaintances, "You get no sympathy from me: you knew what you were getting into." I have to remind myself that no parent knows what parenting will be like, and there is no predicting how challenging systems, schools, healthcare, finances and disability support could be. This bite-sized view of our morning routine is just a glimpse into our lives. We are so busy that we do not have much time to reflect, think, or plan for our children's futures, although the thoughts of their long-term needs contribute to my lack of sleep. Yet I am thrilled to be a mother to these two, who are exuberant, joyful, and so much fun. Despite never imagining I would mother two children with complex needs, it suits me. I cope well with it. Mothering seemed right from the moment I met them.

Worries and Concerns about the Future

It is the early morning hours, and dark outside. I fell asleep after cozy sessions of reading to L and T and made it into my bed several hours ago and have had a few disruptions already; one child has awoken and stealthily emptied all milk cartons and juice bottles, despite our cupboards and refrigerator being locked. I cleaned that up and cleaned the child. She is now in my bed, and I can hear her soft snore. I'm fretting. I'm thinking about the papers on my desk. They are not the papers I will be teaching from or drafts of my most recent journal articles or research statistics; the papers I am worried about are our tax forms, wills, applications for welfare benefits my 16-year-old son now needs, and my annual letter of intent I must revise, which explains all about my two children, their histories, routines, likes and dislikes, our wishes for their future and contact details of all of the distant relatives and nearby friends we hope will stay in their lives after my husband and I are gone.

Thoughts of who will care for them send electric waves of fear and anxiety through me as my daughter sleeps between my husband and me. Are we doing enough? Have we done a disservice to these precious children by adopting them when we were so old? Will they be safe? Will they be loved? Will they be able to live together, or are their needs too different? Who will understand their speech like I do? Can I save enough money for them to have a good life for the rest of their lives? I want them to be able to have a service dog, which is such a comfort to my son. I want them to have a decent home, loving caregivers, and somebody who can tell when they are in pain. Who will keep them involved in their church and make sure they can vote? I need them to have up-to-date technology and clothes that help them to look and feel nice and put together. I want them to have ongoing speech therapy and funds to transport them to Special Olympics events. I want them to live in small family-like homes rather than an institution. The news is filled with announcements of cuts to disability services and about abuse of disabled people in care. My research highlights that disabled people are physically and sexually abused at horrifyingly high rates. I'm fiercely protecting them now, but who will do this when I'm gone? Depending upon which government is in power at any given time, my children and other disabled adults and children will get more or less protection, support, healthcare, housing, and more. It's too painful to think about, so I put in my earbuds and listen to a funny podcast at 4:00 a.m. for a while. And then my daughter giggles and kicks and tickles me. She is awake. Time to start our day. I will adapt to what the day brings and enjoy L and T's exuberant antics. Despite the worry, I love my mothering roles. I am grateful I can manage many of the things I think and worry about. I can experience the joy of parenting, alongside the worry and the work.

Planning for the Future

For me, the way to alleviate worry is to plan. Fortunately, as a long-time disabled woman and a disability and disaster researcher, I am a good planner. I work at it as if it is my third full-time job. Here, I present some of the emotional, practical, and systemic aspects of planning for the long-term future of my children.

Regarding their cultural and familial futures, we keep trying to integrate L and T into the church of our upbringing in hopes that our church will provide a lifelong supportive community for them. But it is not currently terrifically accommodating. I work with our church to be more welcoming and diverse. The rituals and traditions I grew up with are important, and my husband and I want to pass these on. We also work hard to maintain contact with L's and T's first families and cultures. We maintain long-distance relationships with relatives back home as well as continuously cultivating friends of all ages to be family to our children in the future. I feel like just hunkering down with my little family at home sometimes, where we feel safe and secure together. This longing for security is paired with a sense of responsibility and a sense of awareness about the need to reach out, stay engaged with the outside world, and keep others a part of our lives for the benefit of L and T and me, too.

Part of the planning is that I keep records of my children's lives. As one child is mostly nonspeaking, and the other is difficult to understand, I keep their stories, our family stories, their adoption stories, and their adventures at school and beyond. We keep records of celebrations, milestones, and achievements, which can be so exhilarating to revisit, despite the challenges. This is for their future and for those who will love and care for them when I can no longer do that. Sharing my children's successes is not just telling their story—I am advocating for change. Their achievements help challenge stereotypes, expand possibilities, and push society towards greater inclusion and understanding.

We stay on top of L's and T's medical conditions and keep good records so these can easily be passed on when necessary. Children with Down syndrome can experience a myriad of health issues throughout their lives. So, we stay on top of eye health, oral health, hearing, neck instability, heart health, the possibility of celiac disease, diabetes, leukaemia, and thyroid issues. We protect them from falls and injuries to their unstable necks. We pay for private health insurance in hopes that this will help them in the future. We have introduced L and T to sport and exercise, and gyms, and we hope and plan to create a lifelong love for activity in them.

Legal and financial considerations take up a lot of time. My husband and I write wills and update the information yearly. We have set up family trusts and appointed legal guardianship. We consult with financial planners and tax experts. It is a constantly shifting space, and it's hard to stay on top of things and reassure ourselves that we can only try our best. We are saving like fiends, as we have to save for our retirement and for our children, for the rest of their lives—not just for the rest of my life. We try to teach the children about money and savings, and how to use their debit cards.

L's and T's education takes continuous effort, with IEPs, communication with the school, and ongoing home education, because they cannot possibly get all they need at school. We are so fortunate to finally be in a good space, with a great school.

We nurture L's and T's skills and abilities, and from a very early age, we have explored with them possibilities for future paid, meaningful work. We hope and advocate for supported employment schemes that will help give meaning to our children's lives in the future.

We continuously nurture our networks for the sake of L's and T's futures. But friendships shift and change, and sometimes we find our only support is what we pay for. We hope and trust L's and T's charm will win them friendships and support throughout their lives.

Institutional and professional support creates frustration. The disability support system in Aotearoa New Zealand is currently under attack by our new conservative government. We have fought alongside other parents and disabled persons to gain funding for essentials, flexible spending, and individual funding. These are all currently under threat, not just in Aotearoa New Zealand but in Australia and other parts of the world, too. So, we rely on our resources and our friendships, which are mostly with other parents of disabled children.

The emotions that come with managing complex health, legal, and financial matters can include overwhelm, anxiety, frustration, and exhaustion, along with determination, pride and hope. Our plans evolve as L and T grow, and we now also think about future living situations, future jobs, and most importantly, the future happiness of our two precious charges. We are tired. And we continue to grow and learn. I'm very fearful for the future of my children, but mostly, I marvel at their growing personalities, skills, and strengths.

Discussion

Although the vignettes depict the challenges of mothering disabled children, the overarching themes reflect my evolving perspective—one shaped by love, resilience, and the ways we navigate these experiences. The overriding themes that emerge from the analysis of the autoethnographic vignettes are coping, hoping, and loving. Coping with day-to-day life with disabled children can be challenging, but not because of the children. Our children are our primary sources of joy and fulfilment. The challenges we and our children cope with, according to the social model of disability, are not impairments. It is the barriers and attitudes within society that are disabling: "The idea behind the social model of disability stemmed from the Fundamental Principles of Disability document first published in the mid-1970s (UPIAS, 1976) which argued that we were not disabled by our impairments but by the disabling barriers we faced in society" (Oliver 1024). Disabling barriers we cope with include dealing with bureaucratic financial issues, noninclusive social constructs in our schools and society in general, legal challenges, and logistics of finding and maintaining support. These are the day-to-day challenges that can be unique to mothers of disabled children with long-term support needs. Complex mothering can enhance the barriers we encounter, such as racism, ableism, and ageism. Our responsibilities can include working to dismantle these barriers for our children, families, and others.

One way to manage is to operate with a semblance of hope—hope that our planning and hard work will benefit our children in the future. Hope can be a sustaining force; it is not just optimism or wishful thinking but action in the face of ongoing challenges. Hope has been known to help caregivers by reducing burnout and increasing motivation; it can help us find joy and meaning in caregiving tasks (Jones). Communities of support we find with other mothers of disabled children can play an important role in fostering hope as we share experiences and collectively problem solve. This support can help us acknowledge challenges to maintaining hope in the face of systemic barriers to inclusion, lack of resources, and the stigma our children face.

We call for and fight for social justice in our country and communities; I write letters, do public speaking, support other mothers, and involve my children in events, sports, and activities, working to make inclusion happen at camp, school, church, and community events. Systemic change is slow, infuriatingly so. But who better to work for this than a mother who knows her children's gifts and limitations and what is needed for inclusion?

Finally, perhaps most importantly, the love we share with our children sustains us. Few studies discuss the more positive aspects of family strength, resilience, growth, and the love shared with disabled children (Bossert et al.; Canam). However, we have found that a lens of love with our children helps us to express the emotional depth of the mothering experiences. When mothering is complex, love can strengthen resilience and foster empathy, patience, commitment, and connection—all of which can help us sustain our families, help others, and change society. With love at the core of our stories, our children's voices and perspectives can be respected and protected. I challenge deficit models of disability as tragedy or burden and wish to emphasize the value and richness of diverse family experiences.

These autoethnographic vignettes, which have addressed various themes, position this story within a larger academic discourse on motherhood. Personal reflection can expand the storytelling into a critical analysis of societal structures, policies, and cultural influences on the experience of mothering disabled children. Marie Porter writes about her personal experience of mothering a profoundly disabled son and reflects upon not only her loss of identity and marginalization but also the intense love shared. Although I as an older, adoptive mother, mothering in the 2020s with a husband who is a hands-on parent, have not experienced a similar refraction of self in my mothering, as expectations of mothers have changed, I have been able to continue to enjoy and find fulfilment at work, and disability was already a core aspect of my life before I became a mother. But our stories share similarities of intense love, strength, confidence, and identity, which can grow in the face of exhaustion, marginalization, social injustice, and exclusion due to disability. There are crucial lessons from motherhood scholars who have shared their experiences. There are limits to our ability to cope; we need support. Mothers do not have to manage alone, and we can flourish in our paid work and our families. Yet mothering disabled children can be lonely, isolated, and alienating.

Decades ago, Sara Ruddick explored the ethics of care, relationship dynamics, and the labour involved in caregiving, both emotional and intellectual. She wrote about mothering and the knowledge, skills, and expertise we can gain through caregiving roles. Through the lens of feminist thought and with an examination of ethics, Ruddick's work has powerful lessons for mothers raising disabled children in the 2020s. Andrea O'Reilly revisited Ruddick's earlier work with a profound quote: "We have no realistic language in which to capture the ordinary and extraordinary pleasures and pains of maternal work" (515). My autoethnographic piece attempts to capture with words some of the pleasures and pains of the maternal work of mothering disabled children.

Conclusion

This autoethnographic study on caring for disabled children with long-term support needs contributes to the body of knowledge on this subject with some unique perspectives. Unlike many studies that predominantly focus on the challenges and difficulties faced by parents and the struggle for normality and normalization, with these narratives and their analysis, I wish to highlight a hopeful and affirming perspective and embrace a view with some more positive lenses. Although I acknowledge the challenges and sometimes overwhelming worry that come along with caring for my children, these narratives centre on the empowerment found in proactive planning and the vital support mother networks provide. The profound reciprocal love we have with our children allows us to embrace the hardships and develop resilience, solidarity, and deep emotional bonds and enchantment with our children that enrich our lives. By sharing these experiences and telling and reflecting upon personal stories, perhaps there can be a broadened understanding of caregiving beyond the burdens and difficulties to endure and an emphasis on the empowering aspects and strengths that can arise from our journeys as mothers.

The closing vignette illustrates the practical, emotional, and intellectual journey explored in this chapter, offering a lived example of how I cope with day-to-day problem solving, hope for remarkable outcomes, and enjoy the love that is a part of my mothering experiences.

My son just had his sixteenth birthday. All he wanted was a cell phone. I researched what phone and apps would work for a nonverbal, vision-impaired, and learning-disabled teen. I bought the phone and got it set up with the help of a few technicians who were open to learn about what was needed. I taught my son about safely carrying it around and have set up multiple parental controls. I coped with all the technology I had to get on top of for this phone, the problem solving, and the cost. I'm proud of learning what I did and even advocating with the technicians. Then I hoped L would be safe with it, and it might allow for a bit of independence and social inclusion, now and in the future. This phone has allowed him to text overseas family and classmates.

Yesterday, while I was at work, I got a text from my son: I love you, Mom.

I was flooded with pride and delight, as I had not heard those words from my son before. It was such a relief we found a tool for him to communicate with, and he grasped it so quickly.

This loving message from my son grounds me and reminds me why I cope, manage, plan, worry, and love.

Appendix: Checklists to Help with the Planning for Parenting Disabled Children

Parenting disabled children demands love, resilience, and practical knowledge. This appendix lists key tasks to be considered—things I have learned and others that have been shared with me by other mothers over time. While the list may seem overwhelming, it simply reflects our reality. Seeing it all written down is both daunting and validating, affirming the work we do. Yet a list is also finite; it offers structure, reassurance, and a way to bring order to the chaos.

Daily Care Checklist:

- Morning routine (bathing, dressing, and preparing breakfast)
- Medication administration
- Physical, occupational, and speech therapy, or other therapy-related exercises
- Maintenance, care, and use of specialized disability-related equipment (e.g., hearing aids, augmentative communication aids, wheelchairs or other mobility aids, and glasses).
- Educational activities and school preparation
- Mealtime preparation and feeding
- After-school care and activities, rest, and homework

- Evening routine (dinner, hygiene, and bedtime)
- Allow time and planning for flexibility and adaptability, and manage moods, meltdowns, and physical or emotional crises
- Daily observations and notes, and communication with teachers, schools, therapists, and other carers
- Time devoted to the social and emotional needs of the children
- Self-care for caregivers, if there is a spare moment
- Visits to doctors, therapists, schoolteachers, specialists, and case managers
- Phone calls regarding medical issues, insurance, benefits, and legal documents
- Checking on and communicating with carers, advertising, training, contracting, and paying carers

Support Needs Checklist:

- Medical appointments and follow-ups
- Prescriptions and maintain devices
- Therapy sessions (physical, occupational, and speech)
- Documentation of medications, effects, and changes
- Educational support (IEP meetings and special education services)
- Social and recreational activities
- Respite care arrangements.
- Parent support groups and networks
- Family and extended family communication and relationship building
- Plans with our church and recreational supports

Financial Planning Checklist:

- Budget for daily and monthly expenses
- Bank accounts, debit cards, and online banking for children
- Long-term savings plans (be aware of the limit your child can have in their name to be eligible for government programs)

- Special needs trusts
- Insurance coverage (health, life, and disability)
- Government benefits and assistance programs
- Financial advice and planning services

Future Living Situations Checklist:

- Researching residential care options and funding
- Visiting potential living facilities
- Discussing future plans with family members
- Obtaining legal documentation for future care preferences
- Planning for transitioning from the current home to the future living arrangement
- Planning for future living costs
- Exploring potential relationships with other families for cooperative living

Legal Issues Checklist:

- Guardianship and conservatorship arrangements
- Healthcare proxies and advance directives
- Wills and estate planning
- Disability rights and advocacy resources
- Legal consultations for specific issues
- Updating legal documents regularly

Coping and Self-Care Checklist for Moms:

- Regular self-care activities (e.g., exercise, hobbies, and relaxation)
- Mental health support (e.g., therapy and counselling)
- Building a support network (e.g., friends, family, and support groups)
- Stress management techniques (e.g., meditation and mindfulness)

- Seeking respite care and taking breaks
- Setting realistic goals and expectations

Emergency Preparedness Checklist:

- Emergency contact list
- Medical information summary and passport (e.g., medications, allergies, and medical history)
- Emergency plan for natural disasters or other crises
- Backup power supplies for medical equipment
- Emergency supplies (e.g., food, water, medical supplies, and go bags)
- Communication plan with family and caregivers

Educational and Advocacy Checklist:

- Staying informed about disability rights and legislation
- Participating in advocacy groups
- Attending workshops and conferences on special needs care
- Educating others about disability awareness
- Collaborating with schools and educators for the children's benefit
- Keeping updated records of the children's progress and needs

The Most Important List

- Spend time with your children
- Take a moment to be present and attentive
- Foster their strengths and unique personalities
- Embrace and celebrate their abilities and disabilities
- Enjoy what they have to offer you and others
- Rest and help your child rest, relax, and have fun
- Remember the unconditional love and radical acceptance you have for your child and that they have for you can go a long way to alleviate worries

- Express love verbally and nonverbally and receive the love they offer
- Communicate in many ways to find what works best for you and your child
- Share activities and watch how these beloved shared times change as your child becomes an adult
- Encourage autonomy
- Celebrate milestones
- Be patient and understanding, and ask them to do that for you, too
- Offer comfort and reassurance
- Involve your children in your life by sharing your interests and creating an environment where they know they are cherished members of the family and community
- Take care of yourself
- Build and nurture your support network
- Make time for play and laughter
- Capture memories

Works Cited

Bossert, Elizabeth, et al. "Strategies of Normalization Used by Parents of Chronically Ill School-Age Children." *Journal of Child and Adolescent Psychiatric Nursing*, vol. 3, no. 2, 1990, pp. 57–61.

Cameron, S. J., et al. "Emotions Experienced by Mothers of Children with Developmental Disabilities." *Children's Health Care*, vol. 21, no. 2, 1992, pp. 96–102.

Braun, Virginia, and Victoria Clarke. *Thematic Analysis: A Practical Guide*. Sage, 2022.

Comerford, Susan A. "Advancing Social Work Education: The Transformative Power of Critical Autoethnography." *Qualitative Social Work: Research and Practice*, vol. 18, no. 5, 2019, pp. 772–86.

Gibbs, Anita. "Ethical Issues when Undertaking Autoethnographic Research with Families." *SAGE Handbook of Qualitative Research Ethics*. Edited by Ron Iphofen and Martin Tolich. Sage, 2018, pp. 148–60.

Good, Gretchen, et al. "Older, Professional Mothers: Identity and Disability." *Where Did I Go? Reflections on So-Called Late Mothering.* Edited by S. Mitchell and O. Sanmiguel-Valderrama. Demeter Press, 2022, pp. 53–64.

Good, Gretchen, et al. "Parenting during a Pandemic: Mothers and Disabled Children in Aotearoa/New Zealand: A Hidden Minority." *Journal of the Motherhood Initiative. Learning from the Pandemic. Possibilities and Challenges for Mothers and Families*, vol. 14, no. 1, 2023, pp. 45–64.

Good, Gretchen, et al. "Social Model Mothers: Disability, Advocacy and Activism." *Counterfutures—Navigating Activism and Academia*, vol. 4, 2017, pp. 107–35.

Johnson, Barbara Schoen. "Mothers' Perceptions of Parenting Children with Disabilities." *MCN, The American Journal of Maternal/Child Nursing*, vol. 25, no. 3, May 2000, pp. 127–32.

Jones, Darolyn, *The Joyful Experiences of Mothers of Children with Special Needs: An Autoethnographic Study*. 2011. Ball State University, dissertation. ProQuest Dissertations & Theses A&I, Sociological Abstracts, 869748620, https://www.proquest.com/dissertations-theses/joyful-experiences-mothers-children-with-special/docview/869748620/se-2.

Kewanian, Alina, et al. "Fierce Parenting: An Autoethnographic Study of Disability, Inclusion, and 'Othering.'" *International Journal of Qualitative Studies in Education*, vol. 37, no. 6, 2024, pp. 1736–51.

Lowenstein, Elisabeth, and Darolyn J. Jones. "Mother-Teacher-Scholar-Advocates: Narrating Work-Life on the Professorial Plateau." *Journal of Organizational Ethnography*, vol. 10, no. 2, 2021, pp. 132–46.

Oliver, Michael. "The Social Model of Disability: Thirty Years On." *Disability & Society*, vol. 28, no. 7, 2013, pp. 1024–26.

Porter, Marie. "Lost in Disability: Dis-abled by Love". *Mothers at the Margins: Stories of Challenge, Resistance and Love*. Edited by Lisa Raith, Jenny Jones, and Marie Porter. Cambridge Scholars Publishing, 2015, pp. 123–139.

Ruddick, Sara, and Andrea O'Reilly. "A Conversation About Maternal Thinking. *In (M)Other Words: Writings on Mothering and Motherhood, 2009–2024*. Edited by Andrea O'Reilly. Demeter Press, 2024, pp. 507–32.

Ruddick, Sara. *Maternal Thinking: Toward a Politics of Peace*. Beacon Press, 1989.

Runswick-Cole, Katherine, and Dan Goodley. "'The Disability Commons': Re-thinking Motherhood through Disability." *Palgrave Handbook of Disabled Children's Childhood Studies*. Edited by Katherine Runswick-Cole et al. Palgrave, 2017, pp. 231–46.

Runswick-Cole, Katherine, and Sara Ryan. "Liminal Still? Unmothering Disabled Children." *Disability & Society*, vol. 34, no. 7–8, 2019, pp. 1125–39.

Zibricky, Dawn C. "New Knowledge about Motherhood: An Autoethnography on Raising a Disabled Child." *Journal of Family Studies*, vol. 20, no. 1, 2014, pp. 39–47.

5.

Homeschooling, Cancer, and Letting Go: A Parenting Journey

Anne Borden King

Introduction

In 2012, when Ben was three, we tried preschool. It lasted one day.

Midway through the morning, according to the teacher, Ben tapped her leg. "We're done," he announced, in an echolalic rendition of a phrase I often used. I was thrilled by this story—he had initiated a conversation!—but Mrs. Markos was not impressed. She said he didn't listen, he didn't play right, he took off his shoes. He'd spent the morning trying to line up toys, creating a snaking, one-lane traffic jam through the classroom. She sighed in exacerbation: "He needs to share the toys."

It was more than that, of course. They wanted him out. That afternoon, my husband, Roger, and I sat on a bench as Ben raced across the deck of a playground pirate ship. It was time for a big decision. We'd heard stories from our friends about the school district's segregated special education classrooms, where Ben would have been streamed. Our friends' children had been restrained, locked in seclusion rooms, and faced capricious cruelty by staff. Meanwhile, the schools often banned parents from visiting the classrooms, even during pickup times. That day, we chose homeschooling.

It takes a village to raise a child, they say. Could we find this village outside of the world of school?

When Schools Fail Our Families

Schools play three roles in society: academic learning, social opportunities, and childminding. As Allison C. Carey and colleagues point out in the disability parenting book *Allies and Obstacles*, schools are supposed to contribute to the child's and the parent's wellbeing (13). Schools are more than a place of learning; they are a community institution.

When a child is denied a safe education and their family has to homeschool, they scramble to fill the school's role. First, at least one parent will lose income, and families must figure out a plan for financial security. They also must develop or adapt curriculum (a steep challenge for parents of kids with exceptionalities). Finally, homeschooling parents must find or create social opportunities outside of school, usually through a network of homeschooling families in their area. My family faced all these challenges.

But there is another challenge we seldom speak about: identity crisis. When our kids cannot go to school, we lose the neighbourhood community. School events, after-school hangouts… we are excluded from nearly all that. The parent who stays home is also losing their workplace community. Before we decided to homeschool, I had been a writer and editor, with success and opportunity in my field. Now, who was I? That fateful day at the playground, I had walked away from an income and an identity.

My new identity as "just a mom" was by the standards of some of my middle-class peers a status downgrade. *But,* I thought, *isn't being a mom an important job, too?* Not one to dwell, I quickly decided to make it my mission to represent Team Stay-Home. When people asked me what I did for a living, I stopped saying I was a writer. Instead, I kept it simple: "I'm a stay-at-home mom." While many folks reacted with a bored expression, others showed enthusiasm and curiosity. In a world where frazzled parents raced to pick up their kids from after-school care at 6:00 p.m. and had a hard time imagining any other kind of life, the idea of slowing down and staying home had a certain intrigue to them.

In the early days, I struggled with loneliness. I remember some days we would be all alone at the playground, and I would find myself jabbering away to an errant crossing guard or a nanny busy on her phone, just to get some adult conversation going. Luckily, my husband worked for himself and had the flexibility to be part of Ben's and my nine-to-five life. Where I had reverted to a more traditional role as mother, Roger was eschewing tradition by being a part of the hearth and home in the middle of a workday. Together, we launched sports and clubs to bring together Toronto homeschoolers. Being activity leaders had another advantage: There was no room for the club or team to exclude our child because we were the organizers.

My son and I also immersed ourselves in the city—learning the transit system and urban geography and visiting museums, libraries and endless new parks, all during the quieter hours when most kids were in school. We even got in some off-season travel. It took some time to appreciate the impact of what we were doing. We were preparing our autistic son for the real world by being in the real world instead of at school. By accepting that our son was different and adjusting our expectations, we benefited, too. We got to live life outside the box. And that was amazing.

In the early days, I felt like we were some of the only people in Canada homeschooling an autistic child. Most homeschoolers were religiously observant or freethinking unschoolers (two different approaches to child-rearing, as it happens!). But as years went by, more and more families like ours were choosing home education, often after a series of traumatic incidents in special education. When concerned friends and families told us only special education could serve Ben's needs, we could now point to the successes of that handful of other families.

But we did not have proof to back our leap of faith. Other than anecdotes, there was almost no supportive data about families like ours.

Homeschooling Autism Families: Happier, but Broke

In the past few years, there have been a few small studies about families that homeschool their autistic kids. In 2021, Siobhan O'Hagan and colleagues published a thematic review of ten articles about autistic homeschooling families (in the United States, the United Kingdom, and Australia). It focussed on the few, mostly qualitative, studies of small groups of homeschooling autism families. O'Hagan's review confirmed the experience of our family and of those we had met. We were homeschooling for the same reasons parents in the studies chose to, including "lack of flexible and inclusive practices" (O'Hagan et al.) at school, children being bullied, and "school staff's insufficient understanding of and attitude towards autism" (O'Hagan et al.), as well as lack of educational support at school.

We were getting the same results, too—mostly positive. "[Parents] report being able to provide flexible, balanced and individualized education leading to positive outcomes," O'Hagan's team writes. Parents reported a significant decrease in their children's meltdowns and self-harm once they were pulled from school. There was an increase in motivation and a decrease in stress for most homeschooled children.

Like us, parents across the studies reported feelings of relief that their kids no longer experienced high levels of anxiety, and they were flourishing. They reported that their children's social skills improved with regular extracurricular activities, as they had energy and flexibility because they were not burned out by the school day. That was our experience, too. "He is now happy, healthy and confident," said one parent. "He is showing an interest in a huge range of subjects. He is socializing more and full of energy, just like a child should be" (qtd. in Taylor et al.).

But none of these positives erase the economic hit of homeschooling. As the review notes, homeschooling families typically lost 50 per cent of household incomes because one parent was now staying home, with most eschewing even part-time work. In Ontario, families like mine are left with no financial or educational support; to add insult to injury, we are expected to continue to pay taxes for the school systems that excluded our kids.

Given this, you might assume that only wealthy parents homeschool their autistic children, but that is not the case. In our home education community in Toronto, countless working poor parents live precariously, barely making rent, to homeschool their autistic kids. The level of education and nurturance homeschooled kids receive in my community is not class stratified. Regardless of income, some parents act like naturals and are relaxed in the role. Still other parents, no matter their income, struggle with resentment and distractions.

Parents in O'Hagan's review reported feeling "resentment that they were forced into [homeschooling] to protect their child." In none of the studies did any parents report receiving financial support. (Only a few states and provinces provide stipends to homeschooling parents.) Yet "despite the financial implications, [parents reported they] were less stressed and happier home educating, as their children were less stressed and happier."

I felt the same way. Despite financial, professional, and social losses, I was still glad we chose to homeschool. I was not putting up a front anymore: I did feel proud of being a stay-at-home mom.

Something changed in me, mostly because my world had slowed down in those years. When I joined Ben in his special interests, when we broke away to wander for hours along the trails, I got a chance to take a breath from the rat race of the neurotypical world. I started seeing the world and my life goals differently. There was nothing more rewarding than finding those moments of connection and enjoying something together, quietly. Meanwhile, our concerned friends and family began to put away their skepticism and see the positive results.

Homeschooling was working out well. Until suddenly, it did not.

The Pandemic, Cancer, and Life Speeding Up

In 2019, I began to take on freelance gigs that I could do on my own time. Often, I would be cramming it in, like while waiting on a bench during swim lessons or early in the morning. I remember once penning a *New York Times* magazine feature while seated on the ground at the splash pad, hammering away at my laptop and trying not to get wet. A lot of my work from that time, including my volunteer advocacy on autism issues, was done in the late evening at my kitchen table, and more than once, I found my head dropping onto my keyboard, telling me in no uncertain terms: time for sleep.

Life was shifting. My son, now a tween, was doing more on his own. He got some new friends who went to school and decided he wanted to go to school, too. How that would all play out, I was not sure. We did have some time to make a plan, as it happened, because he had made his choice to go back to school during the pandemic shutdowns—at the same time that I was battling synchronous bilateral breast cancer.

My cancer diagnosis jolted me with concerns every mother would understand. Every thought or worry about whether I would be able to enjoy and live a long life was paired with an abiding anxiety: How would this affect Ben?

As lockdowns increasingly displaced many of our routines, Ben and I found ourselves wandering through the empty city, searching for... something. After each chemo session, I would spend days in a dreamy fog on the couch, as Roger and Ben searched for something new to do. Roger cofounded a pandemic biking club, and they played games at the soccer field with the neighbourhood kids (the same kids who'd always been too busy with school and extracurriculars before the school closures). Ben was building a new life—a new identity in some ways—and I was sleeping my way through much of it!

As schools reopened, we found an alternative school for grade nine. Despite the school's promises of being open minded, I girded myself for the work of advocacy. Roger and I knew we would have to deal with what Carey and colleagues describe as balancing autonomy from state control and receiving public support by entering into a social contract with the school. Predictably, in the first weeks of semester one, the scarlet letter of Ben's autism diagnosis was immediately flagged by the school administration. The vice principal and the guidance counsellor strongly encouraged us to enroll Ben in segregated special education classes at a large high school where he could, according to them, "thrive." But he seemed to be doing well academically and socially, and we saw no need to change anything. So, I contacted a disability law firm and had them help me to ensure that we would not be getting any more friendly recommendations to put him in a segregated program.

I became chair of the Parent Council and threw myself into advocacy for disabled students. I had never wanted to deal with schools, yet there I was, going through levels of bureaucracy to try to make a change for students. By the end of the year, I was exhausted; luckily, we found a better school for grade ten.

Now that Ben's settled in school, I have to rediscover my identity beyond "stay-at-home mom." With a fourteen-year gap in full-time employment, my resume looks weird—lacking any recent experience for jobs I might have had a decade ago yet overqualified or too old for entry-level jobs. I understand now why my mom would go to the salon to "paint her hair," as she put it. I will soon be doing the same thing, not out of vanity so much as to create a patina that places me ten years younger for a better chance in the workforce.

There is another huge thing—one I cannot forget, although I wish I could. I am considered a high-risk cancer patient, meaning the cancer may come back, metastasized. If that happens, my family will have to support and care for me, to be *my* advocate and interpreter. And it is also possible we may have to figure out a plan B for our son's adulthood, one that might not include me at all.

It has been therapeutic for me to volunteer to help with advocacy campaigns to get better support for autistic adults in my province. A few years ago, I cofounded Canada's autistic self-advocacy organization, and we are doing policy work and education. I also recently colaunched the autistic-led Autistic Health Access Project to educate health providers on how to communicate with autistic patients. I want my son to be able to go to the ER and be cared for as well as anyone else. It took a cancer diagnosis for me to understand I will not always be there beside him.

Life Transitions and the Work of Advocacy

When Ben was little, my neighbour used to call him my "shadow." Our togetherness was forged with love, to be sure, but also through necessity. We were exiled together at times, feeling the sting of exclusion and ableism. We ran to find spaces for recharging, together.

He is a teenager now, and his thoughts have turned to friends, girls, and the future... not so much hanging out with Mom. This, of course, is true for every autistic young person, no matter what their support needs are. Still, I am sometimes surprised to notice the new, bigger, and taller version of him before me, and it is in those moments that I see the teenage urge for autonomy and pride in self-reliance. I hope that what Roger and I provided in the early years can be scaffolding for his independence.

Getting on with life is my son's gig now, for sure. Mine is to figure out what life looks like without my shadow.

Greek mythology tells the story of Demeter, the goddess of the harvest. Through a twist of fate, each year as summer turned to autumn, she had to let her daughter Persephone be taken away from her to a colder and darker world for half the year. Demeter grieved every winter and was exultant in the springtime when reunited with Persephone.

The myth of Demeter and Persephone is not just about agriculture and seasons. It is a metaphor for parenthood. It has special meaning for parents of autistic young adults as we seek to shield them from the dark institutional spaces that still exist, where they are not truly free or supported. The joy we feel when we connect in the light signifies our closeness, but we also have to be sure we know how to let go. As parents, we must advocate for better options for our children's lives so we will not have to grieve like Demeter because we helped create spaces where our children can remain in the sunshine, feeling safe, happy, and free.

Works Cited

Carey, Allison C., et al. *Allies and Obstacles: Disability Activism and Parents of Children with Disabilities.* Temple University Press, 2020.

O'Hagan, Siobhan, et al. "What Do We Know about Home Education and Autism? A Thematic Synthesis Review." *Research in Autism Spectrum Disorders*, vol. 80, 2021, https://doi.org/10.1016/j.rasd.2020.101711.

Taylor, Elizabeth, et al. "No School Like Home and No Home Like School: Parents' Responses to the Badman Report and Its Recommendations." *British Education Research Association Annual Conference*, Institute of Education, London. 2011, https://www.researchgate.net/publication/292551535_No_school_like_home_parents'_responses_to_the_Badman_Report_and_its_recommendations. Accessed 12 Apr. 2025.

Section III

Intersectionality-Intersections

6.

Navigating the Intersections: The Complexities of Black Mother Caregivers of Division I Student-Athletes with Chronic Illnesses

Yvette C. Latunde

Introduction

This chapter explores the complexities of Black motherhood, career aspirations, and caregiving for Black female Division I student-athletes with chronic illnesses. Through an autoethnographic study, it highlights the challenges and strategies utilized in caring for my daughter, a Division 1 student-athlete with a chronic illness. The study emphasizes systemic barriers related to gender and race, including ignored requests, slow responses, and fragmented care within broader systemic oppressions. It underscores my use of education, mentorship, and empowerment to overcome these issues, advocating for systemic change to ensure equitable care and support for caregivers.

This chapter focusses on how I and other Black mother caregivers advocate for female student-athletes with chronic conditions. Using an intersectional lens, informed by Kimberlé Crenshaw's framework, the chapter examines how overlapping identities of race, gender, and socio-economic status create unique barriers to accessing quality healthcare.

It also draws on Patricia Hill Collins's Black feminist framework, which emphasizes the significance of lived experiences and the necessity of elevating the voices of Black women in discussions about systemic oppression. The intersectional approach reveals how I navigated complex educational, athletic, and healthcare systems while managing my career obligations, offering a nuanced perspective on the triumphs and challenges Black mothers face as caregivers to Division 1 athletes.

Although Black mothers have historically been influential advocates in education, health equity, and athletics, there is a gap in the literature focussing on their roles as caregivers to daughters with chronic illnesses or disabilities in competitive sports. This chapter addresses that gap, providing valuable insights for scholars, practitioners, and policymakers dedicated to supporting division student-athletes.

To understand the multifaceted roles of Black mothers in caregiving and advocacy, this chapter reviews existing literature on Black motherhood, health advocacy, and the intersection of race, gender, and socioeconomic status in caregiving. As the researcher and participant with lived experiences referenced in this study, I draw on my background as a daughter, mother, and university scholar on inclusion, diversity, equity, and community engagement to inform my perspectives and approach.

Review of the Literature

Historically, Black mothers have been pivotal in advocating for educational and health equity, often under challenging circumstances (Lovelace et al. 3). As family caregivers—adults informally caring for another adult, usually a relative or chosen family member (John Hopkins, "Being a Caregiver" 1)—they have been central figures in ensuring the wellbeing of their children. Mary McLeod Bethune and Fannie Lou Hamer were instrumental in promoting educational access and desegregation for Black youth through their advocacy (Britannica, "McLeod-Bethune" 1). Health advocates like Dr. Dorothy Height led efforts to improve healthcare access for Black women and children, addressing systemic disparities (Height). In athletics, pioneers like Althea Gibson and Wilma Rudolph broke barriers and promoted inclusivity, setting the stage for future generations of Black female athletes, including student-athletes—individuals recruited by colleges for intercollegiate athletics (NCAA 1) (Gibson 130; Rudolph 150).

In contemporary times, leaders such as Marian Wright Edelman, founder of the Children's Defense Fund, continue to champion policies supporting disadvantaged students, emphasizing early childhood education and nutrition programs (Edelman 116). Additionally, Omie Mills Cormier's efforts in Central California have been instrumental in addressing educational disparities through community-based initiatives (Latunde, *Equitable* 1).

Current Research Gaps

Despite these achievements, the literature reveals a fragmented and often outdated understanding of Black motherhood and caregiving, particularly in the context of supporting student-athletes with chronic illnesses—long-term health disruptions from communicable or noncommunicable diseases, conditions, syndromes, or disorders (American Psychological Association 1). For instance, a meta-analysis (Cousino and Hazen 809) of thirteen studies and a qualitative analysis of ninety-six studies examined the parenting stress experienced by caregivers of children with chronic illnesses. While results showed these caregivers reported significantly higher general parenting stress compared to caregivers of healthy children ($d = .40$; $p \leq .0001$), little is known about the intersections of race, class, and gender in these experiences for parents and children.

Moreover, most scholarship on Black Division I athletes focusses on males, revealing a significant gap in research on female athletes (Leonard 317). Many of these studies were published between 1980 and 2006, highlighting the need for updated research addressing current challenges and dynamics (Harrison and Lawrence 280).

Caregiving Roles, Responsibilities, and Challenges

Caregiving—providing short- or long-term care for those experiencing illness or disability (John Hopkins, "Being a Caregiver" 1)—encompasses a spectrum of responsibilities varying in duration and intensity, from medical decision-making and medication management to coordinating appointments and advocating across health, educational, or athletic systems (John Hopkins 1). These roles intersect with social factors, such as race and gender, significantly influencing the caregiving experience

(Taylor 3). Studies show women generally assume more caregiving tasks and experience distress (Pinquart and Sorensen 33–45). Many caregivers do not identify themselves as such, despite about forty million Americans providing care for family or friends (John Hopkins, "Being a Caregiver" 1). The family caregiver concept is increasingly recognized as vital alongside healthcare professionals and care recipients (Dilworth-Anderson et al. 208).

Race and Caregiving

In African American families, daughters often take on caregiving responsibilities, whereas in white families, spouses typically do (Carter et al. 1). African American women caregivers frequently face higher socioeconomic challenges, compounding their caregiving stressors (Taylor 3). Differences in values, beliefs about aging, role expectations, and religious practices may explain why African American caregivers experience less stress and find more fulfillment in caregiving than white caregivers (Dilworth-Anderson et al. 208). African American caregivers often perceive caregiving as a familial obligation and draw strength from faith and community support, enhancing their resilience amid challenges (Cox 164). Despite confronting greater socioeconomic disparities, African American caregivers exhibit comparable or lower depressive symptoms than their white counterparts, underscoring the complex dynamics of caregiving experiences (Smith et al. 571).

Caregiving and Division Athletes

The intersection of race, gender, and chronic illness compounds challenges for Black mother caregivers (Ockimey 54). Systemic barriers and discrimination in healthcare, athletics, and education exacerbate difficulties in managing chronic illnesses, affecting academic and athletic performance (Lewis et al. 420–40). Addressing these challenges requires empowering Black women through advocacy efforts that promote awareness, culturally competent healthcare, mentorship, and systemic reforms (Bowleg 1267; Crenshaw 1241).

Laws like HIPAA, FERPA, and ADA protect student-athletes with chronic illnesses, ensuring privacy and accommodations (US Department of Health and Human Services 1; US Department of Education 1; US

Department of Justice 1). However, these laws also emphasize the need for student-athlete autonomy in healthcare and educational decisions, which can impact parental involvement and caregiving, including that of Black mothers advocating for their children's needs (US Department of Education, Office for Civil Rights 1).

Hannah Cardoso Barbosa et al. emphasize that patient education is key to empowering individuals with chronic illnesses, leading to better decision-making, health outcomes, and sustained behaviour change (Barbosa et al. 689–702). For Division 1 student-athletes managing chronic conditions, empowerment is equally essential. Balancing academics, athletics, and health challenges requires an environment fostering education and support, enabling them to thrive both on and off the field (Walton et al. 2).

Impacts, Coping, and Caregiving

In a groundbreaking study examining Black mother caregivers, Sandy Magana et al. investigated the mental and physical health of older Black mothers caring for adult children with schizophrenia compared to their peers without such caregiving responsibilities (712). The study hypothesized that caregiving mothers would experience higher emotional distress and more physical health issues due to the stress of caregiving. However, findings showed no significant differences in mental and physical health outcomes between the two groups. Yet differences emerged in physical health indicators, highlighting the unique stressors associated with caregiving.

Caregiving and Stress

Research shows caregivers of children with chronic illnesses face higher stress (Magana et al. 711). These illnesses include asthma, cancer, cystic fibrosis, diabetes, epilepsy, juvenile rheumatoid arthritis, and sickle cell disease. The results indicate these caregivers reported significantly higher general parenting stress compared to caregivers of healthy children ($d = .40$; $p \leq .0001$). This stress was linked to the greater parental responsibility for treatment management and was unrelated to the duration and severity of the illness across different populations (Cousino and Hazen 809). Additionally, higher parenting stress was associated with poorer psychological adjustment in both caregivers and children with chronic illnesses.

Stress and Black Women

Black feminism, according to Collins, is a critical social theory examining how race, gender, and class intersect to shape Black women's experiences, emphasizing their unique standpoint, lived knowledge, and resistance to oppression (Collins 200). Stress and health disparities are prominent themes in the literature on caregiving, particularly among Black women. They often face compounded stressors due to caregiving responsibilities, career context, and societal expectations (Cox 164). Studies highlight how Black mothers, who predominantly assume caregiving roles, face unique challenges in managing stress.

A Caregiver's Journey

The journey of becoming a caregiver for my daughter, Ebony, began with a slow but undeniable shift in her health. In the spring of 2020, at just eighteen years old, she embodied vitality—intelligent, athletic, and full of life. But beneath the surface, something was changing. Her health began to decline, casting uncertainty over the bright future she had worked so hard to build.

When schools abruptly shut down due to the pandemic, Ebony found herself isolated during her final year of high school, cut off from the structure and energy of in-person learning and athletic training. As a dedicated athlete with collegiate aspirations, the disruptions were devastating. Her training schedule was thrown into disarray; her education shifted to an unfamiliar online format, and the once-clear path towards college athletics became clouded with confusion and doubt.

Soon, Ebony began experiencing troubling symptoms—night sweats, extreme fatigue, and more. Seeking medical help during the height of COVID-19 was a frustrating and disheartening process. Routine doctor visits led to repeated trips to the ER and urgent care centres, where her concerns were too often dismissed. The systemic barriers within healthcare, compounded by the challenges of being a young Black woman seeking medical attention, left us feeling unheard and powerless. After persistent advocacy, multiple grievances, and a long wait, a referral was finally granted—but by then, the damage, both physical and emotional, had already taken its toll.

There was no denying something was seriously wrong, and I had no choice but to step into the role of caregiver. But caregiving did not mean I could put everything else on hold. My career, my professional responsibilities, and my family's financial stability all demanded my attention. As Ebony's health deteriorated, I became her fiercest advocate, fighting for answers while navigating an often-indifferent healthcare system. At the same time, I was amid a critical tenure review, facing mounting professional pressures, and carrying the full financial burden of our household. Despite being married, I was the sole income earner, working three jobs to keep us afloat. The relentless juggling act—balancing my daughter's health crisis, my career, and our financial survival—was exhausting, stretching me to my absolute limits. Yet I had no option to pause. Ebony needed me, and I had to keep pushing forwards.

Despite the overwhelming challenges, I remained steadfast in my commitment to her. I focussed on her recovery, supported her dreams of becoming a healthy student-athlete, and held onto hope even when I felt like I was barely holding myself together. The journey was infuriating and, at times, depleting, but it deepened my resolve and strengthened our bond. Ebony's determination to fight through her health struggles became my inspiration. Together, we faced every challenge head-on and drew strength from each other, navigating her health and future with resilience, love, and unwavering faith.

Methodology

The following questions guided this autoethnographic case study:

1. What were the experiences of a Black mother caregiving for her daughters through the combined pressures of high-level athletics, academics, and chronic illness management?

2. What strategies do Black mothers use to navigate those challenges?

Setting and Context

The study focused on my experiences of caregiving for my daughter, a Black female Division 1 student-athlete with a chronic illness. This study takes place in the United States (US). At the time of this study, I was a full professor at a teaching university, an adjunct at another, a consultant with county offices of education, and undergoing a tenure review, all while serving as my daughter Ebony's primary caregiver. Balancing these professional responsibilities with caregiving required careful management of time and resources, as I navigated multiple roles simultaneously. The demands of my career, coupled with the urgency of supporting Ebony's health and wellbeing, created an ongoing tension between professional obligations and personal responsibilities.

Ebony, a Black female student-athlete, was enrolled in a rigorous academic health sciences program, carrying fifteen to eighteen units per semester. In addition to her coursework, she maintained an intense schedule of athletic practices and games, which required significant travel. Without a car or employment, she relied solely on public transportation to meet her academic and athletic commitments, adding another layer of difficulty to an already demanding schedule. As her health declined, these challenges became even more pronounced, forcing her to balance medical appointments, coursework, and athletic responsibilities while managing the physical and emotional toll of illness.

The study spanned two states and included one private four-year degree-granting institution in the East, as well as two major health insurers. These settings provided the context for examining the multiple responsibilities Ebony and I navigated as we worked to maintain stability in her academic and athletic pursuits while addressing her health concerns.

Autoethnographic Approach and Intersectional Framework

Autoethnography serves as the most effective method to foreground my personal experiences and reflections on Black mother caregiving. I use this approach to describe and critique prevailing beliefs about Black individuals and practices concerning Black Division I student-athletes and their caregivers. This method allows me to provide insights into issues and contexts that would be nearly impossible to convey through other research approaches. Since autoethnography is infused with cultural norms related to Black women and caregivers, as well as the treatment of Black people in healthcare and academia, it is an ideal fit for this study. Scholars utilized autoethnography to document and analyze the lived experiences of marginalized individuals, particularly Black women (Collins; Crenshaw; Griffin; Toyosaki; Pensoneau-Conway). Intersectionality shapes the analytical lens of this study by emphasizing the interconnectedness of various social identities and systems of oppression. Rather than isolating a single factor, such as gender or race, intersectionality provides a framework for examining how these identities interact and shape lived experiences in complex ways. Although not all these scholars explicitly employ intersectionality as a framework, their work demonstrates a shared interest in understanding the complexities of identity and the role of social structures in shaping these experiences.

Crenshaw's intersectionality framework highlights how overlapping systems of oppression—such as race, gender, and class—interact to create distinct experiences for individuals at the intersections of multiple marginalized identities. This theoretical approach informs the autoethnographic analysis in this study by guiding a nuanced examination of the experiences of a Black mother in the contexts of academia, healthcare, and caregiving. Collins also contributes to this understanding through her concept of Black feminist thought, which emphasizes the interconnectedness of race, gender, and class, as well as the role of communal support in Black caregiving. Though not explicitly framed in terms of intersectionality, both frameworks provide a critical lens for examining how these overlapping systems of power affect the caregiving experience.

Satoshi Toyosaki and Sandra L. Pensoneau-Conway argue that writing autoethnographies can be seen as the "praxis of social justice" (558), as they allow the researcher to critically reflect on personal experiences and engage with the broader social structures shaping them. This praxis is essential for challenging dominant narratives and offering an alternative to traditional research methods that often overlook marginalized voices. Similarly, Rachel Alicia Griffin uses autoethnography to document her justified anger as a Black woman, illustrating how emotions like anger are not merely personal reactions but are deeply informed by systemic oppression and racialized experiences (413). These scholars' approaches underscore the power of autoethnography as a form of resistance against dominant social structures, which aligns with my purposes and intent for this study.

Data Collection and Analysis

In this study, the application of both autoethnography and intersectionality serves as a powerful tool for analyzing the experiences of a Black mother navigating the complexities of caregiving, race, and gender. The data collection process focussed on documents providing insight into these layered experiences, beginning with 139 emails exchanged with various stakeholders, including state health insurance providers, medication distributors, and university healthcare services. These emails provide a crucial record of the advocacy efforts required to navigate healthcare and academic systems for my Division I student-athlete daughter, highlighting the intersection of race, gender, and institutional barriers in my caregiving role.

Additionally, sixty-five emails related to my health and professional responsibilities were analyzed. These emails reflect the emotional and logistical challenges of balancing caregiving with professional and personal obligations while also highlighting the intersection of my identity as a Black mother and a professor. Journal entries from 2020 to 2023 were also included in the analysis, offering a more personal and emotional insight into my caregiving experiences and the psychological toll they took. Text messages, phone logs, and notes from 2022 to 2024 provided further data on the daily dynamics of my advocacy for my daughter's autonomy and health, adding depth to the understanding of the relational aspects of caregiving.

The data analysis process was shaped by the principles of intersectionality, recognizing the systems of power shaping caregiving experiences cannot be understood in isolation. As Crenshaw notes, race, gender, and class intersect to create unique challenges for individuals, and this study sought to document how these overlapping factors influenced my experiences as a Black mother and caregiver. In coding the data, the focus was on identifying themes and patterns revealing the complexities of navigating multiple systems of power, including healthcare, academia, and athletics. These themes were explored with a critical eye towards how race and gender shaped responses, interactions, and emotions.

In presenting the data, intersectionality and autoethnography allowed for a narrative honouring the complexity of the caregiving experience. Rather than reducing the experience to isolated factors, such as race or gender, this approach highlighted the interconnectedness of these factors and the ways they shaped my advocacy and resistance. As Griffin demonstrates, justified emotions, such as anger, are not personal flaws but responses to systemic injustice, and this study similarly positions my caregiving experiences within the larger context of social and institutional inequality (411). By using intersectionality as a framework, this autoethnographic analysis provides a holistic understanding of the challenges faced by Black mothers in caregiving roles while also resisting the reductionist tendencies of traditional research methods.

A Discussion of the Findings

The themes emerging from this study shed light on the complex and multifaceted nature of caregiving for Black mothers, particularly those navigating the intersections of race, gender, and systemic barriers. Through the lens of my personal experiences as a Black mother, several significant themes emerged: gendered caregiving and systemic barriers, complexities within healthcare systems, empowerment (both self and for my daughter), and mentoring and wellbeing.

Gendered Caregiving and Systemic Barriers

As a Black woman in the US, I assumed primary caregiving responsibilities, navigating intersectional gender expectations that were compounded by systemic barriers in accessing healthcare (Taylor 1). In analyzing the data collected from multiple sources, I noticed many of my interactions highlighted concerns around healthcare access. I noted a recurring theme in my journal and email communications where I expressed frustrations about my daughter's healthcare needs being dismissed or overlooked. This finding was particularly significant, as my advanced education and professional networks played a crucial role in helping me overcome these challenges. However, these same factors underscore systemic inequities that disproportionately burden women of colour, many of whom may not have access to similar resources (Dababnah et al. 333).

Juggling multiple income-generating activities further emphasized the intersectional pressures I faced, as I balanced caregiving with professional demands, often in environments hostile toward Black women (Alexander 1030; Collins 9). For instance, managing a full-time job, consulting work, and additional tasks to support my daughter out of state highlighted the economic burdens I navigated daily (Carter et al. 5;

Taylor 3). This complex juggling act exemplifies the multifaceted nature of caregiving responsibilities and the additional hurdles faced when dealing with systemic barriers. These experiences, however, also left me feeling powerless at times and emotionally drained. The overwhelming demands of caregiving, combined with systemic inequities, often left me in a state of low energy and frustration, as I was continually required to advocate for my daughter's needs while facing recurring institutional barriers. This emotional toll reflected the ongoing struggle of navigating societal systems that fail to recognize the structural racism and social inequities baked into the fabric of US society and the intersectional nature of Black women's caregiving roles.

Complexities of Navigating Healthcare Systems

Despite the emotional toll, there was little time to dwell on these frustrations, as I had to remain proactive in navigating these complex systems to ensure my daughter received the care she needed. My experiences revealed significant challenges in accessing primary healthcare services, especially due to new insurance networks and state regulations after relocating to a different state (a blue state). I detailed in my communications how navigating the new insurance network was a daunting task, requiring numerous emails and phone calls to understand the coverage options and how to access them. Specialist referrals and long wait times only further complicated healthcare access, requiring a proactive approach to advocacy and leveraging networks for timely intervention (Carter et al. 5). In my journals, I documented instances where I collaborated with a nurse advocate to bypass referral requirements and expedite specialist appointments. This strategy was crucial in navigating bureaucratic hurdles (Carter et al. 5). Additionally, I encountered issues with laboratory tests that were requested in one state, conducted in another, and nearly impossible to relay back to the requesting specialist. This issue, detailed in my emails to both insurance companies and the university athletic department, further disrupted my daughter's access to medication and created significant challenges in understanding her health status. At times, these systemic barriers left us feeling powerless.

Empowerment

Although there were moments of hopelessness, we never completely lost hope. Our faith in God sustained us during these difficult times. We took pauses, when necessary, prayed for wisdom, and sought clarity for the next steps. We began tackling these challenges with empowerment through education. Throughout my caregiving journey, I took an active role in managing healthcare decisions and securing medication approvals across state lines by collaborating directly with healthcare providers and insurers. I made it a priority to educate myself about healthcare requirements and communicated persistently to ensure my daughter received the timely care she needed. This proactive approach aligns with caregiving literature, underscoring the importance of understanding the individual, the illness, and available care options to ensure continuity of care. My experience empowered me to navigate bureaucratic challenges and helped empower my daughter to advocate for herself in healthcare and educational settings (Barbosa et al. 689).

To secure optimal care, I worked closely with nurse advocates and filed grievances when necessary, which made me realize I had partners. These partnerships have been associated with improved health outcomes and greater satisfaction with the care process (Carter et al. 1). It gave me hope. My communications with health insurance companies, advocates, and university officials spanned a range of topics, from compliance inquiries to requests for support, highlighting the persistence required to ensure comprehensive healthcare access (Cousino 809; Cox 164).

My Daughter's Agency

Hope played a vital role in my caregiving journey, not only for me but also for my daughter. I needed to share that hope with Ebony, helping her understand its power in shaping her future. A central goal of my caregiving approach was to empower her to advocate for herself and build her agency. I consistently delegated tasks and responsibilities to her, encouraging a reciprocal relationship where she could also guide and support me. Involving her in decision-making processes was key. I encouraged Ebony to lean into her strengths—her relationships, hobbies, and interests—and to educate herself about her medication options, treatment plans, and health management strategies. Through modelling these actions, I helped her develop the skills and confidence needed to actively participate in decisions that would shape her life (Carter et al. 1).

Watching Ebony take ownership of her health and decisions was deeply rewarding. It was empowering to see her embrace challenges with a renewed sense of control and purpose. She found her voice not only in healthcare decisions but in other aspects of her life as well. Her growth was a testament to the transformative power of self-advocacy, and it brought us closer as a team, reinforcing our shared commitment to empowerment.

In addition to fostering her self-advocacy, I encouraged Ebony to seek mentorship, which played a crucial role in her health and wellbeing. One of her teachers introduced her to health literature and lessons on using food for healing, sparking an interest in cooking for herself. Her grandmother's advice, often conveyed through texts, emphasized the importance of eating and thinking well and praying. This mentorship contributed to Ebony's personal growth and enhanced her ability to take charge of her health. It was inspiring to watch as she internalized these lessons and began teaching me about well-being and health, demonstrating her increasing agency (Barbosa et al. 700).

Mentorship

The mentorship dynamic between Ebony and me was reciprocal, extending far beyond healthcare and into her social, academic, and career aspirations. While I guided her through the complexities of NCAA requirements and the intricacies of selecting courses aligning with her long-term goals, Ebony also mentored me in navigating the university context and its associated regulations. As we worked together, I helped Ebony identify suitable coursework, initiate conversations with academic advisors, and communicate with coaches. In turn, Ebony's insights into university policies, regulations, and systems played a pivotal role in helping me advocate for her health, academic, and athletic needs. This reciprocal mentorship empowered Ebony to advocate for herself and deepened my understanding of the higher education system as she navigated these challenges with agency and determination (Carter et al. 689; Collins 9).

This shared learning process became a source of empowerment for both of us, particularly as I observed Ebony taking charge of her educational and athletic paths. I saw firsthand how her advocacy and communication skills grew stronger as she became more active in addressing obstacles within academic and athletic settings. With each challenge, her sense of agency expanded, and it was inspiring to witness her assert herself in these spaces, always focussing on justice and equity and shaping the future for other student-athletes.

However, the data also revealed significant challenges, particularly when Ebony faced academic transitions between institutions. One major frustration involved her being required to retake health courses and labs she had already completed at a previous institution. This experience, documented in my journal entries, highlighted systemic inequities that Black students often face when navigating institutional bureaucracies. It was disheartening to witness Ebony's frustration with these repeated hurdles, which further emphasized the broader disparities in academic advising and the barriers that students of color regularly encounter when moving between institutions (Harrison and Lawrence 280; Ockimey 54).

Throughout this process, Ebony and I supported each other by affirming one another and learning together. We refined our strategies for addressing these challenges, deepening our shared commitment to empowerment. As she navigated these hurdles with fortitude and determination, the reciprocal nature of our relationship became a source of strength for both of us, reminding me that even in the face of systemic obstacles, we had the tools to advocate for change.

Wellbeing

I believe effective advocacy can only be sustained when attention is paid to the wellbeing of those involved, and other Black women thought leaders believe the same (hooks 35; Woods-Giscombe 338). Balancing caregiving, career, and personal health challenges was no small feat. The experience of teaching during the COVID-19 closures in 2020 and 2021, where students questioned the need for Black teachers in my class, revealed the broader systemic issues at play: anti-Black racism and misogynoir (Collins 9; Walton et al. 3). Despite these challenges, I felt supported enough to share my experiences with colleagues, supervisors, and organizational leaders.

Through this study, I discovered that many Black women, myself included, emphasize the importance of integrating mind, body, and spirit to maintain balance amid familial and professional pressures (Evans 269). Practices such as yoga, running, prayer, and church attendance were essential for managing mental health during stressful times (Evans 269;

Walton et al. 2). These practices aligned with the rituals and routines of radical care I documented in my journaling, which included quiet time, writing, prayer, and meditation. These rituals played a crucial role in helping me stay centred and hopeful during challenging periods.

My engagement in BIPOC writing groups and commitment to wellness activities, such as walking, journaling, and connecting with loved ones, was also a central aspect of my wellbeing. I dedicated approximately two hours each day to these activities, which were essential for relaxation and stress relief. This commitment to self-care reflects a broader theme of holistic wellness among Black women, as described in the literature (Panton 117; Walton et al. 1).

Lastly, I established work boundaries and communicated openly with supervisors and colleagues. This approach helped me manage my work-life balance and ensured I had the necessary support to maintain my wellbeing (Latunde, "Walk with Me").

Empowering My Daughter's Wellbeing

Throughout my caregiving journey, I prioritized empowering my daughter to care for her wellbeing. I encouraged her to explore her interests and hobbies while emphasizing the importance of maintaining her physical, spiritual, emotional, and mental health. With the support of my husband and her grandparents, we ensured she had access to the resources she needed to thrive. She found joy in arts and crafts, plants, and the outdoors, and we nurtured those passions.

This support was deeply rooted in Black feminist thought, which values community, empowerment, and collective action in challenging oppressive systems (Collins 9). Our relationship centred on facilitating Ebony's access to resources, guiding her through obstacles, and cultivating strong bonds. Even in difficult times, when our conversations on FaceTime were sparse, the quiet yet unwavering presence we shared underscored the deep connection that sustained us both (Ockimey 55).

Study Considerations

As an autoethnographic study, this research is inherently subjective, reflecting my experiences as a Black mother caring for a Division I athlete with a chronic illness. While not universally generalizable, it aligns with broader societal patterns of Black women caregivers, as documented in existing literature (Custer 47). By situating my narrative within these systemic realities, this study contributes to the discourse on caregiving, race, and gender, highlighting individual complexities and shared structural challenges (Esposito and Evans-Winters 109; Gannon 43).

Conclusion

This study illuminated the systemic and gendered barriers my daughter and I faced while navigating the intersections of healthcare, athletics, and education. Through an autoethnographic and intersectional lens, I examined the challenges of advocating for her wellbeing within institutions that often dismissed our concerns. The findings reveal the structural inequities embedded in these systems and the fortitude, resourcefulness, and advocacy required to overcome them.

Beyond identifying these challenges, this study underscores the crucial role of Black mother caregivers in shaping the experiences of Black female Division I student-athletes with chronic illnesses. It highlights the power of education, mentorship, and collective empowerment in challenging systemic injustices.

Despite the obstacles we faced, we emerged whole. My daughter graduated on time and in good health, a testament to her resilience and the support we fought to secure. I, too, persevered, earning tenure amid uncertainty while remaining steadfast in my commitment to my career, my well-being, and, equally importantly, my daughter's. More than her academic and athletic achievements, I am most proud of her dedication to advocacy and activism, particularly in championing the rights and wellbeing of fellow student-athletes, especially women. Her journey, and mine, affirm the necessity of continued advocacy. Inspired by her strength and unwavering commitment to justice, I remain steadfast in my pursuit of equitable policies, compassionate care, and institutional accountability for Black student-athletes and the caregivers who walk this path beside them.

Considerations for Policy and Practice

Gendered Caregiving Issues and Structural Racism

Recognizing not everyone has equal access to support, privilege, and resources, I take this moment to reflect on the need for more equitable and just educational and health systems, advocating for changes in policy and practice to ensure fairness for all. To support Black mothers' caregiving for Division I athletes with chronic illnesses, educational and health systems must tackle structural racism and improve social support (Leonard 317; NCAA 2). The Weathering Framework highlights racism's impact on health disparities, especially during COVID-19, urging expanded programs and policies for health equity (Wakeel and Njoku 145). This includes combating stigma through media, culturally tailored health initiatives, and national healthcare for the underinsured (Cousino and Hazen 809). Recommendations include universal healthcare, better care coordination, and data-driven strategies to address racial health inequities (Wakeel and Njoku 1).

Improve Educational and Health System Coordination

Educational institutions should train staff, coaches, and administrators on the unique challenges Black female athletes face (NCAA 2; Ockimey 54). Schools need to enhance coordination between health and educational services to manage studies and healthcare effectively (Carter et al. 1; Taylor 3). Healthcare professionals should show cultural competence, support Black mother caregivers, and provide resources for navigating healthcare systems (Alexander 1021; Ford et al. 1). Culturally informed community support groups are essential for sharing experiences and building resilience (Alexander 1021; Lovelace et al. 3).

Enhance Social Support Networks

Strengthening social supports reduces stress and empowers both Black student-athletes and Black mother caregivers (Sapolsky 200). Peer networks and community groups offer vital emotional and practical assistance (Bell 23–42). Safe spaces for sharing success stories foster resilience (Čolić et al. 1032; Dababnah et al. 322). Providing information on relevant programs and activities like dance, travel, and yoga helps alleviate stress (Sapolsky 200). Ongoing training for culturally competent advocates is crucial (Alexander 1021; Carter et al. 2).

Works Cited

Alexander, Karah, et al. "'Falling Between the Cracks': Experiences of Black Dementia Caregivers Navigating U.S. Health Systems." *Journal of the American Geriatrics Society*, vol. 70, no. 4, 2022, pp. 1021–30.

Barbosa, Hannah Cardoso, et al. "Empowerment-Oriented Strategies to Identify Behavior Change in Patients with Chronic Diseases: An Integrative Review of the Literature." *Patient Education and Counseling*, vol. 104, no. 4, Apr. 2021, pp. 689–702.

Bell, Kanika. "Sisters on Sisters: Inner Peace from the Black Woman Mental Health Professional Perspective." *Black Women's Mental Health: A Black Woman's Perspective*. Edited by Stephanie Y. Evans, et al. SUNY Press, 2022, pp. 23–42.

Bowleg, Lisa. "The Problem with the Phrase Women and Minorities: Intersectionality—An Important Theoretical Framework for Public Health." *American Journal of Public Health*, vol. 102, no. 7, 2012, pp. 1267–73.

Britannica, The Editors of Encyclopaedia. "Mary McLeod Bethune." *Encyclopedia Britannica*, 22 Jul. 2024, https://www.britannica.com/biography/Mary-McLeod-Bethune. Accessed 5 Apr. 2025.

Bryant-Davis, Thema, et al. "Surviving the Storm: The Role of Social Support and Religious Coping in Sexual Assault Recovery of African American Women." *Violence Against Women,* vol. 17, no. 12, Dec. 2011, pp. 1601–18.

Carter, Nancy, et al. "Navigation Delivery Models and Roles of Navigators in Primary Care: A Scoping Literature Review." *BMC Health Services Research*, vol. 18, no. 96, 2018, pp. 5–10.

Chinn, Juanita J., et al. "Health Equity Among Black Women in the United States." *Journal of Women's Health*, vol. 30, no. 2, 2020, pp. 212–19.

Čolić, Marija, et al. "Black Caregivers' Perspectives on Racism in ASD Services: Toward Culturally Responsive ABA Practice." *Behavior Analysis in Practice*, vol. 15, no. 4, 2022, pp. 1032–41.

Collins, Patricia Hill. Black Feminist Thought: Knowledge, Consciousness, and the Politics of Empowerment. 2nd ed. Revised Tenth Anniversary Edition, Routledge, 2000.

Cousino, Melissa K., and Nancy L. Hazen. "Parenting Stress Among Caregivers of Children with Chronic Illness: A Systematic Review." *Journal of Pediatric Psychology*, vol. 38, no. 8, 2013, pp. 809–28.

Cox, Michelle R. "A Black Autoethnography of Grief and Racial Trauma during the COVID-19 Pandemic." *Journal of Humanistic Counseling,* vol. 63, no. 2, 2024, pp. 160–79.

Crenshaw, Kimberlé. "Mapping the Margins: Intersectionality, Identity Politics, and Violence Against Women of Color." *Stanford Law Review*, vol. 43, no. 6, 1991, pp. 1241–99.

Custer, William L. "Autoethnography as a Research Method: A Review of the Literature." *Qualitative Social Work*, vol. 16, no. 1, 2017, pp. 47–59.

Dababnah, Sarah, et al. "'We Had to Keep Pushing': Caregivers' Perspectives on Autism Screening and Referral Practices of Black Children in Primary Care." *Intellectual and Developmental Disabilities*, vol. 56, no. 5, 2018, pp. 321–36.

Dilworth-Anderson, Peggye, et al. "Aging and Caregiving in African American Families." *Gerontologist*, vol. 60, no. 2, 2020, pp. 208–18.

Edelman, Marian Wright. "You Are Never Alone." *Good Housekeeping*, vol. 215, no. 6, Dec. 1992, p. 116.

Esposito, Jennifer, and Venus E. Evans-Winters. Introduction to Intersectional Qualitative Research. SAGE Publications, Inc., 2021.

Evans, Stephanie Y. Black Women's Yoga History: Memoirs of Inner Peace. SUNY Press, 2021.

Forde, Andrea T., et al. "The Weathering Hypothesis as an Explanation for Racial Disparities in Health: A Systematic Review." *Annals of Epidemiology*, vol. 29, 2019, pp. 1–9.

Gibson, Althea. I Always Wanted to Be Somebody. Harper & Brothers, 1958.

Griffin, Rachel Alicia. "I AM (Still) an Angry Black Woman: Black Feminist Autoethnography, Voice, and Resistance." *Handbook of Autoethnography*. Edited by Tony E. Adams, et al. 2nd ed. Routledge, 2022, pp. 411–20.

Harrison, C. Keith, and Shannon M. Lawrence. "The Role of Race in the College Athletic Experience: A Comparison of Black and White Student-Athletes." *Journal of Black Studies*, vol. 35, no. 3, 2004, pp. 280–301.

Height, Dorothy I. Open Wide the Freedom Gates: A Memoir. Public Affairs, 2005.

hooks, bell. Teaching Community: A Pedagogy of Hope. Routledge, 2003.

Jackson, J. S., and M. R. Johnson. "Religiosity and Coping Among African Americans." *Journal of African American Studies*, vol. 22, no. 2, 2018, pp. 107–20.

Johns Hopkins. "Being a Caregiver." Johns Hopkins Medicine, https://www.hopkinsmedicine.org/health/caregiving/being-a-caregiver. Accessed 5 Apr. 2025.

Jones, Lani V., and Beverly Guy-Sheftall. "Black Feminist Therapy as a Wellness Tool." Black Women's Mental Health: A Black Woman's Perspective. Edited by Stephanie Y. Evans, et al. SUNY Press, 2022, pp. 201–14.

Latunde, Yvette C. "Walk with Me: The Ways Black Women Use Values-Based Practices to Thrive and Lead in Hostile Environments." African American Leadership and Mentoring Through Purpose, Preparation, and Preceptors. Edited by Henrietta Williams Pichon and Yoruba Mutakabbir. IGI Global, 2022, pp. 60–87.

Latunde, Yvette C. Equitable by Design: A Guide to Utilizing the Abundance of Resources Within Black Families and Communities to Support Students. Vibrations Publishing, 2021.

Leonard, David J. "The Black Male Athlete and the Politics of Race: Revisiting the 'Problematic' and the Role of the Black Athlete in American Society." *Journal of Sport and Social Issues*, vol. 38, no. 4, 2014, pp. 317–37.

Lewis, Tiffany T., et al. "Self-Reported Experiences of Discrimination and Health: Scientific Advances, Ongoing Controversies, and Emerging Issues." *Annual Review of Clinical Psychology*, vol. 11, 2015, pp. 407–40.

Lovelace, Temple S., et al. "Experiences of African American Mothers of Sons with Autism Spectrum Disorder: Lessons for Improving Service Delivery." *Education and Training in Autism and Developmental Disabilities*, vol. 53, no. 1, 2018, pp. 3–16.

Magana, Sandy M., et al. "The Health and Well-Being of Black Mothers Who Care for Their Adult Children with Schizophrenia." *Psychiatric Services*, vol. 55, no. 6, 2004, pp. 711–13.

Morsi, Yassir. "Using 'Auto-ethnography' to Write about Racism." Handbook of Autoethnography. Edited by Tony E. Adams et al. 2nd ed. Routledge, 2022, pp. 505–12.

NCAA. "Mental Health Best Practices: Understanding and Supporting Student-Athlete Mental Wellness." *National Collegiate Athletic Association*, 2023, https://www.ncaa.org/sport-science-institute/mental-health-best-practices. Accessed 5 Apr. 2025.

Ockimey, Breanna. "K Girl Magic: Exploring and Understanding the Academic and Athletic Experiences of Black Female Student Athletes at Predominantly White Division I Universities." 2019. Temple University Graduate Board, dissertation.

Panton, Rachel. "My Body Is a Vehicle: Narratives of Black Women Holistic Leaders on Spiritual Development, Mental Healing, and Body Nurturing." *Black Women's Mental Health: Balancing Strengths and Vulnerability*. Edited by Stephanie Y. Evans et al. SUNY Press, 2017, pp. 101–18.

Pinquart, Martin, and Silvia Sorensen. "Gender Differences in Caregiver Stressors, Social Resources, and Health: An Updated Meta-Analysis." *The Journals of Gerontology Series B: Psychological Sciences and Social Sciences*, vol. 61, no. 1, 2006, pp. P33–45.

Rafferty, Katherine A., et al. "Spirituality, Religion, and Health: The Role of Communication, Appraisals, and Coping for Individuals Living with Chronic Illness." *Journal of Religion and Health*, vol. 54, no. 5, 2015, pp. 1870–85.

Rudolph, Wilma. Wilma: The Story of Wilma Rudolph. New American Library, 1977.

Sapolsky, Robert M. Why Zebras Don't Get Ulcers: The Acclaimed Guide to Stress, Stress-Related Diseases, and Coping. 3rd ed., Henry Holt, 2004.

Shahin, Wejdan, et al. "The Impact of Personal and Cultural Beliefs on Medication Adherence of Patients with Chronic Illnesses: A Systematic Review." *Patient Preference and Adherence*, vol. 13, July 2019, pp. 1019–35.

Smith, Ashley. B., et al. "Racial Differences in Depressive Symptoms among Caregivers: The Role of Social Support." *Journal of Gerontological Social Work*, vol. 62, no. 5, 2019, pp. 571–84.

Smith, Jennifer. L., and K. M. McKinney. "Caring for Black Elders: The Role of Community and Social Support." *Journal of Applied Gerontology*, vol. 34, no. 4, 2015, pp. 539–57.

Taylor, Jamila. "Racism, Inequality, and Health Care for African Americans." The Century Foundation, 19 Dec. 2019, https://tcf.org/content/report/racism-inequality-health-care-african-americans. Accessed 5 Apr. 2025.

Toyosaki, Satoshi, and Sandra L. Pensoneau-Conway. "Writing Autoethnographies as Praxis of Social Justice." *Handbook of Autoethnography.* Edited by S. Holmes Jones et al. Left Coast Press, 2013, pp. 557–75.

US Department of Education, Office for Civil Rights. *Protecting Students with Disabilities,* 2021, https://www2.ed.gov/about/offices/list/ocr/504faq.html. Accessed 5 Apr. 2025.

US Department of Education. *FERPA General Guidance for Students,* 2023, https://www2.ed.gov/policy/gen/guid/fpco/ferpa/students.html. Accessed 5 Apr. 2025.

US Department of Health & Human Services. *Summary of the HIPAA Privacy Rule,* 2022, https://www.hhs.gov/hipaa/for-professionals/privacy/laws-regulations/index.html. Accessed 5 Apr. 2025.

US Department of Justice. *A Guide to Disability Rights Laws,* 2022, https://www.ada.gov/cguide.htm. Accessed 5 Apr. 2025.

Wakeel, Fathima, and Anuli Njoku. "Application of the Weathering Framework: Intersection of Racism, Stigma, and COVID-19 as a Stressful Life Event among African Americans." *Healthcare,* vol. 9, no. 2, 2021, article 145.

Walton, Queen L., et al. "Mind, Body, and Spirit: A Constructivist Grounded Theory Study of Wellness Among Middle-Class Black Women." *International Journal of Qualitative Studies on Health and Well-Being,* vol. 18, no. 1, 2023, pp. 278–288.

Williams, David R., et al. "Religious Attendance and Spirituality as Protective Factors for Mental Health in a Longitudinal Study." *American Journal of Epidemiology,* vol. 165, no. 6, 2007, pp. 646–54.

Wimberly, Tina. The Lived Experiences of Black Women Frontline Supervisors (Deemed Essential Workers) in Transportation (Bus & Rail) During the COVID-19 Pandemic. 2024. University of La Verne, dissertation.

Woods-Giscombé, Cheryl L. "Reflections on the Development of the Superwoman Schema Conceptual Framework: An Intersectional

Approach Guided by African American Womanist Perspectives." *Meridians,* vol. 16, no. 2, 2018, pp. 333–42.

7.

When Carework and Paid Work Intersect: Challenges and Learnings of Lifelong Caregiving in Mothers' Professional Trajectories

Ana Carolina Rodriguez

Introduction

Mothering an individual with a disability or complex health needs is an experience that transforms one's beliefs, family relationships, social connections, financial stability, and professional trajectory. These mothers engage in what scholars define as "exceptional care"—caregiving that is usually intense, cyclical, crisis driven, and lifelong (Stewart and Charles 1537). Exceptional care involves a considerable amount of dedicated time and often requires considerable financial resources, given the elevated healthcare costs and the usual need for additional paid caregiving support. Moreover, it can be emotionally draining, given the intense and crisis-driven nature of exceptional care (Jang and Appelbaum 320; Stewart 116). For most mothers with a professional life, the additional demands of exceptional caregiving frequently conflict with their paid work demands, often affecting their participation in the workforce (Brown and Clark 869; Stewart 116). However, care and caregiving are topics mainly discussed in the private spheres of our lives and kept apart from professional domains (Tronto 118).

Nevertheless, maintaining paid work can be critical for these families to ensure a stable source of income and, in some cases, access to health insurance benefits (Jang and Appelbaum 331; Scott, "I Feel as If" 675). Having paid work and a professional career also enables many women to keep their financial independence from their partners (Rodriguez 17). Furthermore, maintaining a professional activity has been shown to provide a buffer for these mothers to cope with the emotional strain of exceptional caregiving, offering distraction and respite from their intense care demands, allowing them to keep their social connections, and preserving their sense of self (Rodriguez 135; Scott, "I Feel as If" 676; Scott, "Mother-Ready Jobs" 2662). Research has shown a positive relationship between paid work and mothers' mental health, wellbeing, and quality of life (Morris 115; Olsson and Hwang 968). Therefore, many of these mothers attempt to keep their professional lives, often following nontraditional career trajectories, with challenges and learnings along the way.

This chapter explores how lifelong caregiving shapes the career trajectories of exceptional mothers. It highlights how societal beliefs about gender roles impose challenges to these mothers' careers and discusses how the way most workplaces operate reinforces gender roles, further complicating this situation. Vignettes with the career trajectories of three mothers of young adults with lifelong caring needs in Brazil, collected through interviews[1], illustrate this reality. This work draws on an extensive literature review of the professional lives of exceptional caregivers and in-depth interviews conducted for previous research using the constructive grounded theory method. As a mother of two young adults, one of them with a rare syndrome, my career choices have been strongly influenced by my kids' caregiving demands. As a human resource development professional, I observed that although caregiving is an essential part of adult lives, it is a topic overlooked in the workplace. My work intends to bring attention to caregiving and self-care as critical aspects shaping most adults' professional experiences.

The stories of Andrea, Gail, and Susan[2] narrated in this chapter are exemplary case studies of some of the main themes found in my previous research. Case studies offer a rich and thick description of the phenomenon under study (Yazam 139). These women were selected from a large sample of caregivers interviewed because they had adult kids and long career trajectories; two were already retired. They could look back at their careers and reflect on their decisions from a different perspective. Although paid work was an essential part of their lives, and they had similar caregiving demands, their career decisions were influenced in different ways by their relationship with their partners, their family income, and the characteristics of their jobs and employers. Notably, despite these mothers' experiences being located in Brazil, a country with a strong patriarchal society, the literature shows their experiences are similar to working mothers with lifelong caregiving demands in other countries (Brekke and Nadim 405; Olsson and Hwang 967).

Women Care, Men Work

Andrea

Andrea is a retired paediatrician. She is married and has three sons. Her youngest son, Will, has Down syndrome and was twenty-five years old when this interview happened. Andrea was born in a working-class family and was a first-generation college student. At the beginning of her career, she worked five jobs at the same time, including being on emergency duty during weekends and working in her private clinic with a colleague. She enjoyed her work. She shared that it defined her identity. Nevertheless, Andrea always wanted to be a mother.

When Andrea got pregnant for the first time, she decided to have a more balanced workload. She quit her work at one hospital, which required weekend shifts, and started working at a state clinic with fixed part-time hours and on her private practice. Two years later, she had her second son. Andrea's mother helped her with the kids so she could keep working. When her third son, Will, was born with Down syndrome, it was a big shock. Andrea organized her life and work around her kids' activities. She would drive sixty miles daily, commuting her three kids to different activities, including several health and therapeutic appointments for Will. She kept working at the state clinic four hours a day but reduced the number of patients she saw in her private practice. Andrea confessed that considering caregiving and paid work, she worked a lot. The flexibility with her working schedule at the state clinic and the possibility of hiring a paid caregiver helped her to keep her professional life.

Andrea shared that her husband, a well-established physician, suggested she could stop working, but she refused: "At work, I'm Dr. Andrea, I'm not

Neal's wife, or Joe, Mark, and Will's mother... Here [at work], I'm myself." Reflecting on her career decisions, she said she made all career decisions by herself because she knew from the start she could not count on her husband. At the beginning of their careers, she had a higher salary, but, in her own words, "in our case, the contract was signed at the moment I got pregnant, women care, and men provide." Andrea added that she sought to educate her sons not to be sexist and to become more engaged fathers.

Andrea retired and confessed she did not miss working: "It was time to take care of myself." She would like to have done more things, studied more, and learned English. She never took care of herself; her needs always came last. Despite her career sacrifices, she feels content. Her husband's career has not suffered any impact, though. He is still working as a physician. Andrea believes she made the best decisions she could at that time. She prioritized her kids because there was no other way, and she always knew that was what she would have to do when she became a mother.

In most patriarchal societies, women are seen as being primarily responsible for caregiving, particularly for the disabled, elderly, and severely ill. Society often assumes women are naturally nurturing and skilled caregivers. In contrast, men are expected to be rational, decisive, and the primary financial providers (Acker 152; O'Brien 5). In families dealing with exceptional caregiving, the mother is seen as an even more competent caregiver compared to the father (Scott, "I Feel as If" 691; Shearn and Todd 117). Moreover, it is not uncommon for mothers to believe they are responsible for their kids' condition and for family members and other care providers to insinuate the same (Baker and Drapela 582; Rodriguez 86). As a result, mothers of individuals with lifelong caring needs often carry a strong sense of guilt, which is exacerbated when their children's needs clash with their professional aspirations or when they need to maintain their professional careers for financial reasons (Rodriguez 116; Shearn and Todd 123).

Gendered social norms framing women as primary caregivers are deeply entrenched in family structures and the community. For example, education, health, and therapeutic services often assume the mother is the main caregiver and will be available anytime (Lewis et al., "Managing Work-Family" 426; Shearn and Todd 116). Societal expectations for women as primary caregivers also influence public policies. Although maternity leave policies are well established in most countries, paternity leave is often nonexistent or is brief and unpaid. Moreover, even though policies to protect parenthood and early childcare are of utmost importance, by focussing only on women and not incorporating paternity leave and accessible childcare options, these policies reinforce gender norms and contribute to maternal overload (Addati et al. 125).

Although social norms reinforce men's primary responsibility for financially providing for their families, in most cases, women's employment represents an essential contribution to the family's income. This is particularly relevant for these families, given the elevated healthcare costs (Baker and Drapela 580). Mothers of individuals with disabilities and other lifelong conditions often assume carework while also keeping their employment, even if partially (DeRigne and Porterfield 587; Scott, "Mother-Ready Jobs" 2662). As a result, working mothers provide significant hours of physically and emotionally intense carework on top of their paid working hours, facing high levels of conflict between their family and professional roles (Stewart 116). Conversely, since men are expected to be the primary income provider through their work, fathers of individuals with lifelong caring needs prioritize their paid work and, consequently, experience less conflict between their roles as professionals and parents (Lewis et al., "Dual-Earner Parents" 1052; Rodriguez 158).

How families organize themselves around carework is often shaped by a complex combination of social, structural, economic, and ideological elements. Yet these decisions are regularly viewed through a gendered lens. Studies show that even though mothers and fathers consider their salaries, employment status, and career potential when debating who will assume a larger portion of, if not all, carework, established gender roles weigh strongly in these decisions (Lewis et al., "Dual-Earner Parents" 1053; Rodriguez 163). Even though women may prefer or choose to be the primary caregivers, this decision is often constrained by beliefs around appropriate gender roles and institutional norms reinforcing their role as caregivers (Baker and Drapela 582, 590; Scott, "Mother-Ready" 2679). Due to the emotional burden of receiving a diagnosis and the intense nature of exceptional caregiving, families report not having the time or mental availability to challenge expected gender roles, which contributes to their pervasiveness (Lewis et al., "Dual-Earner Parents" 1053). Consequently, mothers of individuals with lifelong care needs are disproportionately affected in their careers, with longer periods of unemployment or underemployment compared to their male partners

(Brennan et al. 4). Andrea's narrative illustrates how gender roles and exceptional care affect career trajectories and women's lives in general.

Uncaring Workplaces: Ideal Workers and Unsupportive Leaders

Gail

Gail is a retired audio-visual professional. She is married and has two adult sons; the older one has a disability. She started working on television soon after college and had a stellar career. In just a few years, she was the production manager for a live daily television show. After almost a decade of working in television production, she was unhappy with her employer and quit her job at the station. At that time, she had started teaching a television production course at a professional school, and she thought that would be an excellent time to get pregnant. She explained, "I had to benefit from this interval [from television] because in television [working at a station], it is hard to be pregnant; it is too much work, too intense." Gail got pregnant, but her son, Roni, was born prematurely and stayed for three months in the neonatal intensive care unit. During this period, Gail kept working part-time, and the work helped her distract from her worries about her son's health. Her son became severely disabled due to his birth complications. He was twenty-three years old at the time of this interview and depended on her or another adult for most daily activities.

Gail's husband was a lawyer and managed his small legal firm with an unstable income. Consequently, Gail's paid work was crucial to the family's ability to pay for Roni's caring needs. The couple organized their schedules so they both could keep their jobs. Gail would care for her son during the day and teach in the evening when her husband was back home. Her husband has always been a good partner, but she has naturally taken more responsibility as a mother. Six years after Roni was born, the family's financial reserves were almost gone, and Gail decided to look for a full-time job. They had a second son during this period, which amplified the need for additional income. Moreover, Roni was then starting his verbal communication, and she felt more comfortable hiring an aide to help care for him and his brother so she could work full-time.

Gail had an excellent professional reputation and quickly found a job at a large station. Although her new job was in a lower position than her *previous experience, she had a supportive leader, allowing her to grow professionally and attain an excellent salary. She felt comfortable sharing her son's caring needs with her supervisor and had flexibility when needed. She organized carework around her flexible schedule, took her son to therapies early in the morning, and worked until late evening. She also had support from her husband and a paid caregiver.*

Nevertheless, Gail's employer did not have formal family-supportive policies implemented or a family-friendly culture. When a change in leadership happened, she lost the flexibility and support she used to have. Her new supervisor had a toxic leadership style, and she experienced an increase in her workload, high levels of pressure, micromanagement, and a lack of recognition for her work. Since Gail was close to her retirement age, she decided to endure a couple more years in the job to guarantee her pension. After five years, she was diagnosed with burnout and took a medical leave. Gail was then dismissed a couple of months after returning to work.

When our interview happened, Gail had not worked for a year and had an ongoing legal process to access her retirement funds. Reflecting on her career, she claimed she had always worked more than was expected in her roles to avoid any questioning regarding her motherhood and flexibility needs. She said she felt guilty for working all day, but at the same time, her job helped provide good doctors and cutting-edge treatments for her son. She was experimenting with new things, producing a podcast, and considering whether she would return to formal work.

The professional experiences of mothers engaged in intense and lifelong caregiving are complicated by the combination of societal beliefs about appropriate gender roles and how organizations traditionally design working processes and set expectations about their employees (Scott, "I Feel as If" 693). The deeply rooted idea that women are responsible for household duties and caregiving and men should be completely dedicated to work generates the image of an ideal worker—a man with no family commitments—that many organizations uphold as a necessary criterion for professional growth and career success (Acker 149).

Due to these societal and organizational beliefs, caregiving is often overlooked as part of the human condition in the workplace. Instead, jobs and organizational practices to support families are usually designed with the image of the ideal worker in mind, disregarding the needs of caregivers in general, particularly lifelong caregivers (Scott, "Mother-

Ready Jobs" 2679). For example, organizations implementing formal family-supportive policies usually target women as the main users of such policies, reinforcing societal gender roles and often restricting men's options to request and use these policies and to participate in carework (Lewis et al., "Dual-Earner Parents" 1046). Additionally, family-supportive policies are usually designed around the birth or adoption of a child or temporary illnesses but often do not consider lifelong caring needs (Addati et al. 160).

Studies with mothers of individuals with disabilities and other conditions requiring lifelong care show that flexibility in working hours, schedule, and location is critical to their ability to provide adequate care while maintaining their employment (Brown and Clark 868). Although the care demands of these individuals can be different over time, they often require multiple visits to healthcare providers, therapies, and school meetings, all of which generally happen during regular working hours (Brennan et al. 6; Brown and Clark 868). Moreover, because health or behavioural crises can be common occurrences for these individuals, caregivers need to be able to respond to such situations. Therefore, mothers often negotiate their working schedules and locations and request last-minute flexibility (Brennan et al. 12; Lewis, "Managing Work-Family" 421).

Unfortunately, studies also show that women face challenges finding workplaces that offer such flexibility, family-friendly cultures, and supportive leaders and co-workers (Brown and Clark 868–69; Scott "Mother-Ready Jobs" 2678). Unsupportive leaders and organizational cultures significantly affect the ability of mothers in lifelong care situations to sustain carework and paid work. Even when formal supportive policies are available, unsupportive leaders may hinder access to these policies and influence the consequences of adopting them (Brown and Clark 868; Crettenden et al. 258). Many mothers fear that disclosing their caregiving needs will affect their career opportunities, as they become less than ideal workers (Stewart and Charles 8). The flexibility stigma—a perception that those employees who ask for flexibility because of family needs are less committed to their work and careers and less deserving of growth opportunities—is a reality in many workplaces (Stewart and Charles 4). Research shows these mothers may face courtesy stigmatization—"judgment and exclusion due to their relationship to the child or youth with a disability" (Brennan et al. 5). Thus, exceptional caregivers frequently consider the risks before deciding to disclose their family caring needs and ask for organizational support and flexible working arrangements (Brennan et al. 12; Stewart and Charles 14). Despite these concerns, mothers are often compelled to disclose their needs at some point when having some flexibility becomes critical (Crettenden et al. 257). Moreover, some mothers confess they overwork to show competence and avoid discrimination (Rodriguez 108).

As pointed out in the previous section, couples consider their salaries and career prospects when determining who will sacrifice their professional lives to assume a large portion of carework (Lewis et al., "Dual-Earner Parents" 1047). Therefore, the persistent wage gap between women and men and discrimination against women in the workplace strongly affect a family's decision about how to distribute carework. Historically, men receive higher salaries, hold more leadership positions, and are promoted at higher rates than women. Thus, men are often judged as having better career potential than women (Kossek et al. 230). Unfortunately, bias against women is a reality in many workplaces, particularly in the case of mothers working in flexible arrangements (Crettenden et al. 260).

Although care is a natural part of most adults' lives and an essential part of what makes our society survive and thrive, unpaid carework and paid work are subjects discussed in separate spheres of our lives: the personal and professional realms (Tronto 96). This artificial separation is necessary to maintain the idealized image of devoted mothers and committed professionals upheld by Westernized societies (Acker 149). Social gender expectations are deeply rooted in how organizations operate, how jobs are designed, and how work standards are defined (Acker 145). For mothers caring for individuals with lifelong care needs, this separation comes with high emotional costs and is often challenging to sustain (Scott, "Mother-Ready Jobs" 2662). Consequently, these gendered expectations contribute to these mothers' lower participation in the workforce and reinforce women's primary role as caregivers. Gail's experience illustrates the effect of organizational cultures and unsupportive leaders on the career trajectories of lifelong caregivers.

While extensive research demonstrates the multiple challenges mothers with lifelong caregiving demands face in accommodating care and professional demands, this process also results in significant learning and transformation, particularly when these mothers find supportive working environments and have access to resources.

Challenges to Accommodate Carework and Paid Work

Susan

Susan is a divorced woman and mother of a young adult with a rare syndrome. Her daughter, Lila, was nineteen when this interview happened. Susan comes from a family where women have always worked. She values her professional life, and not working was never an option for her. Susan has a bachelor's degree in public relations and has worked in several companies and different roles. She enjoyed most of her working experience and had many opportunities to learn and travel.

When Susan decided to get pregnant, she had a good job at a large corporation but had few prospects to grow in her career. During her maternity leave, she received a job offer to work for a large bank. At that time, her daughter had already received a diagnosis of a rare condition, and Susan was apprehensive about starting a new job. Still, she accepted the offer. The new employer's office was closer to her house and daycare, and organizing her daughter's caring logistics would be easier. Her new employer had a supportive human resources department, so she disclosed her child's situation from the beginning.

In this organization, Susan grew in her career but at a high cost. She would leave her daughter at school early in the morning and pick her up late in the evening. She would schedule therapies and medical appointments during the weekends or late in the day to avoid missing work. She built a network of paid care workers that allowed her to keep her job. Susan shared that she worked twice as hard so nobody would consider it a cause for pity or doubt her competence. At that time, she was the main income provider for the family because her husband had an unstable job. Yet she still assumed most of the carework.

After seven years of working in this organization, Susan was exhausted. Her daughter was missing her, and she felt guilty for not spending more time with Lila. She understood she would need to, in her own words, "work forever" to support her daughter, but she feared her career would end in that company due to ageism. She needed a job where age would not be an issue. When Susan was forty-five years old, she had a good financial reserve and her former husband had stable employment, she decided it was time for a change. She quit her job and started a master's program in her field. While in the program, she began teaching and got excited about the perspective of an academic career. She then started a doctorate focused on diversity and inclusion and was promoted to course coordinator. In her academic career, Susan had the flexibility and autonomy to manage her work and could better accommodate her daughter's care needs. During this period, she engaged in activism, launching a social media page and creating a group to support mothers with lifelong caring needs who wish to develop their small businesses. She also started a consulting business focused on helping organizations to be more inclusive.

Motherhood and exceptional care changed Susan's professional trajectory. She learned to put problems into perspective, became more resilient, and developed excellent problem-solving skills. She redefined several things in her life, including the meaning of happiness, work, and success. For Susan, success is doing work she likes, earning honest money, and positively impacting the world. She was excited about starting her postdoctorate program.

Work-family conflict occurs when demands from work and family collide and become mutually incompatible. These conflicting demands can be related to time, emotional availability, and skills (Greenhaus and Beutell 77). Studies show that mothers of individuals with lifelong caring needs experience high levels of work-family conflict (Stewart 124). Their levels of work-family conflict are usually higher than those of exceptional fathers and mothers and fathers of individuals without exceptional care needs (Brekke and Nadim 404).

For these mothers, the elevated levels of work-life conflict tend to persist in the long term, given the intense, cyclical, and lifelong aspects of exceptional caregiving. At the beginning of their caregiving experience, these mothers usually face a long path of medical appointments with specialists and multiple exams to receive a diagnosis for their kids. Besides the time and financial resources required for this process, the tension and anxiety of waiting for a diagnosis can be excruciating (Jang and Applebaum 320; Rodriguez 82). Receiving the diagnosis of a disability or a chronic or severe health condition can also be emotionally challenging. Although some parents report feeling relieved to have some answers about their child's condition, they typically also worry about what will happen next, how the future will look, and whether they will be able to care for their kids (Jang and Applebaum 320).

The initial years of managing exceptional caregiving and professional life can be particularly challenging. Although the intensity might change as parents learn more about a child's condition, in most cases, the caring demands will continue throughout their lives (Brennan et al. 6). Mothers describe their intense caring routine as full-time work (Jang and Appelbaum 322). Besides providing direct support, which can be emotionally and physically demanding when caring for an individual with cognitive, behavioural, and physical disabilities, these mothers talk about the intense coordination exceptional care requires. They manage appointments for multiple medical and specialized service providers, organize calendars, arrange transportation, administer health insurance claims and battle health coverage denials, learn about their kids' conditions to educate others, and advocate for their kids' rights (Jang and Appelbaum 321; Crettenden et al. 259). Moreover, because of the crisis-driven aspect of exceptional caregiving, mothers report being constantly on call in case of an unexpected crisis, which can sometimes frustrate their work commitments (Scott, "I Feel as If" 688; Stewart and Charles 11). Not surprisingly, these mothers are, therefore, more likely to have work absences (DeRigne and Portfield 398). Furthermore, the emotional strain caused by the conflicting demands between paid work and exceptional caregiving can lead to depression and burnout, affecting these mothers' abilities to perform satisfactorily in their paid work (Crettenden et al. 256; Rodriguez 88).

Generally, because emotional stakes are high and care demands intense, many mothers will make drastic career decisions soon after receiving their child's diagnosis or following an event leading to their child's disability. Unfortunately, the decisions made at those initial moments will likely affect these mothers' future career trajectories as they set the tone in the family regarding who will assume the primary caregiving role. In the aftermath of a diagnosis, many mothers quit their jobs entirely or negotiate extended leaves or reduced working hours if they can. Mothers also report changing jobs to have more flexibility, better health benefits, or to ease the demands of their new caring routine, even if these changes require taking positions outside their professional interests, below their qualifications, or with lower wages (Crettenden et al. 256; Jang and Appelbaum 322; Rodriguez 104).

Unlike mothers who care for individuals without lifelong caring needs, exceptional care affects a mother's return to full-time employment in the long term, often leading to career disruption and financial impact for the family (Crettenden et al. 259; Rodriguez 89). Although in many countries, employment rates for mothers and fathers with lifelong caregiving needs are not significantly different, mothers are less likely to have full-time jobs, are more likely to be paid hourly based wages, and have a smaller average income than fathers (Crettenden et al. 254; Stewart 129). These mothers will often temporarily quit their jobs if their salaries are lower than the costs associated with caregiving or if they have a partner who can provide income (Scott, "I Feel as If" 674). Moreover, mothers also report sometimes declining job offers or promotions due to their kids' care needs (Baker and Drapela 597). Although the impact on mothers' employment is stronger in patriarchal cultures (Chou et al. 141; Rodriguez 66), even in countries with an established gender equality ideology, mothers of individuals with lifelong care needs are still more affected in their work lives than fathers (Brekke and Nadim 405; Olsson and Hwang 967). Maintaining employment is also particularly challenging for single mothers, those who are less educated, and those from lower social classes (Scott, "I Feel as If" 691).

For those mothers who manage to maintain their employment, their need to reduce working hours or adopt flexible working arrangements can negatively affect their careers. Several mothers reported feeling discriminated against and not receiving good job opportunities or promotions because of their part-time or flexible work status (Crettenden et al. 260; Lewis et al., "Managing Work-Family" 421). The career interruptions and undesired changes that happen to many of these mothers can also affect their mental health and wellbeing. Many women grieve the loss of their professional identities and feel unproductive and undervalued despite all the carework they provide (Rodriguez 91; Scott, "I Feel as If" 676). That many societies attribute low value to carework and high value to productive work further magnifies these feelings. This perspective devalues caregivers and the people needing care, ultimately marginalizing both groups (Tronto 120).

Despite all these challenges, because paid work is vital to these mothers' mental and financial health, with time, most mothers will rearrange their working lives and care schedules to maintain their professional lives. Moreover, some mothers worry about their kids' future independence and employment, as well as their own ability to provide care in the future, prompting them to consider their long-term employability. As a result, some of these lifelong caregivers also become lifelong learners (Rodriguez 167). Susan's trajectory is a good example of this transformation.

Integrating Carework and Paid Work: Learnings and Career Development

Although women with lifelong caregiving needs face multiple challenges as they attempt to accommodate care and professional demands, there is also significant learning and transformation that comes from this process (Scorgie et al. 105), particularly when they find supportive working environments (Rodriguez 167). As the stories of Andrea, Gail, and Susan reveal, these women created strategies to accommodate carework and paid work in the best way possible, often reassessing their professional and personal aspirations and renegotiating their working arrangements and caring schemes. For these mothers, managing the interfaces between their personal and professional lives becomes their primary objective and influences their career decisions (Rodriguez 160).

After some years of providing exceptional care, these mothers described their career goals as working with something they like, coordinating the care structure their kids need, and, when possible, having time for themselves. Importantly, these women highlighted the need to invest in their professional development and to look after their own health so they could provide care in the long term (Rodriguez 167). In their endeavours to accommodate carework and paid work, these mothers went through some job changes trying to find a working arrangement that would enable them to perform their family and professional roles as satisfactorily as possible. In this process, mothers with lifelong and intense caregiving demands reported developing self-awareness, resilience, flexibility, empathy, openness, tolerance, and respect for what is different (Scorgie et al. 85). They also reported improving their problem-solving and time-management skills (Rodriguez 168). Many mothers applied these new abilities in their working settings, including pursuing new professional paths outside of their original areas of expertise and crafting new work opportunities, as well as leveraging their care experience and making career transitions to work in organizations supporting individuals with exceptional care needs and their families (Rodriguez 117; Scott, "Mother-Ready Jobs" 2678).

Although some mothers may have found a balance between caregiving and paid work, it was not without challenges. Frequently, these mothers underwent several adjustments until they attained a job with more acceptable levels of work-family conflict. These mothers' stories also show a satisfactory balance between their professional and personal demands is rarely permanent and requires frequent reassessment and rearrangement of priorities (Rodriguez 145). Moreover, although mothers acknowledge the importance of caring for themselves so they can care for their kids and not worry about who would care for their children if they got sick or died, many declared self-care remains a last priority (Rodriguez 140). Furthermore, for mothers with lower socioeconomic status and less education, attaining a balanced relationship between paid work and carework can be impossible without supportive policies (Rodriguez 73; Scott, "Mother-Ready Jobs" 2681).

In conclusion, mothering an individual with intense and lifelong caring needs has a profound impact on these women's professional lives, including effects on their mental and financial health. Even though some women, often those from more privileged backgrounds, find ways to integrate their caring and professional demands, the role of family-supportive policies in the workplace and supportive public policies is critical. Finally, understanding care as central to the human condition and as a moral responsibility (Tronto 101) is paramount to the wellbeing of these caregivers and the individuals they care for.

Endnotes

1. Interviews were conducted and analyzed in Portuguese, the native language of the participants and the researcher. They were later translated into English.
2. All names in the vignettes are fictional to preserve anonymity.

Works Cited

Acker, Joan. "Hierarchies, Jobs, Bodies: A Theory of Gendered Organizations." *Gender and Society*, vol. 4, no. 2, 1990, pp. 139–58. JSTOR, http://www.jstor.org/stable/189609.

Addati, Laura, et al. "Care at Work: Investing in Care Leave and Services for a More Gender Equal World of Work." 1st ed., International Labour Organization, 2022, https://www.ilo.org/wcmsp5/groups/public/---dgreports/---dcomm/documents/publication/wcms_838653.pdf. Accessed 5 Apr. 2025.

Baker, Dana Lee, and Laurie A. Drapela. "Mostly the Mother: Concentration of Adverse Employment Effects on Mothers of Children with Autism." *The Social Science Journal*, vol. 47, no. 3, Sept. 2010, pp. 578–92. Elsevier, doi:10.1016/j.soscij.2010.01.013.

Brekke, Idunn, and Marjan Nadim. "Gendered Effects of Intensified Care Burdens." *Work, Employment and Society*, vol. 31, no. 3, 2017, pp. 391–408. Sage, doi:10.1177/0950017015625616.

Brennan, Eileen M., et al. "Challenges and Supports for Employed Parents of Children and Youth with Special Needs." *The Oxford Handbook of Work and Family*. Edited by Tammy D. Allen and Lillian T. Eby. Oxford University Press, vol. 1, 2016, pp: 1–34., doi:10.1093/oxfordhb/9780199337538.013.14.

Brown, Theresa, and Christine Clark. "Employed Parents of Children with Disabilities and Work Family Life Balance: A Literature Review." *Child & Youth Care Forum*, vol. 46, no. 6, 2017, pp. 857–76. Springer, doi:10.1007/s10566-017-9407-0.

Chou, Yueh-Ching, et al. "Making Work Fit Care: Reconciliation Strategies Used by Working Mothers of Adults with Intellectual Disabilities." *Journal of Applied Research in Intellectual Disabilities*, vol. 26, no. 2, Mar. 2013, pp. 133–45. Wiley, doi:10.1111/jar.12005.

Crettenden, Angela, et al. "Mothers Caring for Children and Young People with Developmental Disabilities: Intent to Work, Patterns of Participation in Paid Employment and the Experience of Workplace Flexibility." *Community, Work & Family*, vol. 17, no. 3, 2014, pp. 244–67. Routledge, doi: 10.1080/13668803.2014.923816.

DeRigne, LeaAnne, and Shirley L. Porterfield. "Employment Change Among Married Parents of Children with Special Health Care Needs." *Journal of Family Issues*, vol. 38, no. 5, Apr. 2017, pp. 579–606. Sage, doi:10.1177/0192513X15572368.

Greenhaus, Jeffrey H., and Nicholas J. Beutell. "Sources of Conflict Between Work and Family Roles." *Academy of Management Review*, vol. 10, no. 1, Jan. 1985, pp. 76–88. Academy of Management, doi:10.5465/amr.1985.4277352.

Jang, Soo Jung, and Eileen Appelbaum. "Work-Life Balance in Extraordinary Circumstances." *Journal of Women, Politics & Policy*, vol. 31, no. 4, 2010, pp. 313–33. Taylor & Francis, doi:10.1080/1554477X.2010.517156.

Kossek, Ellen Ernst, et al. "'Opting Out' or 'Pushed Out'? Integrating Perspectives on Women's Career Equality for Gender Inclusion and Interventions." *Journal of Management*, vol. 43, no. 1, Jan. 2017, pp. 228–54. Sage, doi:10.1177/0149206316671582.

Lewis, Suzan, et al. "Dual-Earner Parents with Disabled Children." *Journal of Family Issues*, vol. 21, no. 8, Nov. 2000, pp. 1031–60. Sage, doi:10.1177/019251300021008005.

Lewis, Suzan, et al. "Managing Work family Diversity for Parents of Disabled Children – Beyond Policy to Practice and Partnership." *Personnel Review*, vol. 29, no. 3, June 2000, pp. 417–30. Emerald, doi:10.1108/00483480010324797.

Morris, Lisa A. "The Impact of Work on the Mental Health of Parents of Children with Disabilities." *Family Relations*, vol. 63, no. 1, Feb. 2014, pp. 101–21. Wiley, doi:10.1111/fare.12050.

O'Brien, Karen M., et al. "Women's Experiences of Managing Work and End-of-Life Care: Challenges, Rewards and Recommendations for Vocational Psychologists." *Journal of Career Assessment*, vol. 29, no. 1, Feb. 2021, pp. 3–17. Sage, doi:10.1177/1069072720933556.

Olsson, Malin B., and C. Philip Hwang. "Well-Being, Involvement in Paid Work and Division of Childcare in Parents of Children with Intellectual Disabilities in Sweden." *Journal of Intellectual Disability Research*, vol. 50, no. 12, Dec. 2006, pp. 963–69. Wiley, doi: 10.1111/j.1365-2788.2006.00930.x.

Rodriguez, Ana Carolina. *Integrating Care and Paid Work: The Career Development of Parents of People with Disabilities in Brazil*. University of Minnesota, 2024.

Scorgie, Kate, et al. "The Experience of Transformation in Parents of Children with Disabilities: Theoretical Considerations." *Developmental Disabilities Bulletin*, vol. 32, no. 1, 2004, pp. 84–110.

Scott, Ellen K. "'I Feel as If I Am the One Who Is Disabled': The Emotional Impact of Changed Employment Trajectories of Mothers Caring for Children with Disabilities." *Gender & Society*, vol. 24, no. 5, 2010, pp. 672–96. Sage, doi:10.1177/0891243210382531.

Scott, Ellen K. "Mother-Ready Jobs: Employment That Works for Mothers of Children With Disabilities." *Journal of Family Issues*, vol. 39, no. 9, June 2018, pp. 2659–84. Sage, doi:10.1177/0192513X18756927.

Shearn, Julia, and Stuart Todd. "Maternal Employment and Family Responsibilities: The Perspectives of Mothers of Children with Intellectual Disabilities." *Journal of Applied Research in Intellectual Disabilities*, vol. 13, no. 3, Sept. 2000, pp. 109–31. Wiley, doi:10.1046/j.1468-3148.2000.00021.x.

Stewart, Lisa M. "Family Care Responsibilities and Employment." *Journal of Family Issues*, vol. 34, no. 1, 2013, pp. 113–38. Sage, doi:10.1177/0192513X12437708.

Stewart, Lisa M., and Avelina Charles. "To Disclose or Conceal? Workplace Disability and Eldercare-Related Disclosure Decision-Making Strategies." *Journal of Family Issues*, vol. 43, no. 6, 2022, 1536–1554. Sage, doi:10.1177/0192513X211026965.

Tronto, Joan C. *Moral Boundaries: A Political Argument for an Ethic of Care.* Routledge, 1993.

Yazam, Bedrettin. "Three Approaches to Case Study Methods in Education: Yin, Merriam, and Stake." *The Qualitative Report*, vol 20, no. 2, 2015, pp. 134–52. DOAJ Directory of Open Access Journals, doi: 10.46743/2160-3715/2015.2102.

Section IV

Caregiving Children with Disabilities beyond Mothering

8.

Siblings of Children with Medical Complexity

Hanae Davis, Samantha Bellefeuille, and Linda Nguyen

Introduction

Across the myriad of relationships we encounter in our lives, the sibling-to-sibling relationship is often the longest and most enduring. The dynamics of sibling relationships are often layered and complex, as they change across the lifespan. These dynamics are of particular significance for siblings wherein one (or more) individual(s) has a disability or complex medical condition. Between 15 and 18 percent of youth have a chronic health condition, disability, or both in North America (Newacheck 118; Perrin 2755). While there is limited statistical data about siblings, the Canadian census data from 2016 indicate that approximately 31 percent of couples have two or more children, and approximately 39 percent of lone parents have two or more children.

Being a sibling to an individual with a disability, unlike becoming a parent to one later in life, is a core influence during the formative childhood and adolescent years (Nguyen "Being a Sibling" 5–6). The sibling without the disability (henceforth referred to as "sibling") often traces their special-needs siblings through life stages more closely than their parents do, and both siblings often experience transitions together. This proximity within a family ecosystem may drive the sibling to embody different roles over the lifespan, serially or even simultaneously, such as a companion, an advocate, or a caregiver to their special-needs sibling (Nguyen "Being a Sibling" 5–6; Nguyen "Filling in the Gap" 1363).

These roles can then shape a sibling's self-perception and development beyond the immediate family ecosystem, including their mental health, chosen vocation, financial well-being, and residential proximity to their family.

Being a sibling can be an enriching experience. Still, it also entails many challenges that are not receiving enough attention, including in healthcare (Nguyen, "Canadian Resources" 10–12). The "sandwich generation" concept colloquially refers to parents who care for their aging parents and their children. In this chapter, we highlight another type of "sandwich" generation: siblings who care for their special-needs sibling, their parents or caregivers, and eventually their children. Caregivers are a key pillar in the healthcare system, and some siblings will choose to have this active and longitudinal role.

Using lived and living experience as the foreground, this chapter illustrates the unique experiences and needs of siblings through the perspectives of two adult siblings and a researcher specializing in siblings and patient-oriented research partnerships. Taken together, our experiences suggest increased recognition and support for siblings to be a priority, as they are central figures in the family-centred approach to care.

What Happens Next? A Sibling's Perspective

Samantha Bellefeuille

What happens next? This is the question I find myself constantly asking—trying to gauge what will happen in the future to bring me some sense of certainty or clarity. Navigating unpaved roads with little information and no blueprint creates a sense of fear and anxiety about what will happen next. Along my journey as a sibling, I have tried to forge a path that works for my family and myself while still being ready for the next step.

My younger brother was born when I was nine, and I was so happy to be the older sister. I always wanted to hold him, cuddle with him, and just love him. At two months old, he had his first seizure. I remember being confused and terrified about what these looked like, and a big part of the next few years all blended into a kaleidoscope of memories filled with happiness, heartbreak, sadness, and love. At such a young age, I started to realize he needed more attention and assistance and frequently went to the hospital with my mom. I realized how others perceived our family and how they perceived him. It was almost as if I could feel their fear of being left around him or could hear their panicked thoughts when a seizure occurred. Oftentimes, I was left feeling anxious about what was happening and scared about what would happen next. There were whispers about the duration of his life as medications, therapies and doctors changed throughout the years. I was too young to understand the gravity of the situation, but I did know one thing: I wanted to protect him at all costs. He was the most important person in my life; he provided many lessons that strengthened our sibling bond. With each memory we shared, I knew I loved him unconditionally and would always be there for him no matter what. I insisted on going to his therapies when I could and was often told to wait in the waiting room. I quickly learned he was on this path that I could not walk beside him because there were never any opportunities for siblings to be a part of their world. I was often told to wait in the waiting room or that the room could only accommodate two people (my mom and dad), and no one ever stopped to explain what was going on. Siblings were never a concern or seen as part of the circle of care. Instead, we were viewed as more of a hindrance, especially in the early years when we were not needed for anything due to age or lack of knowledge.

I wish that had been different. I felt like an outsider looking in on my little brother, who was in so much pain. I felt like I was constantly trying to string together what little understanding I had of the situation based on whispers, murmured conversations, and what I saw happening. I would then come up with my own conclusions about what was happening and looking back I think that is where my anxiety first stemmed from: the fear of the unknown and the fear of what would happen next. I became extremely good at the "what if" game and started to create scenarios that could happen, so it would lessen the anxiety of what was coming next. Reflecting on this, I wish someone had helped me feel seen. I wish I could have been understood and made a part of the conversation in any way. To be a part of the discussion with ways I could help, instead of being told to not worry about it or to focus on school. All I wanted was to help him feel better in any little way I could. It caused me so much pain and anxiety, which was extremely hard to process, especially from an early age.

In my teens, I started to understand what "medically fragile" meant. He was trying out new diets, had an NG tube, was put on new medications, and his seizures were constant. He went on frequent hospital trips, got sized for his first wheelchair and was deemed nonverbal. There are so many lingering memories about just how medically fragile he was. The worst feeling in the world is knowing someone is hurting, and there is nothing you can do to help them. It was terrifying to see my best friend and brother in so much pain, and all you want to do is hold him close and sing to him—to hug him and tell him that everything is going to be okay. So many heartbreaking memories play on repeat in my mind, but I have long since tried to replace them with good memories. All our memories, good and bad, have moulded me into who I am today. It is because of them that I have learned valuable life lessons, including how to be grateful for every day. I have memories of us singing and dancing in our kitchen, spinning him around while both of us were laughing, and of him walking and playing in the leaves in the fall. I remember the snowmen we built in winter and his radiant smile and spirit with everyone he crossed paths with. Over the years, I was not just his sister. Somewhere along the way, he became my best friend. I wanted to do everything with him and create all these memories with him. I wanted to love life with him and go on many adventures together.

As more years passed, I noticed I had naturally become an advocate for my little brother. When I noticed something was off or different, I would tell my parents. When he was kept in his highchair for too long at daycare or had seizures, I would let them know. When he was not treated the same way as others, I would ask, "Well, why not?" I wanted him to be included in all areas and activities because I did not see any limits. I did not understand why someone would say he could not do something. I always looked at him as a whole person, yet all around me, others would dissect what he could not do instead of stating what he could. They would lead with the negative and leave out the positive. Seizures did not define him. His developmental delays did not define him. With some accommodations and a little creativity, he could do anything.

In my twenties, I learned the art of accommodation. I learned what it meant to think outside the box and create scenarios that worked for him. I learned how to best organize activities or trips that were fun-filled and, most importantly, inclusive. I started to look for more opportunities for him, like sit-skiing and music therapy. Naturally, I progressed into more of a carer role and started to understand more about the medical side. I started to ask more questions and receive more answers as time went on. I voiced my opinions and shared my thoughts on different situations like drug trials, studies and programming, and so much more.

Now, at twenty-nine, I am one of his legal guardians. When I was eighteen, it was well known that if anything happened to my parents, I would have custody. We had discussed it, and it was an easy decision. I loved him and always wanted what was best for him. It took a few conversations with my parents before that was decided because it was important to them that I "lived my life". Yet I knew my choice, and I believe every sibling should be able to make their own choice and choose their level of involvement with their sibling with exceptionalities. There should be multiple age-appropriate conversations regarding the roles they would like to have over the years and opportunities where they could choose to be involved. Sometimes, these roles change as life develops, and that is okay. One of the biggest challenges I had to overcome was accepting my limits. I would ask myself what I could do at the moment and what needed to be accomplished or achieved. This would then help to dictate my role at that time, and I worked on accepting that I could not always meet the expectations others had for me.

To this day, I continue to struggle with being kind to myself and setting aside the guilt when I have reached my limits and cannot take on more responsibilities. I have learned to have more open communication about what my brother needs and what needs to happen to feel prepared for what comes next. He is at the centre of my world and is a big part of my life. I do not see that changing. Over time, my role in his life has shifted, as I have supported him in many roles, such as friend, sister, advocate, teacher, and guardian. To be one of his legal guardians as an adult is such an honour, as I can continue to serve as his voice, advocate, and anything else he needs while continuing to be his best friend. This new role has already taught me so many lessons and will continue to do so. It has not been easy as we navigate the adult world one lesson at a time, and it has created a new level in our relationship. Our bond is so unique. It makes me so proud to have him as my little brother. I would not be the person I am today without him in my life, and I will always be forever grateful for that.

Our Normal: A Sibling's Perspective

Hanae Davis

Growing up as the oldest of five children, I did not perceive my role as the eldest as being distinct from my role as a sibling to my brother with special needs. I do not remember whether my sense of responsibility, acute awareness of others' needs, heightened vigilance, and empathy were due to one role or the other. To this day, in my thirties, I still have difficulty teasing them apart. The answer, of course, is that it is both. The influences on my perceptions and behaviours—being the eldest and a sibling to someone with special needs—speak to an experience I believe all siblings like me share.

We use language to communicate with others, and labels are often helpful, albeit inexact, to categorize our experiences, especially for those who do not share our own. As a sibling, labels are tricky because our roles are always changing. Am I a companion? A playmate? A friend or advocate? A caregiver? My label depended on my age at the time, the chapter in my life, and most importantly, what my family and brother needed from me. To those on the outside, I used to withhold these qualifiers for fear of taking too long to explain. So, I would simply say, "I am his sister."

But "sister" is a loaded term. It could mean as little or as much as the listener can understand. Only when I found the sibling advocacy community did I feel I had the verbal scaffolding to describe my experiences. The importance of my ability to reflect on and categorize my experiences is twofold. First, our experiences as families with exceptionalities are different from others. We were often the anomaly, asking for accommodations and needing more time or resources to get from A to B. Second, my development necessarily traced our family's journey by being close in age to my brother, in contrast to my parents, who were already adults when they entered the disability world. What others, even my parents, saw as an anomaly was my normal. It was often confusing for me to grow into adolescence and adulthood, being part of two different worlds.

To help those in our lives better understand the role(s) that we have as siblings, I would like to offer the following messages in the hope they help siblings like me and families like mine.

To healthcare workers: We are the nurses on the ward growing up, understanding what is going well and what is not working. We should be heard and valued for our perspectives, as they are sometimes different from those of our parents, who are the "physicians". Our parents are often too focussed on getting through the day to engage us in these clinical appointments the way we may want to be. Help them by asking questions about the bigger picture. If you see us at an appointment, please ask how we are doing. If you do not see us at an appointment, ask our parents how we are doing. Working with us is an investment in our family's future, even through a brief conversation. Include us in it.

To researchers: Partnering with us is not the same as partnering with parents. We are experts in our own experiences. We thus have different needs that ought to be met to effectively and comfortably participate in research, especially child, youth, and young adult siblings. For instance, these subgroups are in a particularly dynamic phase of their lives. Some may be transitioning between new schools, jobs, and geographic locations. Accommodation and good offline communication are critical to ensuring that ongoing work is accessible for this population. Some of us may have never discussed our experiences with a researcher or clinical team. The more novel this experience is and the greater the age gap between partners and researchers, the more difficult it will be to disclose. We may not always feel comfortable sharing details about our family because we do not feel as though we have a right to, unlike our parents. To help with this, take your time to explain what informed consent and confidentiality mean in the context of your research and create a supportive environment.

To our parents: We are all figuring this out together. It is okay that you do not know everything, but let us work on it with you in an age-appropriate way, especially if we say we want to. We are active participants in our family, and we can feel helpless if we do not have a role. We feel the tie to our sibling in some shape or form. Some parents may say, "Go live your own life" to reduce their feelings of guilt. Statements like this invalidate our norms, which you may perceive as abnormal. Our sibling is part of our lives, and we are trying to navigate our lives with them. This constant navigation and learning of our different roles can be overwhelming to think about, particularly if there is a possibility that we will absorb the caregiving role in the future. But your acknowledgment of our efforts and support in that journey would make it easier for us. Because we feel an added responsibility, we may struggle to ask for help for ourselves. The mental health of the family includes siblings, too, so please reach out to us. Encourage our resilience by giving us space to be vulnerable.

To our sibling with a disability: You are our centre point, and we have learned so much from you. Your resilience grounds us, and your optimism inspires us. Being your sibling has sharpened our priorities early in our lives, and we are thankful for it. We may act frustrated at times, but that is because we care. We are growing up alongside you and working hard to figure ourselves out fast enough. It is scary not to know the future, and our future is intertwined with yours. Some of us may be your caregivers or cohabitants someday. We want the best for you and the best for us, and sometimes preparing for both is overwhelming. But we are here with you always and would not have it any other way.

As special-needs siblings, we are acutely aware of the value of our relationships. Fostering stronger foundations and common ground is a group effort, and we feel strongly about collaborating towards our families' collective wellbeing and future.

Roles and Responsibilities: A Researcher's Perspective

Linda Nguyen

In research that began during my doctoral studies, I established and partnered with the Sibling Youth Advisory Council (SibYAC) for over six years. The SibYAC has grown and is comprised of young adult siblings who have a sibling with a disability, two of whom are co-authors of this chapter (HD and SB). In qualitative research, reflexivity is done by researchers to reflect on how their personal lived and living experiences influence how they view and conduct research (Finlay 531–33; Koch and Harrington 888). Within our team, including the SibYAC, we reflect on our personal experiences and values, which shape how we conduct our program of research. We have held ongoing conversations about the roles of siblings in a family and recognize the value of these roles as Hanae and Samantha share in their stories above.

I grew up in an immigrant family, and I recognize how my personal and familial values influenced the development of my identity. I was motivated to pursue the research topic on siblings—including understanding their experiences and co-developing resources in partnership with siblings with lived experiences—based on my personal experiences. My sister is eighteen years older than me, and she was like a second mother to me when I was growing up. She supported me during times of stress and encouraged me to pursue my interests and passions. As I grew up and now as an adult, she has the role of a mentor and companion, as I often confide and share updates about my life with her. My niece (my sister's daughter) has a different relationship with me as we are seven and a half years apart; we have more of a sibling relationship. My niece was completing her undergraduate program at the same time I was pursuing my graduate studies, and we lived together like we were sisters. Throughout my childhood and even today, I continue to be a translator for my parents. My parents are aging, and I translate for them when they attend healthcare appointments. We have had family discussions to plan our roles, such as when I moved away from home for postsecondary education and employment. These personal experiences motivated me to support siblings and to partner with the SibYAC to understand the needs of siblings.

In our partnership with the SibYAC, I have had ongoing conversations with each member. We shared stories of our personal and professional experiences and identified knowledge gaps and support that could be studied in research for siblings. I have connected with the SibYAC by sharing my own experiences on how I have supported my family, and the SibYAC shared their experiences in how they supported their siblings and family. We also reflected on our partnership together and identified how we have worked well together and how we can improve. We further discussed the direction of the SibYAC and where we would like to see future research to support siblings.

Each sibling will develop values based on their personal experiences and familial and cultural values (Nguyen, "Being a Sibling" 8). The roles siblings choose to have, as shown in the previous two sections, are often influenced by many factors, such as age, birth order, gender, and cultural background. Sisters who are older than their sibling with a disability often choose to become caregivers to their sibling with a disability and begin to take steps to prepare for this future role, such as asking questions about health management and the healthcare team (Nguyen, "Canadian Resources" 12; Nguyen "Being a Sibling" 10). Siblings also begin to ask questions about the legal and financial aspects of how to care for their sibling with a disability.

As youth experience transitions in their life, including finding employment, pursuing postsecondary education, and developing friendships and romantic partnerships, they begin to develop their identities. Young people have different roles in the family, and siblings who have a sibling with a disability must consider how their role can evolve and change during the transitions in their lives. During childhood, siblings are often playmates; they can simply play and get to know each other's preferences, hobbies, and interests. During adolescence, a sibling may experience role changes, such as becoming a role model, mentor, advocate, supporter, or protector of their sibling with a disability (Nguyen, "Being a Sibling" 5). Some siblings have described how they begin to recognize how their sibling relationships are similar or different from their typically developing peers. They may begin to protect their sibling with a disability from feeling negative emotions, such as during instances of bullying. As siblings transition into adulthood, they are considering how their roles can change. Some siblings choose to become caregivers to their sibling with a disability, such as taking them to health appointments.

My messages to those who acknowledge, value, and support siblings are provided at multiple levels.

Healthcare service provision level: Siblings often want to support their sibling with a disability and require information to understand how to be involved with healthcare management, including attending health appointments and securing medications and treatments. Siblings have shared how they have felt ignored by healthcare providers during their appointments. Family-centred service includes providing care to the young patient and the whole family (King 1–3). Each family is unique, and it is important to recognize the diverse structure of families (Phoenix 2). Who is considered to be a part of the family? How can siblings be involved? How might healthcare support and respite services be provided to siblings and family members? How can siblings and family members themselves receive the services they require for their health and well-being?

Community level: Students can have different roles, including as siblings and young carers, within the family while juggling their school responsibilities and commitments. During elementary and high school, siblings construct their identities, which can be shaped by their sibling and family relationships (Nguyen "Filling in the Gap" 1361–62). Siblings have previously shared that they often navigate their identities and identify ways to fill in the gap in the family based on where they feel they are most needed (Nguyen, "Filling in the Gap" 1363). For example, they may plan their schedule around being available to support their sibling with a disability and family when needed. Some siblings have described that they cancelled events with their friends when they were most needed to stay at home to care for their sibling with a disability, and their parents or caregivers are away.

Siblings continue to navigate their commitments to their sibling role when they explore postsecondary education and/or employment opportunities. Siblings grapple with questions about whether to move away from home, stay nearby, or live with their family. They also navigate how to have conversations with their family to discuss the evolving changes in their role. For example, they may be away for some time but want to reevaluate their role when they move closer to home. Conversations with the family can be ongoing to develop plans for how the sibling roles can change over time.

Individuals at the community level, including teachers and employers, can consider how to support individuals who are siblings. What kind of organizations are available in the community for siblings to connect with? What types of accommodations can be provided in school and at workplaces to support siblings in their roles?

Systems and policy level: Families continuously advocate for increased support and services for children and youth with disabilities. Services may exist to support families, such as respite services and parental leave. Yet there is limited information available about the services siblings can access. Siblings are growing up and may become future carers to their siblings with a disability. While there are respite services and parental leave, some siblings may find the language unclear about whether such options are available. Policies and services can incorporate inclusive language to recognize and acknowledge the role of siblings. What are the policies that directly affect siblings? What kinds of services can siblings access to prepare for their current and future roles? How might siblings become advocates for their roles at the systems and policy level?

For all researchers, consider how your research affects the individual healthcare and service provision level, the community level, and the policy level. Studies have often focussed on the child with a disability, parents, and caregivers, but siblings can provide a different yet valuable perspective to inform research. For example, siblings can be included in testing interventions alongside other participants or share their experiences in qualitative studies. As we shift towards including persons with lived experience in participatory action research, siblings (such as the SibYAC) have provided input to shape and guide the direction of research affecting them.

It is critical to create space to include siblings within the family, community, and policy levels. While the sibling role is one role individuals may have, this role can have similarities with other roles, such as a caregiver. Recognizing the sibling role would directly benefit siblings and also highlight the multidimensional identities individuals can have.

Conclusion

It is not always easy to spot a caregiver. The goal of this chapter was to bring to light the experience of one type of caregiver: siblings. Having a multidimensional and evolving identity was a central theme across all our perspectives—the idea that siblings have various concurrent identities and roles over their lifetime, often starting at an early age. This experience may be shared with other sociodemographic groups as well, such as individuals who grew up in immigrant families or multigenerational homes. Siblings are key players in the family unit and in the circle of care for the individual with a disability. The sibling perspectives shared here allude to the uncertainty and responsibility they already experience and foresee in the future. To ensure long-term resilience and sustainability for these families, we must invest in supporting and researching siblings across the lifespan.

Works Cited

Finlay, Linda. "'Outing' the Researcher: The Provenance, Process, and Practice of Reflexivity." *Qualitative Health Research*, vol. 12, no. 4, 2002, pp. 531–45, https://doi.org/10.1177/104973202129120052.

King, Gillian, et al. "Family-Centred Service in Ontario: A 'Best Practice'

Approach for Children with Disabilities and Their Families." *Can Child*, 2002, https://www.canchild.ca/en/resources/175-family-centred-service-in-ontario-a-best-practice-approach-for-children-with-disabilities-and-their-families. Accessed 6 Apr. 2025.

Koch, Tina, and Harrington, Ann. "Reconceptualizing Rigour: The Case for Reflexivity." *Journal of Advanced Nursing*, vol. 28, no. 4, 1998, pp. 882–90, https://doi.org/10.1046/j.1365-2648.1998.00725.x.

Nguyen, Linda, et al. "Being a Sibling of a Youth with a Neurodisability: A Qualitative Study about the Roles and Responsibilities during the Transition to Adulthood." *Child: Care, Health and Development*, vol. 50, no. 2, 2024, p. e13241.

Nguyen, Linda, et al. "Canadian Resources for Siblings of Youth with Chronic Health Conditions to Inform and Support with Healthcare Management: A Qualitative Document Analysis." *Frontiers in Rehabilitation Sciences*, vol. 2, 2021, p. 52, https://doi.org/10.3389/fresc.2021.724589.

Nguyen, Linda, "'Filling in the Gap': A Qualitative Case Study about Identity Construction of Siblings of Youth with a Neurodisability." *Journal of Adolescence*, vol. 96, no. 6, 2024, p. 1354–1367, https://doi.org/10.1002/jad.12353.

Phoenix, Michelle, et al. "Reconceptualizing the Family to Improve Inclusion in Childhood Disability Research and Practice." *Frontiers in Rehabilitation Sciences*, vol. 2, 2021, https://doi.org/10.3389/fresc.2021.710580.

9.

My Life as a Lifelong Sibling Caregiver: An Exploration of Choice and Complex Feelings

Mary Sword

Introduction

I am a lifelong sibling caregiver to two of my three younger siblings. This means I have been caring for my siblings in different capacities throughout my life. My brother and sister are both multiply disabled and have lifelong high-care needs that my mother, my other younger sister and I have attended to since their birth. Our father, an abusive and harsh man, does not, despite a court-appointed custody order, provide any support, financial or otherwise, to my siblings and me.

While my younger neurotypical nondisabled sister and I no longer require our father's financial support, our siblings are another story. Both have been determined to have lifelong care needs, requiring 24/7 care and monitoring. Going by diagnostic standards, my siblings are high-needs autistic (level three) and have additional diagnoses of developmental delays, anxiety, epilepsy, ADHD, and OCD. What this means is that my siblings struggle to communicate verbally and do not appear to have a cognitive age matching their biological one.

I have found that people experience two emotions when they see my siblings: fear and pity. People see them, and a thousand words, stereotypes, and stigmas pass through their brains. When they look at my siblings, they see someone unknown to them, something different, something other.

When I was nineteen months old, my first younger sister was born. At the start, my caregiving towards her was standard and typical of a not-so-much-older sister still not yet out of diapers herself. I fawned over my newborn baby sister; I helped where I could, proud I was caring for the new baby. Often, my mother would wake up to find that my toddler self had crawled into my sister's crib—she was my baby, best friend, and sister. While I cannot remember this time, I like to think that even then, I knew this bond between sisters was one we would always have. This big sister role was one I would always hold above all other positions. I would spend my life caring for my sister.

When she was seventeen months old, and I was just two weeks past my third birthday, my sister and I became joint big sisters to a third sister, my nondisabled and neurotypical sister, who has, in our adulthood, become my sole confidant and support throughout this life we were both born into. Just another seventeen months later, our baby brother was born. In just four and a half years, my mother had had four C-sections and had, luckily, produced four healthy babies.

It was in 1999, when my mother was six months pregnant with her third daughter, that my first younger sister was diagnosed with pervasive developmental disorder and autism spectrum disorder. As my mother tells it, my sister had been developing typically when, around the age of two years old, she appeared to halt progressing in her language and cognitive development (although it was not until she was almost seven years old that she was officially diagnosed with a developmental delay). My sister is now twenty-six years old, and although she does communicate her wants and needs in her own way, she has never held a verbal conversation.

As a child, my sister was full of music, always singing her favourite songs and repeating quotes from her favourite movies. She never spoke directly, but she made it abundantly clear she was aware of the world around her. As an adult, my sister is still full of music, but now her language has all but completely left her, leaving those who love and care for her to coax words out with bribes and songs.

Unfortunately, language is of the utmost importance in our society. If one is unable to communicate verbally, they oftentimes are left in their world, left behind by an uncaring society with only their family to assist. People see my siblings and immediately disregard them; they speak about them as if they are not there, laughing and making snide remarks. Let me be clear: My siblings, in their own way, understand exactly what you are saying. They understand they are outsiders. They understand they are being made fun of. They understand they are other. I have comforted my sister for hours while she sobs because someone has laughed or said something about her as if she were not right in front of them. People look at her and are confused about why she becomes upset seemingly for no reason, but those closest to her see her reasons. We see the pity in their stares and laughs, their moving away when she comes near, being so clearly other. We see everything; people think they hide it well—they do not. My sister and brother understand the world around them, and they recognize this world is not made for them, despite their desire to be a part of it.

It was much easier for my family to exist in the wider world when my siblings were children. When you are a child, the world expects a certain level of unpredictability and loudness. When you are a child, the world is more lenient. As a fully grown, quite large man in his twenties, my brother is not allowed this same leniency. He is treated as a menace, a social pariah, and something unpredictable that needs to be feared.

In a way, I understand people's fear of my siblings and their unpredictability, particularly their fear of my brother. Even though his interests have not changed in over twenty years, and he would still rather see a Wiggles concert than something more age appropriate, he is, physically, a fully grown man with the full strength of a man in his prime. He is bigger and stronger than my mother, sisters, and me. For him, at least, I do understand people's fear; men are feared when they are unpredictable and when they can and do use their strength against you.

My brother's teenage years were a dark time in my family's history. As he was entering puberty, my brother was unable to communicate or process the anxieties, frustrations, and feelings that come with this hormonal change. At fourteen years old, my little brother, the youngest of my mother's four children, was already taller than all three older sisters and his mother, and at least sixty pounds heavier. To put it plainly, this was a dangerous and often alarming time for my family; every day was determined by the uncertainty of a teenage boy's temperament.

It was during this period that I, at around fifteen to eighteen years old, began to feel resentment towards the situation I had been born into. Throughout my life, I had been raised with the knowledge that my siblings needed help with most things, and it was up to me and my mother, sister, and grandmother to make sure they were taken care of. At the time, it seemed logical, something I would do no matter what. I would be there to take care of my siblings. In ways, it still seems logical now. How can I, after twenty-eight years of caring for them stop?

However, this does not mean that I do not often wonder about that alternate life where disability did not enter my world, where my siblings are not my charges but just my siblings, I know them as I know our other sister, and they move out and have lives, just as we have had the opportunity to do. Nor does it mean I do not think about the other alternate life where I have chosen to step away from this responsibility.

It is a choice I have made; it was always a choice, and it will always be a choice. I choose every day to assist my mother with their care. I choose to put them before many of my wants. If I am being honest, sometimes I do not know if I choose this because it is what is expected of me, or if it is something I choose to do because I want to.

During this time, our days were dictated by my brother's mood. Every day, my mother, sisters, and I were in danger of being beaten, punched, hit, kicked, slapped, bitten, screamed at, and pushed into walls. Each day was worse than the last, and here is where my resentment and jealousy, not towards my siblings but towards the apparent unfairness of the universe and to my friends who did not have this overhanging responsibility began.

Resentment is something that in my personal experience appears often in the life of a sibling caregiver and is certainly something I have dealt with throughout my life. I grew up assisting my mother with the care of my siblings while knowing one day my mother would get old and that she would not be able to care for them in the same way she did when we were children. I knew my sister and I would become their primary caregivers. While growing up in this environment, I remember seeing friends and desperately wishing for them to understand my life. I wanted them to experience wiping their siblings' bums clean of feces, having to bathe and dress them, and becoming uncomfortably familiar with their siblings' naked forms. I wanted them to know the meltdowns, fear, and beatings. I wanted them to understand what was happening in my house.

I wanted acknowledgment, understanding, and compassion from my peers. I wanted some sympathetic stranger to see my problems and say, "It's okay, I go through that, too!"

This life, and the responsibility that comes with being my siblings' sister, is not something I would choose for myself. It is not something I would pick out of a lineup and say, "Yes, please!" I do not want to come across as though I feel resentment towards my siblings; I will do anything and everything in my power to make sure they are content, safe, and loved throughout their lives. I will sacrifice my independence, free will, and the ability to make many choices in my adult life to care for them. However, despite this being my choice and the choice I continue to make each day, it has not been an easy one. I did not choose to be born into this life. I did not choose to become a caregiver, to have no separation between work and life and to be terrified of the future and of the unknowns and inevitable deaths and the impossibility of explaining those deaths. It is not a life I would choose. However, it is a life I do choose.

I do not want to demean, judge, or degrade the siblings like me who have made a choice different from my own. My experiences are my own, and I make the choice every day to care for my siblings. I respect your decision and am in some ways jealous of you if this is not the life you wanted for yourself.

How can I judge someone like myself who grew up in the same environment yet made a choice different from my own when it is so abundantly complicated and when so many inexplicable smaller decisions and experiences go into such a choice? As I have said, this is not a life I would choose, but it is a life I do choose. In many ways, however, it feels like it was decided for me, something I chose because it was what was expected of me. This goes back to the abundance of complications with this decision to become a sibling caregiver; it comes with many convoluted feelings.

I see that my friends can make choices unavailable to me. I see them not knowing how to speak to me about my siblings or how to broach the topic. I see their unease about the subject and situation. I see them live as typical adults, and I feel jealous. I am jealous of their ability to make decisions untethered, and I am jealous of their seeming unawareness of their undeniable privileges. They are privileged in a way I will never know and free and untethered in a way I am choosing to never be.

When I was eighteen, I decided to attend a university eight hours away from my hometown and my family. Looking back, it was clear I was trying to escape. At the time, my family was still very much dictated by my brother's frequent and terrifying meltdowns. I would purposefully stay in my university town for as long of a stretch as I could, never wanting to visit because I knew it would only induce a panic attack. I realize now, having since moved back to be a caregiver and having experienced life outside of my family, that what I was experiencing was my first taste of, for lack of a better word, freedom. I was free there. I had friends who did not know about my family and my impending responsibility (although I did eventually disclose this to most people). I could live where I wanted and was not bound by anyone other than myself. I tasted freedom, and it was addictive.

Thinking back on it now, this freedom feels like something I was entitled to and a luxury I took for granted. I still hold a few dear friends from this period, some of whom have since met my siblings. I see these friends go through the motions when I bring them to my childhood home. I see them realize that, simply put, my life has been vastly different from theirs. To this day, I can count on one hand the number of friends who have come to my childhood home and who have genuinely interacted with my siblings and have inquired after them while being honestly interested in the answer. This is not to speak ill of my friends who have not done this; I recognize my life and siblings are simply unknown to them. My siblings and I are other to them.

It is only in these brief moments where I see friends not know how to interact with or even speak about my siblings or my life as a caregiver that I think a part of me does feel resentment. It is in these moments that those convoluted feelings that come with being a lifelong caregiver creep up, with the thought, *Am I doing this because I want to or because it was ingrained into me as a child?* I do not know the answer to this question, and I do not know if I ever will. I think I will always deal with feelings of resentment in my life. I think I will always feel tethered and uncertain about my decision to be a caregiver to my siblings. It is a hard and uncertain life that I have chosen. I often tell my mother that she needs to outlive my siblings for the simple reason that I do not want to have to be the one to explain to my sister and brother where their mother has gone when she passes away.

I see myself in fifty years not being able to grieve my mother's death because I am busy helping my brother and sister understand her death. I see myself pushing aside my grief for years, not allowing myself the time I know I will need because I will be too focussed on making sure my siblings survive this complete shift to their worlds. My mother's death is my greatest fear, not because she is my mother, but because she is their mother. How can I possibly replace her? How can I possibly explain to them where she went?

When my mother leaves the house for even twenty minutes, my brother will ask me, "Mummy, come home soon?" How can I answer that question in thirty or forty years when the answer is that "No, buddy, mummy won't be coming home"? I live in terror of the day I am asked this question by him. Sometimes I think about this and how the only way it would be feasible for my mother to pass away before she is an old woman would be if my siblings somehow passed right along with her— some kind of horrible accident perhaps—and then at least my siblings would never have to know a world without their mother. At least then, my other sister and I would be able to grieve properly.

How horrible is it to think that? How awful is the fact that I would rather most of my immediate family die together than explain my mother's death to my siblings? The world is not built for my siblings, and I live in fear of the day I must navigate it with them without the guiding presence of our mother. I live in fear of the day I will inevitably become her. Even if, God willing, my mother dies a comfortable old woman in her bed, if my siblings are still alive, it will be too much. This day haunts my dreams, and I would be willing to bet similar thoughts haunt the dreams of countless other sibling caregivers like me.

Perhaps if I had made a different choice, I would be content. If I had chosen to stay in my university town, like so many of my friends have done, perhaps I would be content. At least then, I would not have to think about this future horrible day so often. At least then, these thoughts of my entire family dying would not plague me. At least then, I would not be constantly faced with the reality of my family situation.

Honestly, though, I do not think I would have been happy. I would have been consumed by guilt. The responsibility of one day becoming their caregiver has been so deeply ingrained into my being that I do not know how to be without them. I do not know who I am if I am not their sibling. I do not know who I am if I am not striving towards bringing them and people like them more understanding and representation. I am not happy if I am not with my siblings; they are part of me and have influenced most, if not all, of my adult decisions.

I am fascinated and driven by a desire to see families like my own represented in mainstream media and productions. I am determined to leave a lasting impact on the lives of those with high needs and multiple disabilities and on the lives of their families, particularly their siblings. I want to help these families feel less isolated and alone, as my own family has often been made to feel. Growing up, I would be the one the adults came to with questions about my siblings, who they were being paid to care for in their special education classes. These educational assistants would interrupt my classes and come to me with questions that to me had easy answers. They would ask about temperament, about likes and dislikes, about tells—things that to me were so clear because I was their big sister, caregiver, and protector.

My siblings are part of a vulnerable population within society, those requiring assistance in almost all aspects of their lives from their loved ones, family, and caregivers. Being there for my siblings—being their sister and their caregiver and doing my best to make the world more accessible to and for them—is perhaps the biggest part of my identity. This is why even though I do not think I would choose my life, I do choose my life. I have grown up knowing what it is to be a caregiver, and, for me, being their sister means being their caregiver. Being their sister comes before caregiving, but the two often go together. Regularly, the simple acts I do to care for them are just our sibling relationship demonstrating itself. I cannot and will not give up being their big sister, so I will choose to be their caregiver.

I do not resent my position as a lifelong sibling caregiver, but it is not an easy life. I would never change who my siblings are; they are whole as they are, despite what doctors and society may say about them and others like them. If I could do anything to change my life, I would change the world for my siblings. I would eliminate the stares, judgment, and stigma that can be felt emanating from strangers. I would change the world so that my siblings have the services available to them that they need to participate in society. I would make it so that there is an overflowing amount of people who feel the calling of caregiving, individuals who go to school to work with people like my siblings. In this changed world, my family and every family like my own would have access to a team of people to help them care for their family members rather than waiting on endless lists to maybe have access to assistance.

I would change the world so that I and siblings like me do not feel so alone. I would create more services for family members to deal with the inevitable specific anxieties that come with being a lifelong caregiver. I would change it so that there was enough money allocated by our governments towards people like my siblings who require care. My siblings would have friends; they would have fulfilling social lives and would not be constantly othered by an uncaring society.

I would make it so that my sister is not laughed at by teenagers when I bring her to the movies. My family would no longer live in fear of the day my brother does the wrong thing with his strength and winds up in the justice system. I would make it so we feel like any other family. I would change everything for my siblings.

Unfortunately, though, I cannot change the world. I can only care for my siblings and continue my research to bring more representation to people like them and families like my own. I wish society were built to help those most vulnerable members of our communities. I wish there were more resources for siblings like me, such as sibling support groups for adult sibling caregivers. I wish people felt more compassion for families like my own and did not feel uneasy and afraid when we are out in our community. I wish for a lot of things, as I am sure my siblings do, too.

Section V

Mothering and Caregiving with Adult Children with Disabilities

10.

"It Is What It Is": Mothers Caring for Adult Children with an Intellectual and Developmental Disability in Rural Ontario during the COVID-19 Pandemic

Anna Przednowek, Sharon Desormeau, and Sarah Ederer

Introduction

The care and support of adults with intellectual and developmental disabilities (IDD) in Ontario, Canada, have shifted drastically over the last several decades from publicly funded institutions to a private family responsibility. As the last three large-scale institutions closed in 2009 and the waiting lists for residential care have continued to grow exponentially, the care of adults with IDD has fallen on families. While attempts are made to share the care workload through Passport Program funding,[1] which provides funding for families to pay for support, the bulk of care work continues to be performed by mothers well into older age. In 2020, the care workload experienced by these mothers was further exacerbated by the impact of the COVID-19 pandemic and the implementation of associated social and physical distancing measures that reduced access to publicly funded support and services and to public spaces within communities.

Perspectives of mothers of adult children with IDD and the concerns about the current social organization of care are well explored in the literature (Knight 668; Traustadottir 211), including as mothers are aging (Chou and Kröger 482). That said, the experiences of mothers caring for adult children with IDD in rural Canada are relatively underexplored. In turn, our chapter aims to centre the perspectives of rurally located mothers and contribute to a more nuanced understanding of caregiving during the COVID-19 pandemic in Ontario. We ask the following questions. How do they describe the conditions shaping their family caregiving experiences, before and during COVID-19? What can we learn from their work and coping strategies?

In responding to these questions, a relational lens (Rogers 44) helps us illuminate how the conditions of everyday life and care of rurally located adults with IDD are deeply intertwined with the conditions of life of their caregiving mothers. We also elaborate on how the current social organization of care affects the care relationship in ways that "disempower and restrict the autonomy of mothers" (Bryant and Garnham "Bounded Choices" 261).

In what follows, we introduce the importance of focussing on rural families' caregiving experiences, including during the COVID-19 pandemic. We then introduce our study design and methods, which apply a critical ethics of intellectual disability care approach.

A Brief Overview of the COVID-19 Pandemic and Its Impacts

As a response to the global COVID-19 pandemic, on March 17, 2020, the premier of Ontario declared a state of emergency, marking the beginning of the first lockdown in the province (Long 1). Regionally targeted restrictions were implemented with each wave of the pandemic, and more strict lockdown conditions affected the public health regions of Ontario having the highest number of COVID-19 cases (Long 2). People were asked to stay at home and practise social distancing, which entailed avoiding contact with others and wearing personal protective equipment while accessing essential services (Long 2). Businesses deemed nonessential were shut down, leading to more online shopping and the widespread implementation of virtual programming (Long 2, 7).

The global COVID-19 pandemic has had profound social impacts, exacerbating economic and health disparities (McMahon et al. 1). Changes in the labour market and disruptions in global food supply chains led to heightened food insecurity as people struggled to access an overwhelmed healthcare system (Alabi and Ngwenyama 167). There was a significant increase in adverse mental health outcomes, including depression, anxiety, substance use, and suicidal thoughts and behaviours (Jenkins et al. 2). People experiencing preexisting social inequities based on race, gender, sexual orientation, disability status, and socioeconomic status were disproportionately affected by these issues (Jenkins et al. 3).

Across Canada, stigmatizing policies, discrimination from healthcare providers, and stringent lockdown measures in residential care homes and community service delivery have affected the physical, mental and social wellness of people with IDD by limiting their access to support workers, health services, social participation, and vital information for their wellness (Goyal et al. 77; Hansford et al. 2). When seeking mental health support, people with IDD were disproportionately affected by longer wait times and inaccessible care, which left people with new-onset conditions unsupported and produced more adverse outcomes for people who had already been struggling (Jesus et al. 1).

As our research illustrates, issues with policy, stigma, accessibility, and health disparities affected people with IDD and their families, too. Familial caregivers were disproportionately affected by the pandemic, having had their care arrangements disrupted by COVID-19 policies, which isolated them from their loved ones (Goyal et al. 77).

Life in Rural Communities before and during the Pandemic

Depending on one's definition of "rural," up to 90 per cent of Canada's land mass and 30 per cent of its population can be as such (Williams and Kulig 1). Rural life comes with many unique benefits as well as some challenges. For Canadians, rural living is associated with overall higher levels of life satisfaction (e.g. self-perceived psychological wellbeing) compared to their urban counterparts (John et al. 1). However, rural life also comes with issues, such as higher unemployment rates, limited options for social engagement, and a lack of funding for resources promoting health and wellness (Keating et al. 323). These issues disproportionately affect populations facing marginalization, such as people living in poverty or people with significant health issues, who report lower life satisfaction in rural settings (Keating et al. 323).

As a part of the lockdown measures implemented to stop the spread of the COVID-19 virus, international travel became restricted, leading many Ontarians to seek out travel destinations within the province (Long 2). This raised concerns for residents of rural communities, who had seen slower transmission of the virus and wanted to maintain lower infection rates (Long 2). As such, many rural communities asked people from regions with high rates of COVID-19 infection to avoid travelling to their area (Long 2). People living in rural Canada during the pandemic reported less life disruption than their urban counterparts, which may be explained by the reality they were already accustomed to the need for exercising creativity while trying to access resources in remote and northern areas (Goodwin et al. 57; Wang et al. 78). Despite this, rural communities still faced distinct challenges in the wake of the COVID-19 pandemic (Goodwin et al. 57), which worsened health disparities across the lifespan in the north (Maximova et al. 1).

Familial Caregiving in Rural Communities.

People living rurally face barriers to social participation and limited access to healthcare; as such, adults with IDD are also disproportionately affected by these issues (Nicholson 50). Although these intersecting social locations mean people with IDD and their familial caregivers may be affected by dual disadvantages in rural settings, these families strive to provide care through a series of arrangements to compensate for the limited support they receive from the state (Nicholson 50; Pan and Ye 352). For example, as transportation is an ongoing issue in rural communities in Ontario, caregivers are required to transport their children with IDD to most of their activities.

The state's lack of support creates immense stress for families, who already experience a high level of resource strain (Pan and Ye 352). This issue is further exacerbated as people with IDD and their caregivers begin to age, as there are no formal supports to adequately plan for post-parental care (Garnham et al. 836; Wark 1–2).

Our Research Project

Our qualitative research project titled "Impact of COVID-19 and Associated Social and Physical Distancing Measures on Everyday Life and Care of Adults with Intellectual and Developmental Disabilities and Their Supports: A Rural Ontario Case Study" explores the perspectives of mothers,[2] adults with IDD, direct support workers, and program managers about the everyday life and care of adults with IDD and their supports living and caring in rural Ontario under COVID-19. The study was a collaboration between the first author and a rurally located, publicly funded community agency serving adults with IDD.

In this chapter, we draw on semi-structured interviews with three mothers caring for adult children with IDD following the onset of the COVID-19 pandemic. As the research was carried out during the early phase of COVID-19, and the social and physical distancing measures were still in place, the research had to be conducted via telephone or a virtual meeting platform. The first author conducted the interviews via telephone in October 2020, roughly eight months after implementing the social and physical distancing measures. The interviews were shaped by a predetermined set of questions, which generated information about "everyday interactions and occurrences" (Runswick-Cole 79). In our conversations, participants—Amy, Judy, and Kelly[3]—described their material and social situations.

Amy is an employed fifty-year-old married mother of three children living in rural Ontario. Amy works night shifts to provide support throughout the day to her adult child with IDD, Alexa. Before the pandemic, Amy's mother also provided additional support one to two days a week. Due to a lack of transportation services in the rural community, Amy transported Alexa to daily activities. She also volunteered with two local networks serving people with IDD. During the COVID-19 pandemic, Amy reduced her employment hours to help provide care to Alexa as community supports were reduced.

Judy is a retired sixty-five-year-old mother who lives in rural Ontario with her semiretired husband and an adult child with IDD, Jenny. Judy transports Jenny to many of the activities that are available and provides all personal care. During the COVID-19 pandemic, Judy also cared for her grandchildren several days a week.

Kelly is a retired fifty-seven-year-old mother who lives with her husband and an adult child with IDD, Krista, in rural Ontario. The family relocated from a small town to a smaller rural community and discovered an even greater limit to support and services. As a result, Kelly provides all personal support care to Krista and transports her to all activities.

A critical ethics of intellectual disability care (Bryant and Garnahm, "Incorporating" 289; Rogers 44) shapes our data analysis. First, although the care of people with IDD in our study takes place within the context of the family, framing care provision in families supporting adults with IDD as familial caregiving occludes the gendered nature of care. The contemporary models of social organization of care have also assigned a disproportionate moral responsibility for care to mothers, thus ascribing a high standard for mothers in meeting the needs of their children (Bryant and Garnham "Bounded Choices" 260). Second, by employing a relational lens in the study, we aim to make visible how the conditions of life and care of people with IDD and their families—more specifically, their mothers—are deeply intertwined. Finally, building on the work of Lia Bryant and Bridget Garnham ("Incorporating" 289), we discuss how rurality is incorporated into the discussion of the care provision of rurally located mothers.

Results

The results from our interviews with the mothers are divided into two key themes: rural caregiving and imperfect lives before the pandemic and the impact of the COVID-19 pandemic and associated social and physical distancing measures. The second theme has two subthemes: taking on new carework during the pandemic and bounded choices.

Rural Caregiving and Imperfect Lives before the Pandemic

Although families of people with IDD often struggle to access adequate, funded support, those living in rural areas face additional barriers, such as limited resources and a lack of trained workers, thereby further reducing the support available (Wark et al. 429). Kelly, the fifty-seven-year-old mother of Krista, indicated that the rural location influences her family's ability to access support and services for her daughter; she acknowledged the difficulties with accessing resources, since the family relocated to a smaller and more isolated community, including higher financial costs associated with purchasing supports through direct funding. She shared: "I don't have the same quality and quantity of services that were available for my child." When living in a more urban centre, her daughter could access more support and activities, but since moving, Kelly has spent countless hours advocating for her daughter to gain access to social activities. Kelly also noted she was finally successful and had arranged for additional activities for her daughter just before COVID-19; however, the newly secured activities were located thirty minutes outside of their community, and transportation is central to accessing them. This distance would have resulted in additional pressures being placed on her to transport her daughter. Issues surrounding transportation and increased unpaid family care workload were echoed by Judy and Amy, who live ten to fifteen minutes outside of towns where there is no access to public transit.

As Kelly's experiences speak to, before COVID-19, some formal care was available as people with IDD could access support through agencies and the Passport Program. The mothers in our study revealed that before COVID-19, some of their adult children with IDD were actively engaged in daily activities, such as dancing, swimming, skating, and art classes. Others were employed, volunteered, or participated in enriching social gatherings outside of the home. Families could access activities through a local agency and the broader community, and Passport funding allowed them to hire individual supports to help share in the daily care of their adult children.

Impact of the COVID-19 Pandemic and Associated Social and Physical Distancing Measures

Taking on Additional Care Work during the Pandemic

With the onset of the pandemic, caregivers experienced a shift and an increase in their care workload and responsibility alongside a decrease in support and opportunities for respite (Rogers et al. 1421). People with IDD face multiple barriers to healthcare, such as limited transportation options, inaccessible medical facilities, and lower social determinants of health (e.g. increased poverty, unemployment, and social isolation) and are more likely to report having unmet healthcare needs (Goyal et al. 77; Sabatello et al. 187). In emergencies, the geographical distance from healthcare facilities, such as hospitals, presents significant challenges in rural communities, especially when they struggle to access reliable transportation (Pini et al. 224; Sanders et al. 1389). These barriers have created adverse health outcomes for people with IDD, which have been exacerbated during the COVID-19 pandemic, thus increasing the stress levels of mothers who took on more caregiving responsibilities to fill in systemic gaps caused by the pandemic and associated restrictions (Goyal et al. 77; Hansford et al. 1–2). Additional stressors for maternal caregivers came with the rising number of positive COVID cases in rural areas. As the virus spread within communities located closer to the cottage country, which saw an influx of visitors from urban centres, mothers became aware of the heightened risk of contracting the COVID-19 virus and experienced their stress levels increase.

The mothers interviewed in this study described an added cognitive and emotional care workload during the pandemic, as they put work into (1) keeping families safe, (2) making do with limited support, and (3) organizing and overseeing activities.

Keeping families safe. All the mothers discussed how they needed to take the time to explain the COVID-19 pandemic and the effects of the restrictions on their children, such as closing services, support, and even stores they would frequent before the pandemic. They put thought into preventing the spread of the virus and keeping their families safe. Some also highlighted the added stress and challenges of trying to get their family members with IDD to wear personal protective equipment to prevent them from getting sick. Amy shared she needed to educate her daughter Alexa about COVID-19 and make the information accessible and relevant, but not go into too much detail to create anxiety. Judy's daughter experienced many challenges wearing a mask and "wouldn't meet any health standards by any means." Meaning, that her face was not properly covered and therefore would not meet the standard for preventing the spread of the COVID-19 virus.

As we learned, the responsibility to prevent COVID-19 and to provide and oversee the care fell onto the parents.

Making do with limited support. Parents had to worry about who they let into the house and had to trust the care worker who came in to support their child. The worry about keeping the child with IDD and the family safe meant some families even decided to stop receiving support from workers who worked across multiple sites. Amy highlighted this common practice of sharing the support workers before the pandemic: "I had a variety of people, but it didn't mean as much to me. I didn't care what that person did if they weren't with me. I didn't care if they worked in a group home, or if they went into other people's houses and that kind of thing, whereas now, that's all I can't stop thinking about it".

Organizing and overseeing activities. The mothers in our study got creative when it came to planning and participating in their activities, whether by getting outside or helping their children access online services. A notable finding was that rural living helped some families in our study to overcome some of the social distancing measures by providing outdoor space and not limiting them to indoor activities. When weather and bugs permitted, families could engage in activities, such as swimming, walking, enjoying nature, and planning for winter activities, such as adapted skiing, skating, and snowmobiling in the bush. This echoes the research finding that rural living presents advantages and obstacles for people with IDD during the pandemic (Pini et al. 223). The increased access to green spaces and time outdoors associated with rural life can benefit mental wellness by creating opportunities for community engagement (Pini et al. 224).

Mothers also put time and thought into overseeing online activities or dealing with the frustrations of not having reliable internet in rural areas. Regarding the additional work involved, when services began to be delivered through virtual platforms, familial caregivers often had to learn to act as mediators to help make online services accessible for their loved ones with IDD (Jesus et al. 2, 15). One way adults with IDD attempted to cope was through an increase in online connections through social media groups and Zoom activities, such as bingo, to maintain access to support and to promote wellbeing. The use of technology to compensate for a lack of in-person support during the pandemic has had mixed results for people with IDD (Goyal et al. 78; Pellegrino and DiGennaro 1276). Families shared that service accessibility made a key difference in maintaining support. Inaccessible technology resulted in difficulties navigating online resources when seeking support, especially when individuals required text-based communication (Linden et al. 2). Lack of connectivity to services and support was highlighted by mothers as concerning because it created a greater sense of isolation for the daughters and the mothers. This situation, in turn, created a greater sense of worry in mothers regarding the increased mental health effects on their loved ones and the loss of skills and independence that families had to develop.

Speaking about the emotional work involved in organizing activities, Amy said the hardest part was keeping her daughter's spirits up and keeping her busy with activities. Her daughter had just learned to be more independent, which had taken over three years of caregiver support to achieve. Judy's daughter was social. The family had worked hard for over forty years to get her out and promote social participation and social inclusion, and with COVID-19, everything shut down. While Kelly's caregiving responsibilities did not change, she no longer had time away from her daughter, thereby affecting her ability to have a social life. She noted, however, that her daughter's life was more drastically affected. For Kelly personally, the most notable difference was not being able to see her friends.

When adults with IDD were given more accessible options, such as video conferencing, they could connect with resources that benefited their wellness (Linden et al. 2), especially when they connected with services with whom they had a previous connection, such as through a community agency. One of the drawbacks for rural families was difficulties accessing reliable internet connectivity when connecting to check-in calls with support workers or accessing virtual activities. Furthermore, when mothers accessed community or agency connections through social media groups, they expressed concerns about a lack of confidentiality, as information could easily be shared within their small communities.

As illustrated, the mothers in this study adapted to their new routines created by the changes posed by COVID-19 restrictions, such as cancelled programming and social activities that helped support their child with IDD, as well as the unavailability of trained workers. In many cases, this resulted in the mothers "single-handedly fill[ing] in for an entire non-existing 'village' of supports[;] they sacrificed their own personal and professional aspirations and well-being" (Pozniak et al. 15). Such all-encompassing demands for care affected mothers' paid work options, too. While Judy and Kelly were both retired from paid work at the onset of the pandemic, Amy worked a full-time job. At the onset of the pandemic, Amy had to reduce her working hours from full-time to two shifts a week to accommodate the increasing time devoted to care.

Bounded Choices

As we learned from the stories of Amy, Judy, and Kelly, the possibilities and sites of care were bounded and restricted not only by the geographical context (Bryant and Garnham "Bounded Choices" 264) but also by the restrictions posed by the COVID-19 pandemic and associated social and physical distancing measures. Furthermore, as we will elaborate, their choices were powerfully shaped and bounded by gendered dimensions at play and by moral expectations to provide care.

Gendered expectations. With the gendered nature of caregiving, many of the carers affected by the pandemic were the *mothers* of people with IDD (Rogers et al. 1422; Traustadottir 211). Mothers who participated in our research struggled to access educational, professional, and social support due to the lockdown restrictions, which produced difficulties, including increased stress, carer burden, and depression (Rogers et al. 1421). Mothers also reported feeling the loss of daily routines and sources of support (Rogers et al. 1422). Kelly said the only people providing care were she and her husband. The family stayed away from everyone, so there was little interaction because of COVID-19. Judy shared she had a worker before COVID-19 who was providing care to her daughter, but she had to resign because of her fears of getting COVID-19 and caring for her aging mother. For Amy and her family, all the support and services, including typical extended family support, even as small as participating in a birthday party stopped due to COVID-19.

Moral expectations. With a reduction in support and services, high societal and moral standards for mothering, and an increase in the lifespan of people with IDD, mothers continue to be the primary caregivers for their adult children despite their aging and health-related issues (Patel et al. 255). Even though she experiences health challenges herself, Kelly continued to be the primary caregiver of her adult child with IDD: "It is what it is... I just do it because I have to, and I'm sure somewhere down the road that's going to come back to bite me eventually. It hasn't taken its toll yet. I just do what I have to do." Amy felt as if there was no other option when caring for her daughter: "I think you just do it; they just need us to do it." Despite the rural inequities and bounded choices, rural mothers of children with IDD continued to try, albeit ambivalently, and meet societal standards which define "the good mother" as one who is "a resilient and self-less carer" (Bryant and Garnham "Bounded Choices" 263), resulting in a decrease in their health and quality of life (Patel et al. 255).

COVID-19 Shines a Light on the Sustainability and Future of Care

On the periphery of our study sample were adults with IDD being supported by support workers in publicly funded care homes who faced even more strict and frequently changing regulations, which disrupted their routines and isolated them from their families (Standley et al. 271). People with IDD living in these settings were disproportionately affected by care staff's political resistance to COVID-19 protocols (e.g., vaccinations and personal protective equipment) (Standley et al. 271). This resistance created barriers to adequate care despite our knowledge that people with IDD are at higher risk of developing serious illnesses when exposed to COVID-19 (Hughes et al. 206–07). The mothers in our study were affected by these public conversations and tensions with the implementation of strict social and physical distancing measures in paid care homes, many of which resulted in workers being bound to one care home and providing essential services, thus withdrawing from supporting individuals in living in the community and their families. Kelly stated that even before COVID-19, she did not want her daughter living in a care home, as she was concerned about what might happen to her. Judy expressed that although she understood why services and supports had to shut down with COVID-19, she did not have much hope for how they could fix the system.

Although we may see issues and tensions surrounding care provided in care homes as unrelated to familial care provision, these disproportionately affect caregiving mothers due to gendered expectations surrounding care (Bryant and Garnham "Bounded Choices" 260). As rural caregivers age alongside their children with IDD, they face uncertain futures for postparental care due to the normative construction of the archetypal "good mother" (Bryant and Garnham "Bounded Choices" 265). Social responsibility for care is disproportionately placed upon mothers, and relinquishing that care is deeply problematized despite the caregiver's need for support (Bryant and Garnham "Bounded Choices" 263). This dynamic further legitimizes the state's limited provision of support to caregivers in rural communities and increases stress and uncertainty for caregivers with no clear long-term care options for their adult children (Bryant and Garnham "Bounded Choices" 265–66).

Conclusion

Although the general population reported less life disruption in the rural north, this was not always the case for people with IDD and their families (Wang et al. 78-79). The mothers in our study articulated the multilayered effects of COVID-19 and the associated social and physical distancing measures on themselves and their adult children with IDD. They described the challenges of sharing the care workload in rural areas, considering the increased costs of purchasing care through direct funding and the limited availability of support workers. The mothers also highlighted the added cognitive and emotional carework associated with keeping their children safe, as well as the opportunities and barriers afforded to them by rural living in managing the social and physical distancing measures during the pandemic.

At the time of the study and eight months into the pandemic, many cancelled programs were "gone... gone.... gone...," as described by the mothers, and never fully reimplemented as restrictions were being lifted. Unsurprisingly, the maternal care providers of people with IDD were becoming accustomed to the adversities they faced during COVID-19, as they often experienced a lack of resources and services before COVID-19 (Pozniak et al. 12). Although families who care for adult children with IDD are resilient and adapt to the limited or nonexistent services and support for their children with IDD, the mothers in our study questioned how sustainable this was in the long term.

As the chapter draws on the perspectives of a small sample of mothers living in rural Ontario, it offers a snapshot of and a glimpse into the "bounded choices" (Bryant and Garnham "Bounded Choices" 264) and imperfect lives of rurally located mothers and their adult children with IDD during the pandemic. The state has historically disproportionately made mothers responsible for adapting their caregiving approaches to suit conditions of austerity; however, this issue was exacerbated by the COVID-19 pandemic and its policies, which further limited caregivers' access to support (Bryant and Garnham "Bounded Choices" 264; Rogers et al. 1421).

The chapter invites us to consider a gendered and relational lens to care provision under COVID-19 and to take seriously the geographical location of care in the larger landscape of care provision for adults with IDD in Canada. The perspectives shared by the mothers in our chapter also invite us to consider the future and sustainability of care in rural communities.

Acknowledgment

We would like to thank Dr. Anne Wagner and Dr. Janna Klostermann for their feedback on an earlier version of this chapter.

Endnotes

1. The Passport Program is provincially administered direct support funding. One of the primary goals of the program is to support the daily living of persons with IDD and the facilitation of social inclusion.
2. Although we aimed to include the perspectives of familial caregivers more broadly, it was not surprising to us that caregiving mothers expressed interest in our study.
3. We use pseudonyms for the participants' names.

Works Cited

Alabi, Michael Omotayo, and Ojelanki Ngwenyama. "Food Security and Disruptions of the Global Food Supply Chains during COVID-19: Building Smarter Food Supply Chains for Post COVID-19 Era." *British Food Journal*, vol. 125, no. 1, 15 Mar. 2022, pp. 167–85.

Bryant, Lia, and Bridget Garnham. "Bounded Choices: The Problematisation of Longterm Care for People Ageing with an Intellectual Disability in Rural Communities." *Journal of Rural Studies*, vol. 51, Apr. 2017, pp. 259–66.

Bryant, Lia, and Bridget Garnham. "Incorporating Rurality into a Critical Ethics of Intellectual Disability Care 1." *The Routledge Handbook of Critical Social Work*. Edited by Stephen Webb. Routledge, 2019, pp. 289–301.

Chou, Yueh-Ching, and Teppo Kröger. "Ageing in Place Together: Older Parents and Ageing Offspring with Intellectual Disability." *Ageing and Society*, vol. 42, no. 2, 12 Aug. 2020, pp. 480–94.

Goyal, Divya, et al. "Impact of the COVID-19 Pandemic on People with Disabilities and Implications for Health Services Research." *Journal of Health Services Research & Policy*, vol. 28, no. 2, 23 Feb. 2023, pp. 77–79.

Garnham, Bridget, et al. "Policy, Plans, and Pathways: The 'Crisis' Transition to Post-Parental Care for People Ageing with Intellectual Disabilities in Rural Australian Carescapes." *Ageing and Society*, vol. 39, no. 4, 4 Dec. 2017, pp. 836–50.

Government of Ontario. "Passport Program for Adults with a Developmental Disability." *Government of Ontario*, www.ontario.ca/page/passport-program-adults-developmental-disability. Accessed 8 Apr. 2025.

Hansford, Rebecca, et al. "Short Report: The Influence of Congregate Setting on Positive COVID-19 Tests among a High-Risk Sample of Adults with Intellectual and Developmental Disability in Ontario." *Research in Developmental Disabilities*, vol. 122, Mar. 2022, https://www.sciencedirect.com/science/article/pii/S0891422222000087?via%3Dihub. Accessed 13 Apr. 2025.

Hughes, M. Courtney, et al. "The Perspective of Administrators of Intellectual Disability Organizations on the COVID-19 Pandemic." *Journal of Intellectual Disabilities*, vol. 27, no. 1, 17 Jan. 2022, pp. 206–20.

Jenkins, Emily K., et al. "A Portrait of the Early and Differential Mental Health Impacts of the COVID-19 Pandemic in Canada: Findings from the First Wave of a Nationally Representative Cross-Sectional Survey." *Preventive Medicine*, vol. 145, Apr. 2021, https://www.sciencedirect.com/science/article/pii/S0091743520303649?via%3Dihub. Accessed 13 Apr. 2025.

Jesus, Tiago, et al. "Lockdown-Related Disparities Experienced by People with Disabilities during the First Wave of the COVID-19 Pandemic: Scoping Review with Thematic Analysis." *International Journal of Environmental Research and Public Health*, vol. 18, no. 12, 8 June 2021, https://www.mdpi.com/1660-4601/18/12/6178. Accessed 13 Apr. 2025.

Keating, Norah, et al. "Aging in Rural Canada: A Retrospective and Review." *Canadian Journal on Aging / La Revue Canadienne Du Vieillissement*, vol. 30, no. 3, 18 July 2011, pp. 323–38.

Knight, Kathryn. "The Changing Face of the 'Good Mother': Trends in Research into Families with a Child with Intellectual Disability, and Some Concerns." *Disability & Society*, vol. 28, no. 5, July 2013, pp. 660–73.

Linden, Mark A., et al. "Impact of the COVID-19 Pandemic on Family Carers of Those with Profound and Multiple Intellectual Disabilities: Perspectives from UK and Irish Non-Governmental Organisations." *BMC Public Health*, vol. 22, no. 1, 16 Nov. 2022, https://bmcpublichealth.biomedcentral.com/articles/10.1186/s12889-022-14560-4. Accessed 13 Apr. 2025.

Long, Jed A., et al. "Do Regionally Targeted Lockdowns Alter Movement to Non-Lockdown Regions? Evidence from Ontario, Canada." *Health & Place*, vol. 79, 2023, https://www.sciencedirect.com/science/article/pii/S1353829221001647. Accessed 13 Apr. 2025.

Maximova, Katerina, et al. "The Impact of the COVID-19 Pandemic on Inequalities in Lifestyle Behaviours and Mental Health and Wellbeing of Elementary School Children in Northern Canada." *SSM – Population Health*, vol. 23, Sept. 2023, https://www.sciencedirect.com/science/article/pii/S2352827323001192. Accessed 13 Apr. 2025.

McMahon, Meghan, et al. "Informing Canada's Health System Response to COVID-19: Priorities for Health Services and Policy Research." *Healthcare Policy | Politiques de Santé*, vol. 16, no. 1, 20 Aug. 2020, pp. 112–24.

Nicholson, Laura. *The Health, Support Needs, Access to Healthcare Services and Social Exclusion of Adults with Intellectual Disabilities Living in Rural Areas: A Rural-Urban Comparison*. 2012. University of Glasgow, dissertation.

Pan, Lu, and Jingzhong Ye. "Family Care of People with Intellectual Disability in Rural China: A Magnified Responsibility." *Journal of Applied Research in Intellectual Disabilities*, vol. 28, no. 4, 5 Mar. 2015, pp. 352–66.

Patel, Varsha, et al. "The Experiences of Carers of Adults with Intellectual Disabilities during the First COVID 19 Lockdown Period." *Journal of Policy and Practice in Intellectual Disabilities*, vol. 18, no. 4, 15 May 2021, pp. 254–62.

Pini, Barbara, et al. "On making disability in rural places more visible: Challenges and opportunities [introduction to a special issue]." *Journal of Rural Studies*, vol. 51, Apr. 2017, pp. 223–29.

Pozniak, Kinga, et al. "What Supports and Services Post COVID-19 Do Children with Disabilities and Their Parents Need and Want, Now and into the Future?" *Frontiers in Public Health*, vol. 12, 8 Apr. 2024, https://www.frontiersin.org/journals/public-health/articles/10.3389/fpubh.2024.1294340/full. Accessed 13 Apr. 2025.

Rogers, Chrissie. *Intellectual Disability and Being Human: A Care Ethics Model.* Routledge, 2016.

Rogers, Gemma, et al. "The Experiences of Mothers of Children and Young People with Intellectual Disabilities During the First COVID-19 Lockdown Period." *Journal of Applied Research in Intellectual Disabilities*, vol. 34, no. 6, 23 Mar. 2021, pp. 1421–30.

Runswick-Cole, Katherine. "Interviewing." *Qualitative Methods in Psychology: A Research Guide.* Edited by Peter Banister et al. McGraw-Hill Education, 2011, pp. 88–99.

Standley, Krys, et al. "'Just Trying to Adjust to the New Reality That Seems to be Changing Every Hour': Lessons Learned from Nation-Wide Peer Meetings on COVID-19 with Rural Disability Service Providers." *Community Development*, vol. 55, no. 2, 11 Aug. 2023, pp. 271–88.

St. John, Philip D., et al. "Life Satisfaction in Adults in Rural and Urban Regions of Canada—The Canadian Longitudinal Study on Aging." *Rural and Remote Health*, vol. 21, no. 3, 2021.

Traustadottir, Rannveig "Mothers who Care." *Journal of Family Issues*, vol. 12, no. 2, June 1991, pp. 211–28.

Wang, Donna, et al. "Coping with and adapting to COVID-19 in rural United States and Canada." *Families in Society*, vol. 102, no.1, 2021, pp. 78–90.

Wark, Stuart, et al. "Ageing with an Intellectual Disability: Support Issues in Rural Localities." *12th National Rural Health Conference*, Adelaide, 2013, pp. 1–10.

Williams, Allison, and Judith Kulig. "Health and Place in Rural Canada." *Health in Rural Canada.* Edited by Judith Kulig and Allison Williams. UBC Press. 2011, pp. 1–22.

11.

Mothering in a Sandwich Generation

Joy Seguin

Introduction

I live in a small community in Eastern Ontario. Cornwall is located in the traditional territory of the Haudenosaunee, Mohawk, and Huron-Wendat peoples. I am a mother, sister, sister-in-law, aunt, niece, cousin, friend, and granddaughter. I am a caregiver and advocate for my adult son with a developmental disability. I am a caregiver for an elderly uncle and a supportive essential caregiver for several senior family members. I am a member of the new so-called sandwich generation. I care for and live with a disabled son and a senior family member.

Like most caregivers, I had numerous jobs while shuffling daily family responsibilities. My certified professional roles include cosmetologist, accounting assistant, medical receptionist, educational assistant, and teacher of adults. Like many who care for a family member or two, we have a few more unexpected, uncertified, and professional roles, including caregiver, developmental support worker, personal support worker, bookkeeper, managing health appointments, speech-language therapist, unregistered nurse, behaviour therapist, counsellor, occupational therapist, and designated volunteer. And let's not forget an uncertified domestic scientist with culinary expertise and household management (Seguin ix).

Throughout my younger years, I witnessed my mother caring for five children and my father, who had health issues, until his passing. In my middle years, I watched my mother care for her mother, my mémère, until her passing. My mom often worked more than one job to feed the family. Although my father was present, he could not contribute to the family's financial and emotional needs. My mother was basically a single parent raising three sons and two daughters.

When I reflect on my mother's life, I realize that her life was a life of caregiving and mothering. It was a life misunderstood and devalued by her employers, friends, family, and a fractured healthcare system. Mom's employers, friends, family, and healthcare providers could not possibly understand my mom's daily life. I did not understand and appreciate the tremendous responsibilities and struggles my mom had experienced. Yet she never made us feel as though caring for us and my dad was a burden. I had no idea how much she tried to hide her daily distress from her family, employers, and friends. As much as Mom tried, her employers would question her requesting time off. Eventually, there was no way of hiding the numerous requests to manage health appointments for my dad. My mother was mothering and caregiving. She was a member of the sandwich generation decades before it was called that (Wray).

My understanding of my mom's caregiving came from having my child, my son. My son, Andre, was diagnosed with a disability. I soon became my mom. I became a caregiver for a person who depended on me, indefinitely. I began to appreciate much deeper the emotional, physical, and financial stress experienced by my mom. I, too, tried to hide my son's disability from my employer. I wasn't ashamed of my son. I was concerned with disclosing the seriousness of my son's disability for fear of affecting my employment. I acquired part-time employment, which allowed me to work in the morning and manage my son's health appointments in the afternoon. This worked until my employer asked me to extend my hours.

I struggled with the decision to continue working part-time or accept a full-time position. I loved working with adult learners in the literacy program. My husband and I could surely use the extra money. Having a disabled loved one has so many extra associated costs. The extra funds would have helped offset my family's financial pressures.

I knew I could not accept full-time unless I disclosed my son's numerous doctor, specialist, and therapist appointments. I would have to provide my employer with more than "I accept your offer." I would have to have a tête-à-tête with my employer and risk disclosing my personal life.

I explained how I would love to accept a full-time position. However, she may not be willing to accept the likely challenges that would come with working full-time. I explained how my son requires my attendance at health care appointments. Working full-time would mean I would need to be absent, on occasion, from an hour to an entire afternoon. I expressed my concern for my coworkers. They may not be so understanding of my absence. She asked me to try working full-time for a few months. She would deal with my coworkers if needed. We would evaluate in a few months. I was employed full-time for twenty years. I know many caregiving women, mothers like me, who were not so fortunate to have such an amazing employer.

Working full-time and managing dozens of appointments monthly was a challenge. Luckily, my position was from September to June. If I could survive emotionally and physically for nine months, then I would have a few months to cram in appointments for July and August to minimize the number of medical appointments upon returning to work.

I grew to appreciate the tremendous emotional and financial pressures my caregiving mother experienced. Women, like my mother, were primary caregivers. They were unpaid caregivers juggling work and the daunting caregiving responsibilities. They experienced uncertainty in the workplace, witnessed friends and extended family fade into the shadows, and experienced an unforgiving health system. They were devalued, unappreciated, and misunderstood. Mothering and caregiving were seen as a duty, an expectation, and an obligation.

Years later, as a mother and an unpaid multi-primary caregiver, I juggled work along with the unappreciative caregiver expectations. I experienced uncertainty with employment, witnessed friends fade into the shadows, and experienced a disjointed health system.

Asking Questions

A growing number of carers are involved in caring for a vulnerable family member residing at home or in a care facility. We are often given labels, such as difficult, intimidating, aggressive, demanding, volatile, and unpredictable. These titles, given to us by professionals, do not fit our behaviour. These labels usually occur when we ask questions about the care or lack of care for our loved ones. These labels are given to us when our expectations for answers to questions are ignored, and we will not let them go.

Even when we diplomatically ask questions, we are still labelled inappropriately. I consider these labels a badge of honour. They are a testament we are making a difference. We are rattling the spirit of the professionals. Our concerns are challenging their purported values, mission statements, and patient/client bill of rights and exposing the professionals' inaction with a lack of accountability (Seguin x).

I am unaware of any criminal code suggesting that asking questions is a crime. Yet asking the questions of concern can lead to consequences against the loved one and the family.

There are numerous professional and compassionate care providers working tirelessly to care for our loved ones. We need more of these true professionals. These passionate professionals gave me hope to trust other professionals.

I will always remember, with gratitude, the few professionals who chose to do the right thing for my son. I will never forget the professionals who chose what was best for their careers rather than the needs of their students.

I was unprepared to navigate a school system, a social system, and a health sector riddled with inefficiencies. I have experienced the worst, the best, and everything in between with professionals and policymakers at every level.

As my son became a young teenager, my husband and I made the difficult decision to locate a community group home. I was navigating an inefficient special education school system and learning about a fractured developmental sector. My son resided with a Ministry of Children, Community, and Social Services–funded community group home for more than twenty years until he was dropped off at our doorstep unexpectedly and without warning.

My husband and I were asking too many questions about our son's care. Asking the questions, without receiving reasonable responses, led to restrictions on visiting my son. Eventually, formal and informal trespass orders were issued, which led to my son being unlawfully evicted, without due process, from his group home of more than twenty years.

Mothering and Caregiving

My husband's senior uncle, known as mon oncle Felix to family, friends, and the neighbouring farming community, never married. He moved from St. Anicet, Quebec, to Cornwall, Ontario, in 1945, with his parents and three sisters, tante Marianne, tante Laurette, and my husband's mother, Juliette.

Tante Marianne lived and worked on the farm with mon oncle Felix. She spoiled my son rotten with love, attention, and too many cookies. My son's eyes would gleam with excitement when he saw her. Towards the end of my tante Marianne's journey, I needed to assist with her care. I recall her saying I should not have to be taking care of her. I responded that she was right. I did not have to. I wanted to. I mentioned how she took care of my son's care with love and compassion. I was simply returning the love.

I was the primary caregiver for my tante Marianne. I would travel from the city to the farm and prepare meals, manage health appointments, monitor her care and do grocery shopping and housekeeping. Upon her passing, there was no way mon oncle Felix would leave the farm to live in the little big city of Cornwall. It was much easier for my family to relocate to the farm.

After twelve years of living together and calling the farmhouse home, my disabled son was dropped off unannounced at our doorstep. He arrived with his group home's support workers, a manager, two green garbage bags as luggage, and two police escorts. Fortunately, my husband was at the farmhouse. He was upstairs preparing to visit mon oncle Felix at the hospital, who had a bout of pneumonia. My husband was greeted by a manager handing him a discharge from services letter.

This was my last day of employment. A few weeks later, my husband had to leave his employment. My son required 24/7 care. We could not work and care for a disabled adult son who was incontinent and nonverbal and who had frequent injurious behaviours to himself. I planned to care for mon oncle Felix. I had not planned to care for both mon oncle Felix and my son on a full-time 24/7 basis.

Suddenly, I became a member of the new sandwich generation. In the blink of an eye, my son's life, mon oncle Felix's life, and my family's life were turned upside down. We all became isolated ten months before the COVID-19 pandemic and until five years after it.

The Risks Are Real

The agency's egregious act was a consequence of my asking questions about my son's care. Actively involved family carers and advocates are at risk of consequences when speaking up and standing up for a loved one. Exposing an agency's inadequacies and expecting a higher standard of care for a family member is risky.

The risks of doing the right thing for our loved ones are real. The fear of consequences against a loved one and the family is real. The fear of informal and formal trespass orders, visitation restrictions, communication restrictions and possibly a discharge from services is real.

The COVID-19 pandemic exposed the horrific inadequacies in numerous senior care homes, including group homes. The Canadian military gave credence to these courageous caregiving advocates who, for decades, suffered retribution with visitation restrictions and trespass orders from visiting loved ones. Before COVID-19, caregivers and advocates suffered consequences simply for expressing concerns about loved ones and for exposing the lack of accountability from service providers and the complicity of our elected officials. We managed to close the institutions, yet we failed to close the institutional mindset.

Four years after my son's unlawful eviction, there was still no resolution for his reinstatement. Even with a court ruling directing the service provider to immediately reinstate my son, they continued delaying and denying my son's reentry to his group home. Their inaction was seemingly above the law, intentionally breaching the ruling. The agency continued to defy the court's recommendations. They continued placing conditions on my son's return to his group home by restricting visits, prohibiting my presence on the property, and prohibiting my communicating with employees.

I suggested installing a camera system in the group home. I suggested recording conversations between the family and the employees. I suggested encouraging employees to access training modules intended for those who work with disabled individuals. All suggestions were rejected.

Five years after my son was dropped off on our doorstep, he returned to his former group home. His service provider has a renewed mindset of working with families in the best interest of the people they support, which is how it should be.

In preparation for my son's return to his group home, the agency offered to install a camera system, record telephone conversations, implement a mobile phone to share updates between our family and support workers, provide daily updates about my son's day, and welcome my visits to my son's group home. The service provider also mentioned they will mandate all employees to view the *Difficult Family?* training module and incorporate policies and procedures to better work together as partners with families across the entire agency. I graciously accepted and welcomed their innovative ideas.

My disabled son, with the support of his parental caregivers, raised the standard of care for so many others residing with the service provider. The risks were worth it. Change happens with taking risks. Change happens with speaking up, standing up, and expecting excellence, not perfection.

When Does Mothering and Caregiving End?

Mothering and caregiving occur when you least expect it. My mother did not expect to be a caregiver for my father or my grandmother. My mother's caregiving began unexpectedly and ended when my father and grandmother passed. I did not expect to be both a mother and a lifelong caregiver for my disabled son. I did not expect to be a primary caregiver for my beloved tante Marianne and mon oncle Felix. My caregiving for Marianne and Felix ended upon their passing. I did not expect to be an on-call caregiver for my senior mother-in-law and my husband's other two maternal senior aunt and uncle. As much as I was expecting to be a caregiver for my mom, I really was not.

Mothering and caregiving are lifelong. My son will depend on his parents, his only true advocates and caregivers, indefinitely—at least while my husband and I are alive and well.

Most mothers cannot imagine one of their children will pass ahead of them. My mom lost a son, her eldest son, to cancer. The anguish of his passing is seen in her eyes daily. I could not imagine how deeply losing her son, my brother, devastated my mom. My mother would say, "When we were young, we were a handful. When we grew up, we were a heartful. Mothering never ends." She is right.

My heart will break if my son passes before I do. The anguish will be seen in my eyes. However, his passing would bring a sense of peace, calm, and relief. I would no longer worry every minute of the day about his care, about the next strategy to improve his quality of life, about the next unexplainable injury, about the fear of retribution for speaking up, or about blindly trusting healthcare providers. I would no longer have to worry. Caregiving will end with "death do us part."

Caring for a loved one is not for the faint of heart. Caregiving requires strong moral courage. Carers must set aside personal desires, wants and needs in lieu of respecting a loved one's autonomy. Carers may not always agree with a loved one's desires but we must, at the very least, make every effort supporting and respecting our loved one's decisions without their being controlled or influenced. Caregiving is selfless. It requires a strong, loving and patient heart.

Call to Action

Most Canadians are responsible for their journey of life. Other Canadians, like our seniors and disabled, depend on caregivers to be a supportive voice for a meaningful journey. Our loved ones depend on us to make every effort to influence our society to eliminate ableism and promote a life worth living.

In Canada, baby boomers are aging at an exponential rate. Aging baby boomers are caregiving seniors who care for other seniors and often also their children and grandchildren. These baby boomers are a growing sandwich generation. These baby boomers consist of almost 25 per cent of the population across Canada. They, like me, are trying to retire and are putting more pressure on the health and home care system and pension plans (Statistics Canada). Eventually, each of us will be a vulnerable and marginalized person. If we have the privilege to live into our senior years, we will likely have a cognitive impairment or physical disability. Are you ready for this real possibility? The time is now to highlight our moral courage within each of us. Speak up, stand up, and do the right thing. We are all headed towards the same journey. We all deserve to be treated as valuable citizens with respect and dignity.

As caregivers, we are advocates for our loved ones. We must risk speaking up, standing up, and doing the right thing for our family members. Professionals must work together with the caregiver and risk speaking up, standing up, and doing the right thing for the client. Caregivers are trying to support their loved one in their home or the loved one's residence. Yet the government is building new facilities and renovating facilities to house more seniors and people with disabilities rather than fund and support caregivers caring for loved ones.

Caregivers across Canada are filling the inadequacies in our health care system. This continued intentional expectation in our government is unacceptable. Many caregivers are unexpected participants in the new sandwich generation. They are becoming the new "double-layered toasted generation." Remunerating caregivers would be more financially feasible than building meretricious care facilities.

I am witnessing exploitative practices against family caregivers, advocates, and their loved ones. I continue to witness a social attitude culminating in a culture of entitlement and ableism. I am concerned for the future of our loved ones and our caregivers. I am concerned about our seniors and citizens with disabilities and complex medical needs choosing or being referred to the Medical Assistance in Dying (MAID) program because of hardships, homelessness, and lack of support, not because of a terminal illness. In Ontario, seniors with cognitive impairments, without a terminal illness, are considered disabled by our government. Seniors with cognitive impairments are eligible for MAID. Our Canadian government will be expanding the MAID eligibility in March 2027 for people with mental health illnesses, without a terminal illness. I have to wonder if the expansion of MAID to include people with disabilities without a terminal illness, seniors with cognitive impairment, and people with mental health illness is the government's attempt to covertly socially cleanse the vulnerable and marginalized.

Caregiving responsibilities include being informed and advocating for the person we are caring for. Caregivers who also care for a loved one in a care home must know their rights. Knowing your rights and being informed empowers decision-making. The more informed you are, the more questions you ask. The more questions you ask could lead to unforeseen restrictions or trespass orders from visiting your loved one.

Be aware that every province across Canada has a Trespass to Property Act (TPA). In Ontario, this act states the "occupier," the person residing in the care home, may refuse a visitor. The owner, or "deed possessor," of the facility cannot restrict visitors (King's Printer for Ontario). In March 2021, the Ontario Legislative Assembly unanimously voted in favour of Motion 129: Voula's Law, which provides clear direction to owners and operators of care homes to follow the TPA. Three years later, the Ontario premier has yet to comply with the assembly's unanimous vote.

Across Canada, children and adults with disabilities, whose primary caregivers are relentlessly advocating for a better standard of care for their loved one, are being unlawfully evicted from their group homes under the guise of being discharged from services. Owners and operators of care homes complying with the proper use of the TPA will eliminate the misuse of taxpayer dollars by owners and operators of nonprofit and for-profit organizations who are funding illegitimate litigation against the people, families, and caregivers they purport to support and value.

Advocacy is even more crucial in today's continued culture of entitlement, oppression, and ableism to support our caregivers while supporting our seniors and the disabled. I encourage citizens in every province to contact their member of provincial parliament (MPP) and express their healthcare and homecare concerns. If your MPP does not hear from you, then your concerns do not exist in their riding. Silence is not golden.

Works Cited

King's Printer for Ontario. "Trespass to Property Act." https://www.ontario.ca/laws/statute/90t21. Accessed 9 Apr. 2025.

Seguin, Joy-Ann P. *Is Advocating a Crime? Trust Everyone Trust No One.* Self-Published, 2023.

Statistics Canada. "A Generational Portrait of Canada's Aging Population from the 2021 Census." *Statistics Canada,* 27 Apr. 2022, https://www12.statcan.gc.ca/census-recensement/2021/as-sa/98-200-x/2021003/98-200-x2021003-eng.cfm. Accessed March 18, 2025. Accessed 9 Apr. 2025.

Wray, Dana. "'Sandwiched' between Unpaid Care for Children and Care-Dependent Adults: A Gender-Based Study." *Statistics Canada,* 2 Apr. 2024, https://www150.statcan.gc.ca/n1/pub/89-652-x/89-652-x2024002-eng.htm. Accessed 9 Apr. 2025.

Section VI

Reimagining and Restorying Narratives and Care Models for Children with Lifelong Care Needs

12.

Children with Medical Complexity: An Integrated Village Approach to Support Mothers and Their Families

Anneliese de Groot, Yvonne Zurynski, Karen Hutchinson, Jeffrey Fletcher, Amy Hickman, and Raghu Lingam

Introduction

According to social norms worldwide, mothers are typically responsible for many domestic family tasks, including childcare. Childcare is intensified for children with medical complexity (CMC), who have severe long-term medical conditions and require extensive ongoing care from their family and medical professionals (Cohen et al. "Children" 530–31; Woodgate et al. "Intense" 4). Family care can be thought of as carework, referring to the time, energy, and emotional input involved (Armenia 470). However, using the term "carework" is not intended to suggest caring for CMC is a burden (Yantzi et al. 1778). Much carework arises not from direct parenting tasks but from navigating and coordinating healthcare and social services to meet CMC and family needs (Medway et al. 391; Page et al. 1148–49). Mothers often experience physical and mental health issues due to the volume of carework required for CMC survival and wellbeing (Atkins and Padgett 623; Lauder et al. 1552–53, 57). Additional family members, including fathers, siblings, and extended family, are also affected by caring for CMC and often participate in care, supporting mothers (Farrar et al. 3–4; Teicher et al. 637–38; Woodgate et al., "Siblings" 507, 09). Yet research has almost entirely focussed on mothers' caring experiences, and other family members are seldom represented in research or policy to support families caring for CMC.

The challenges faced by families caring for CMC indicate the need for multiple sources of support working together to respond to each family's needs, according to their changing circumstances. Family members are CMC's key care providers; however, because caring for CMC can overwhelm family members and affect their health, comprehensive supports are needed to ensure equitable family health outcomes (Barnert et al., "Experts" 674). The idea of a supportive village has previously been used to refer to a combination of formal and informal support for children and families (Reupert et al. 1). In this case, the village refers to a model of care, including numerous cross-sectoral, interdisciplinary services, which must be integrated to collaborate with and support each family (Turchi et al. 1451, 57). A model of care is a design for delivering care according to theory, evidence, and standards for optimal patient outcomes (Davidson et al. 49). This chapter discusses the need for codesigned family-based research to inform the development of models of care to support families caring for CMC that sustainably meet care demands and optimize the long-term health and wellbeing of the whole family.

Many different types of families are recognized and may be composed of people related by blood, and other significant individuals who share caring and trusting relationships, including single-parent and same-sex families (Murray and Barnes 533). Current evidence predominantly focusses on members of nuclear, heterosexual, two-parent families, and although we recognize there is a greater diversity of family structures caring for CMC (Walsh 12–15), this is not the focus of the chapter. The language used here to describe parents reflects normative gendered roles (i.e., mothers and fathers) to acknowledge differences in experience among parents. However, more inclusive language will be used to refer to parents collectively where appropriate. The family unit refers to nuclear families, and extended family members are referred to where relevant. We recognize parental caring roles vary among families, and these roles may also be fulfilled by siblings or extended family members (Skrobanski et al. 1823). The term "sibling" is used throughout to refer to brothers and sisters of CMC.

Models of Care Should Address the Experiences and Needs of Whole Families

The experience of caring for CMC influences all members of the child's family. Carework commonly becomes the central focus for the family; it requires time, energy, and financial resources, reduces the capacity for employment, and affects the wellbeing and needs of all other family members (Farrar et al. 2–3; Skrobanski et al. 1823, 26; Teicher et al. 637–38). Due to these demands, caring for CMC can reduce family functioning, which refers to how the whole family participates in daily routines and activities to meet each family member's needs and to maintain an overall sense of shared family life (Stein and Riessman 466). Families have varied capacities for adapting to CMC's needs and finding a sense of family functioning that feels normal and sustainable to them, according to the unique context within and surrounding each family unit (Deatrick et al. 20–24). Carework particularly affects mothers (Werner 835) and has been associated with a doubled risk of clinical depression (Toly et al., "Families" 64) and 61 per cent higher likelihood of physical or mental health issues compared with mothers in the general population (Feudtner et al. 3–4). However, when additional family members share responsibility for CMC care and actively participate in caring tasks, mothers' experiences and wellbeing outcomes improve (Angelhoff et al. 376), which increases their capacity to support ongoing family functioning (Toly et al., "Families" 64). Therefore, exploring the experiences, roles, and needs of family members is necessary to understand how to best support mothers and their families.

Families' Adaptation to Caring for CMC

All family members may require support as they adapt to providing care for CMC, individually and together as a family unit. With the onset of CMC's health complications, family members adjust their priorities and behaviours as they learn how to meet CMC's care needs (McKechnie et al. 7–9; Rolland 453). During this time, family members must support one another as they work out how to navigate healthcare services and provide the required level of medical care in their homes (Currie and Szabo, "It Would" 1255; Page et al. 1148–49). Over several years, many families develop a sense of normalization as they find ways to organize their time and resources to meet CMC's ongoing medical, therapeutic, and emotional needs, as well as parents' and siblings' emotional and physical wellbeing needs (Driessens et al. 8–9; Lerret et al. 3–5). Families' capacity for normalization varies according to the severity and prognosis of CMC illness, which influences the level and type of long-term care required, and the circumstances of each family unit (Deatrick et al. 24; Rolland 457–58). Families with strong relationships and a sense of caring for CMC as a team may be more likely to normalize family life around caring for CMC as opposed to families in which mothers carry sole responsibility for CMC care (Knafl and Zoeller 292–93; Pelentsov et al. 213–14). Understanding how to support multiple family members to adapt to their family caring roles and maintain them over time may be considered an important way to strengthen support for mothers within their family unit.

Inequitable Wellbeing Outcomes

Mothers have the greatest responsibility for CMC care and experience less optimal health and wellbeing outcomes compared to their partners (Boettcher et al. 5; Feudtner et al. 4). Even when multiple family members contribute to carework, mothers usually manage CMC's daily in-home care and health service needs (Medway et al. 388; Pelentsov et al. 214). As a result, mothers are more likely than fathers to cease employment (50 per cent of mothers, no fathers), and only 40.6 per cent of mothers work full-time compared with 93.8 per cent of fathers (Atkins and Padgett 628; Walkowiak et al. 5). However, mothers have described the mental health benefits of maintaining employment (John Cherian et al. 10). Evidence of the effect on mothers' health compared with fathers' is scarce. However, Johannes Boettcher et al. show increased psychological distress and anxiety and lower quality of life (5–6), and Chris Feudtner et al. report higher numbers of mental and physical health diagnoses (3–4). Similarly, siblings of CMC have been found to experience greater health disparities compared with their counterparts in the general population (Feudtner et al. 8). Further research is required to better understand the experiences of multiple family members and the long-term impacts on all family members throughout their life course.

Varied Family Contexts Influence Mothers' and Families' Experiences

Different aspects of families' circumstances form the context within which they meet CMC care needs while maintaining the family's expected normal functioning (Deatrick et al. 24). Family contextual factors include support from extended family (Farrar et al. 3), available financial resources and geographic location (Teutsch et al. 705), and beliefs about who in the family is responsible for caring duties (Knafl and Zoeller 294; Rolland 476). Additionally, siblings' ages determine the kind of childcare they require, and their ability to contribute to the family and support their parents as young carers (Toly et al., "Maternal" 404). These factors influence the impact on individual family members and the sources and levels of support mothers receive (Farrar et al. 3, 5; Skrobanski et al. 1823).

Mothers caring for CMC experience better health and wellbeing in families that can share carework. Cultural beliefs around carework are commonly gendered, attributing the majority of responsibility for childcare to mothers (Armenia 469; Glenn 78). In some families, both parents share responsibility for care and support each other practically and emotionally in daily caring activities and during CMC hospitalizations, including navigating healthcare services and making healthcare decisions (Currie and Szabo, "It Would" 1254–55; McKechnie et al. 8; Page et al. 1148; Woodgate et al., "Exploring" 5). Mothers experience numerous benefits from having a partner share their experience and provide respite from CMC care, enabling them to continue part-time employment and engage in social and wellbeing activities (John Cherian et al. 9–10). However, in some families, fathers' capacity to participate in CMC care may be restricted by the need to work long hours to maintain economic stability for the family (Medway et al. 387; Toly et al., "Caring" 6). Other fathers may struggle to accept their child's illness and understand their caring role; therefore, they may use their ongoing employment to escape the daily challenges of meeting CMC care needs (Pelentsov et al. 214). Hence, fathers may only be able to support their partner and family if they receive appropriate support themselves to relieve financial pressures, support their mental and physical health, and provide strategies to assist them in engaging with their parental caregiving role (Woodgate et al., "Exploring" 5, 7, 11–12).

In addition to support from partners, mothers often require support from siblings, extended family members, and formal support services (Skrobanski et al. 1823). Extended family members provide childcare for siblings; however, some families do not have extended family or do not live close enough to receive regular support from them (Medway et al. 386). Additionally, family or friends may not comprehend the challenges of caring for CMC, alienating parents rather than supporting them (Currie and Szabo, "Social" 6–7). Although carer respite and financial support may be available through formal services, families must often navigate complex bureaucratic processes and meet rigorous criteria before support is provided (Farrar et al. 5; Medway et al. 391). Additionally, families in rural areas may have limited access to support services and experience increased difficulties as they must travel long distances to access healthcare and other services for the whole family (Teutsch et al. 705–07). It is important to understand how to provide tailored support responsive to varied family members' challenges, from the initial caring experiences through different stages of family life (Solar and Irwin 18).

How Health Service Interactions Affect CMC's Families

Little is known about how specific family members' roles influence their experiences of healthcare navigation work or the support needs of the whole family when interacting with health services. CMC require frequent healthcare encounters, such as scheduled clinical consultations, pathology tests and medical imaging, emergency department attendances, hospitalizations and surgical procedures (Kuo et al. 5–6; Teutsch et al. 703–04). Much of the work of caring for CMC relates to understanding how to move through the healthcare system to access and attend these encounters (Currie and Szabo, "It Is" 100; Zurynski et al. 5). This healthcare navigation work is often stressful and time consuming (Woodgate et al. "Intense" 7), as it requires parents to understand and work around fragmented and complex health system networks, which are rarely family centred or structured to integrate the complex level of healthcare required by CMC (Currie and Szabo, "Social" 6). Mothers commonly assume responsibility for most healthcare coordination work, including organizing and managing healthcare, as part of their broader carework role (Toly et al., "Caring" 3). However, the whole family is affected by the volume of healthcare coordination work required for CMC and the stress of healthcare encounters (Farrar et al. 4; Price et al. 8). When adequately funded and supported, care coordination services are invaluable in supporting family experiences of interacting with the health system (Satherley et al. 3), but we do not know how these services affect the functioning of families.

The Work of Navigating Healthcare Services

Mothers' healthcare navigation and coordination roles affect their and their families' wellbeing. CMC have high service needs; they often require complex multidisciplinary care from various paediatric medical and surgical subspecialists, and allied health professionals, including physiotherapists, psychologists, dieticians, and occupational and speech therapists (Teutsch et al. 705; Zurynski et al. 4). Coordinating these services involves a high level of complex administration tasks, including researching health information, finding appropriate healthcare providers, obtaining referrals, coordinating appointments, and managing logistics when travelling to access services (Castro et al. 3007–08; Lauder et al. 1556–57; Page et al. 1148–49, 51) To complete these tasks, family carers must develop excellent skills in health literacy and advocacy to ensure the quality of care for CMC's routine and medical crisis needs, which must be delivered promptly across multiple health sectors (Currie and Szabo, "It Is" 98–99; Currie and Szabo, "It Would" 1254–55; John Cherian et al. 8; Price et al. 7–8). This intensive carework often impairs mothers' capacity to spend time with their partners and CMC's siblings, which can alter family dynamics and strain family relationships (John Cherian et al. 3–4; Price et al. 8). Although other family members may engage in carework or other support, the current understanding of how families negotiate and share these caring responsibilities and roles is limited.

High Service Use Affects Parents' and Siblings' Health and Wellbeing

Mothers' stressful and traumatic experiences with CMC's healthcare encounters are well documented (Castro et al. 3004; Dewan et al. 296). However, only limited evidence describes the experiences of other family members, such as siblings' anxiety and stress-related symptoms, family separation during travel to, and lengthy stays in, healthcare facilities, and the need for mutual emotional and practical support among family members (Castro et al. 3005; McKechnie et al. 8; Teutsch et al. 705). CMC with rare conditions may need multiple assessments, investigations, and medical imaging to reach a definitive diagnosis, creating extended periods of uncertainty causing stress and frustration and delays in accessing appropriate care and treatment pathways (Zurynski et al. 5). In addition to interrupting family life, this lengthy diagnosis process may result in worsening symptoms and progression of the child's condition, adding to the family's stress (5). In two-parent families, both parents may be required to advocate strongly for CMC needs during intensive healthcare encounters, relying on each other's support to navigate difficult healthcare decisions for their child (Currie and Szabo, "It Would" 1254–55; Price et al. 8; Woodgate et al., "Exploring" 5, 7). Similarly, single parents may rely on extended family members for advocacy and decision-making support (Woodgate et al., "Intense" 5). Some fathers value being able to advocate for their children, often experiencing frustration when healthcare providers only communicate directly with mothers (Woodgate et al., "Exploring" 5). Additionally, siblings experience anxiety relating to CMC hospitalizations and may benefit from increased inclusion in healthcare communications, particularly if they are primary carers (Skrobanski et al. 1823; Toly et al., "Maternal" 406). Yet little is understood about how multiple family members engage with healthcare services or how the whole family, including siblings, might be supported through these interactions to improve whole family experiences.

Effects of Care Coordination on Families

Paediatric care coordination improves the quality of CMC care (Breen et al. 6, 7; Satherley et al. 3–6; Teicher et al. 639). However, we do not yet understand the impact of care coordination on the whole family or how these support services can encompass broader family needs. Care coordinators are experienced healthcare professionals with access to CMC health information who provide parent and clinician education, facilitate cross-sectoral health communication, and coordinate appointments within health administration systems (Breen et al. 3; Satherley et al. 2, 9). Family carers have reported important benefits when receiving care coordination, including connecting healthcare services, increasing families' trust in healthcare provision, improving access to specialist services, reducing unnecessary hospital admissions, reducing travel, and improving experiences and adequacy of care (Breen et al. 6–7; Cohen et al.; "Integrated" 9; Satherley et al. 11). Despite these positive reports, no significant associations have been found between care coordination and family functioning or quality of life (Cohen et al.; "Integrated" 9; Johaningsmeir et al. 80–81). However, this may reflect the inadequacy of standardized measures to reflect the complex and unique circumstances experienced by families caring for CMC rather than a lack of impact (Barnert et al., "A Healthy" 8–9). Commonly used measures focus on the functioning of the family member filling out the survey rather than on the collective functioning of the family (Mann et al. 24). Furthermore, few qualitative service evaluations have included perspectives of multiple family members (Satherley et al. 3). Therefore, further research is required to understand how care coordination services influence the whole family and to inform future models of care that are broader than simply healthcare navigation.

Integrated Care Models to Address Cross-Sectoral Needs of Whole Families across the Life Course

Future models of care need to be family centred and integrated, ensuring the right types of support are provided in the right way. Integrated care is coordinated across different providers within and beyond the healthcare sector according to patients' needs (World Health Assembly 2) and has been shown to improve the quality of care for children with chronic illnesses (Wolfe et al., "Models" 7). In this case, integrated care must be centred around the whole family's needs to address CMC's needs effectively (Barnert et al., "Experts" 674). Numerous avenues of support are required by families caring for CMC; however, without integration, accessing and navigating support services can be difficult for families without available funding, time, and energy (Farrar et al. 5; Medway et al. 391). As an evidence-based model of integrated care, paediatric complex care coordination establishes an important point of contact with families through which a range of integrated cross-sectoral services can be provided (Cardenas et al. 237–38; Satherley et al. 2). Further expansion of current care coordination services can address broader family needs across sectors, improving health and wellbeing outcomes for the family and supporting a family-centred approach to prioritizing CMC medical outcomes.

Integrating Care to Increase Health Equity

Expanding current integrated care models to proactively include multiple family members' needs can improve care quality, equity, and long-term family wellbeing. Ingrid Wolfe et al. illustrate four dimensions of paediatric integrated care, including integration between primary, secondary, tertiary, and allied health sectors; longitudinal integration to connect age-appropriate care across the life course; care across health, social, not-for-profit, and education sectors; and health promotion and disease prevention ("A Solution" 993–94). A range of unmet family needs can be integrated in addition to CMC healthcare, including linking families with financial, housing, and respite support, providing maternal and family mental healthcare, and delivering training for school staff (Cardenas et al. 238; Ostojic et al. 4; Satherley et al. 6). These comprehensive, integrated models of care are necessary to ensure health equity, meaning all family members should be enabled to have good health and wellbeing, despite needing to prioritize CMC care needs (Weinstein et al. 32). However, healthcare providers can experience immense challenges in providing adequate care for CMC if they are not supported by structures that support multidisciplinary care and decision-making (Donohue et al. 940–42). Therefore, future models of care must support healthcare and other service providers to deliver integrated family-centred care while considering a broad range of family needs.

Family-Informed Solutions to Improve Caring Experiences

Family-centred integrated care should first aim to address core health determinants affecting the whole family (Barnert et al., "Experts" 674). Social determinants are nonmedical factors, such as ethnicity, gender, socioeconomic status, housing, and employment, which influence health outcomes now and into the future (Solar and Irwin 18). Families caring for CMC have a high chance of experiencing these needs, including reduced employment, financial hardship, and housing instability, which can affect families' ability to access or afford healthcare (Barnert et al.,

"Experts" 674; Millar et al. 7–8). These challenges highlight the importance of shifting to more family-centred care with crucial support from government, nongovernment, and not-for-profit social care and support organizations (Barnert et al., "Experts" 674; Farrar et al. 5; Turchi et al. 1457). However, sourcing, applying for, and accessing support is often fraught with challenges, including complex eligibility criteria and bureaucratic processes (Farrar et al. 5). Several new models of integrated care that link families with a social worker enable exploring ways to overcome access barriers (Cardenas et al. 238; Ostojic et al. 4). This important connection between social and healthcare services is critical to support families caring for CMC and should become a core part of care coordination services.

Specialized psychosocial services may be required to support multiple family members through the long-term challenges of caring for CMC. Analyssa Cardenas and colleagues describe a new model of care addressing acute family mental health issues by offering all family members access to psychotherapy and psychiatry services alongside social work and paediatric care coordination (238). In addition to addressing acute anxiety, stress, and emotional trauma, family-based counselling may have the potential to support healthy adjustment to caring roles, such as fostering positive and unique relationships between siblings and CMC (Toly et al., "Maternal" 401). Similarly, individual counselling for fathers may enable healthy engagement with parenting and caring for CMC (Woodgate et al., "Exploring" 14); however, this has not been adequately researched. A workforce of social workers and psychologists is likely to require education tailored to caring for CMC over the life course to enable them to provide holistic, strength-based counselling for multiple family members individually or as a group (Cardenas et al. 238).

Parents have highlighted the critical importance of healthy family functioning, including parental teamwork, in achieving positive CMC health outcomes (Abebe et al. 6; Currie and Szabo, "It Would" 1254). For example, creating routines to share responsibility for administering medication is one strategy that increases treatment adherence and reduces organizational overload on a sole carer (Abebe et al. 5–6). However, it takes time for parents to learn how to develop and maintain routines that cultivate healthy family functioning while caring for CMC (Driessens et al. 8; Lerret et al. 4–5). Further exploration is needed to better understand what practical and emotional support multiple family members may require and how this support can be provided while taking the family's context into account.

Promoting Family Health

To be able to care for CMC, parents must manage their psychosocial and healthcare needs by responding to emergent health issues and engaging in preventative health checks and practices (John Cherian et al. 10; Teicher et al. 635). Looking after their health ensures that parents sustain their capacity to care for each other's and siblings' health and social wellbeing needs, and avoid family relationship breakdown, including sibling resentment and emotional and behavioural issues (John Cherian et al. 9, 10; Teicher et al. 635–36). The time and planning required to manage the whole family's needs often become overwhelming for parents, who predominantly prioritize CMC's and siblings' wellbeing over their own (Farrar et al. 5; John Cherian et al. 10–14). Therefore, future models of care could explore whether and what types of support parents require for their physical and emotional health, including accessing preventative healthcare checks and how this support might vary across the life course.

Codesigning Research Including Multiple Family Members

Despite the undeniable impact on the whole family caring for CMC (Teicher et al. 636–38), most research to date has focussed primarily on the mothers' experiences, underrepresenting the perspectives of additional family members (Atkins and Padgett 622). Many studies predominantly engage with mothers by focussing recruitment on the primary carer role (Cohen et al., "Integrated" 5). Even when fathers are included, they represent only up to 15 per cent of participants in quantitative studies (Cohen et al., "Integrated" 5) or 33 per cent in some qualitative studies (Teicher et al. 635). Siblings and extended family members are represented in research even less frequently than fathers, although several notable studies have focussed solely on fathers' (Woodgate et al., "Exploring" 3) or siblings' experiences (Woodgate et al., "Siblings" 505). This underrepresentation leaves the experience of fathers, siblings, and extended family members largely invisible, perpetuating a culture that places the responsibility for carework on mothers.

Codesigning research with families can support the development of effective models of care and is crucial to ensure these future models are guided by multiple family members' lived experiences (Francis-Auton et al. 2; Slattery et al. 2–6). Codesigned research engages families in research to develop and evaluate health and support services according to their needs and priorities (Vargas et al. 3). Previous research has identified that fathers may decline to participate in research (Lauder et al. 1551), thereby highlighting the importance of using a multipronged approach to engagement that is meaningful and inclusive across the whole family. Adopting codesigned approaches to research can be empowering; it provides families with a voice and can improve understanding of the deeply personal and nuanced nature of families' experiences (Francis-Auton et al. 2; Vargas et al. 5). Additionally, including stakeholders from healthcare and support sectors alongside family members increases the potential of codesigned research to generate outcomes that respond to health system and societal context challenges faced by service providers, including pervasive funding and workforce shortages, alongside families' needs (Vargas et al. 3–4). To ensure a broad range of perspectives are included, families with varied circumstances should be included in codesigned research, including families with diverse structures and from varied cultures (Walsh 12–15) and families at different stages of life-long caring journeys. Building this foundation of knowledge may offer opportunities for improving engagement with hard-to-reach families to better understand how to develop more family-focussed and culturally appropriate services engaging with families who may otherwise fall through the gaps and experience worse health and wellbeing outcomes.

Summary and Conclusion

Despite limited evidence, the benefits of supporting multiple family members caring for CMC are apparent. Developing future models of care that optimize family experience and outcomes requires service providers, researchers, and policymakers across multiple sectors to work collaboratively with families. Care coordinators can provide a solution to overcome the challenges of navigating and connecting care and provide the key point of contact between services and families. However, support addressing the social determinants of health should be routinely integrated with healthcare coordination by connecting social and health services, ensuring families' basic social needs are met. Practical and emotional support should also be provided routinely to safeguard family members' adjustment and ongoing contribution to family and caring roles and responsibilities. In this way, supporting the whole family's wellbeing can help alleviate the demands on the mother. Taking a code-signed approach seeking to understand the specific and diverse needs of multiple family members will help deliver responsive, appropriate, and effective family-centred, cross-sectoral, and integrated support services.

Acknowledgment

This research was supported by an Australian Government Research Training Program (RTP) Scholarship.

Works Cited

Abebe, Ephrem et al. "What Do Family Caregivers Do When Managing Medications for Their Children with Medical Complexity?" *Applied Ergonomics*, vol. 87, 2020, pp. 1–10, doi:10.1016/j.apergo.2020.103108.

Angelhoff, Charlotte, et al. "Sleep of Parents Living with a Child Receiving Hospital-Based Home Care: A Phenomenographical Study." *Nursing Research*, vol. 64, no. 5, 2015, pp. 372–80, doi:10.1097/NNR.0000000000000108.

Armenia, Amy. "Caring as Work: Research and Theory." *Handbook of the Sociology of Gender*. Edited by Barbara J. Risman et al. 2nd. ed. Springer International, 2018, pp. 469–78.

Atkins, Jenny C., and Christine R. Padgett. "Living with a Rare Disease: Psychosocial Impacts for Parents and Family Members–A Systematic Review." *Journal of Child and Family Studies*, vol. 33, no. 2, 2024, pp. 617–36, doi:10.1007/s10826-024-02790-6.

Barnert, Elizabeth, et al. "Experts' Perspectives toward a Population Health Approach for Children with Medical Complexity." *Academic Pediatrics*, vol. 17, no. 6, 2017, pp. 672–77, doi:10.1016/j.acap.2017.02.010.

Barnert, Elizabeth S., et al. "A Healthy Life for a Child with Medical Complexity: 10 Domains for Conceptualizing Health." *Pediatrics*, vol. 142, no. 3, 2018, pp. 1–10, doi:10.1542/peds.2018-0779.

Boettcher, Johannes, et al. "Quality of Life and Mental Health in Mothers and Fathers Caring for Children and Adolescents with Rare Diseases Requiring Long-Term Mechanical Ventilation." *International Journal of Environmental Research and Public Health*, vol. 17, no. 23, 2020, pp. 1–12, doi:10.3390/ijerph17238975.

Breen, Christie, et al. "Significant Reductions in Tertiary Hospital Encounters and Less Travel for Families after Implementation of Paediatric Care Coordination in Australia." *BMC Health Services Research*, vol. 18, no. 1, 2018, p. 751, doi:10.1186/s12913-018-3553-4.

Cardenas, Analyssa, et al. "Caring for the Caregiver (C4c): An Integrated Stepped Care Model for Caregivers of Children with Medical Complexity." *Academic Pediatrics*, vol. 23, no. 2, 2023, pp. 236–43, doi:10.1016/j.acap.2022.06.001.

Castro, Aimee R., et al. "The Day to Day Experiences of Caring for Children with Osteogenesis Imperfecta: A Qualitative Descriptive Study." *Journal of Clinical Nursing*, vol. 29, no. 15–16, 2020, pp. 2999–3011, doi:10.1111/jocn.15310.

Cohen, Eyal, et al. "Children with Medical Complexity: An Emerging Population for Clinical and Research Initiatives." *Pediatrics*, vol. 127, no. 3, 2011, pp. 529–38, doi:10.1542/peds.2010-0910.

Cohen, Eyal et al. "Integrated Complex Care Coordination for Children with Medical Complexity: A Mixed-Methods Evaluation of Tertiary Care-Community Collaboration." *BMC Health Services Research*, vol. 12, no. 1, 2012, pp. 366–66, doi:10.1186/1472-6963-12-366.

Currie, Genevieve, and Joanna Szabo. "'It Is Like a Jungle Gym, and Everything Is under Construction': The Parent's Perspective of Caring for a Child with a Rare Disease." *Child: Care, Health & Development*, vol. 45, no. 1, 2019, pp. 96–103, doi:10.1111/cch.12628.

Currie, Genevieve, and Joanna Szabo. "'It Would Be Much Easier If We Were Just Quiet and Disappeared': Parents Silenced in the Experience of Caring for Children with Rare Diseases." *Health Expectations*, vol. 22, no. 6, 2019, pp. 1251–59, doi:10.1111/hex.12958.

Currie, Genevieve, and Joanna Szabo. "Social Isolation and Exclusion: The Parents' Experience of Caring for Children with Rare Neurodevelopmental Disorders." *International Journal of Qualitative Studies on Health & Well-Being*, vol. 15, no. 1, 2020, pp. 1–11, doi:10.1080/17482631.2020.1725362.

Davidson, Patricia, et al. "Beyond the Rhetoric: What Do We Mean by a 'Model of Care'?" *Australian Journal of Advanced Nursing*, vol. 23, no. 3, 2006, pp. 47–55, doi:10.37464/2006.233.1935.

Deatrick, Janet A., et al. "Family Management Style Framework: A New Tool with Potential to Assess Families Who Have Children with Brain Tumors." *Journal of Pediatric Oncology Nursing*, vol. 23, no. 1, 2006, pp. 19–27, doi:10.1177/1043454205283574.

Dewan, Tammie, et al. "Experiences of Medical Traumatic Stress in Parents of Children with Medical Complexity." *Child: Care, Health & Development*, vol. 49, no. 2, 2023, pp. 292–303, doi:10.1111/cch.13042.

Donohue, Pamela K., et al. "'It's Relentless': Providers' Experience of Pediatric Chronic Critical Illness." *Journal of Palliative Medicine*, vol. 21, no. 7, 2018, pp. 940–46, doi:10.1089/jpm.2017.0397.

Driessens, Corine, et al. "The Impact on Parents of Diagnosing PCD in Young Children." *Journal of Clinical Medicine*, vol. 11, no. 16, 2022, pp. 1–18, doi:10.3390/jcm11164774.

Farrar, Michelle A., et al. "Financial, Opportunity and Psychosocial Costs of Spinal Muscular Atrophy: An Exploratory Qualitative Analysis of Australian Carer Perspectives." *BMJ Open*, vol. 8, no. 5, 2018, pp. 1–7, doi:10.1136/bmjopen-2017-020907.

Feudtner, Chris, et al. "Association between Children with Life-Threatening Conditions and Their Parents' and Siblings' Mental and Physical Health." *JAMA Network Open*, vol. 4, no. 12, 2021, pp. 1–16, doi:10.1001/jamanetworkopen.2021.37250.

Francis-Auton, Emilie, et al. "Exploring and Understanding the 'Experience' in Experience-Based Codesign: A State-of-the-Art Review." *International Journal of Qualitative Methods*, vol. 23, 2024, pp. 1–30, doi:10.1177/16094069241235563.

Glenn, Evelyn Nakano. "Reimagining Care and Care Work." *Care and Care Workers: A Latin American Perspective*. Edited by Nadya Araujo Guimarães and Helena Hirata. Springer International, 2021, pp. 77–92.

Johaningsmeir, Sarah A., et al. "Impact of Caring for Children with Medical Complexity and High Resource Use on Family Quality of Life." *Journal of Pediatric Rehabilitation Medicine*, vol. 8, no. 2, 2015, pp. 75–82, doi:10.3233/PRM-150321.

John Cherian, Dani, et al. "How Families Manage the Complex Medical Needs of Their Children with Mecp2 Duplication Syndrome." *Children*, vol. 10, no. 7, 2023, p. 1202, doi:10.3390/children10071202.

Knafl, Kathleen, and Linda Zoeller. "Childhood Chronic Illness: A Comparison of Mothers' and Fathers' Experiences." *Journal of Family Nursing*, vol. 6, no. 3, 2000, pp. 287–302, doi:10.1177/107484070000600306.

Kuo, Dennis Z. et al. "Variation in Child Health Care Utilization by Medical Complexity." *Maternal and Child Health Journal*, vol. 19, no. 1, 2015, pp. 40–48, doi:10.1007/s10995-014-1493-0.

Lauder, B., et al. "Mothers' Experience of Caring for a Child with Early Onset Scoliosis: A Qualitative Descriptive Study." *Journal of Clinical Nursing*, vol. 27, no. 7–8, 2018, pp. e1549–e60, doi:10.1111/jocn.14301.

Lerret, Stacee M., et al. "Parents' Perspectives on Caring for Children after Solid Organ Transplant." *Journal for Specialists in Pediatric Nursing*, vol. 22, no. 3, 2017, pp. 1–8, doi:10.1111/jspn.12178.

Mann, Kilby, et al. "Health-Related Quality of Life and Family Functioning of Parents of Children with Medical Complexity." *Current physical Medicine and Rehabilitation Reports*, vol. 7, no. 1, 2019, pp. 23–29, doi:10.1007/s40141-019-0208-2.

McKechnie, Anne Chevalier, et al. "Adaptive Leadership in Parents Caring for Their Children Born with Life-Threatening Conditions." *Journal of Pediatric Nursing*, vol. 53, 2020, pp. 41–51, doi:10.1016/j.pedn.2020.03.018.

Medway, Meredith, et al. "Parental Perspectives on the Financial Impact of Caring for a Child with Ckd." *American Journal of Kidney Diseases*, vol. 65, no. 3, 2015, pp. 384–93, doi:10.1053/j.ajkd.2014.07.019.

Millar, Kyle, et al. "The Clinical Definition of Children with Medical Complexity: A Modified Delphi Study." *Pediatrics*, vol. 153, no. 6, 2024, pp. 1–10, doi:10.1542/peds.2023-064556.

Murray, Lesley, and Marian Barnes. "Have Families Been Rethought? Ethic of Care, Family and 'Whole Family' Approaches." *Social Policy* and Society, vol. 9, no. 4, 2010, pp. 533–44, doi:10.1017/S1474746410000254.

Ostojic, Katarina, et al. "Epic-Cp Pilot Trial Study Protocol: A Multi-centre, Randomised Controlled Trial Investigating the Feasibility and Acceptability of Social Prescribing for Australian Children with Cerebral Palsy." *BMJ Open*, vol. 14, no. 7, 2024, pp. 1–10, doi:10.1136/bmjopen-2023-076304.

Page, Bethan F., et al. "The Challenges of Caring for Children Who Require Complex Medical Care at Home: The Go between for Everyone Is the Parent and as the Parent That's an Awful Lot of Responsibility." *Health Expectations*, vol. 23, no. 5, 2020, pp. 1144–54, doi:10.1111/hex.13092.

Pelentsov, Lemuel J., et al. "The Supportive Care Needs of Parents with a Child with a Rare Disease: A Qualitative Descriptive Study." *Journal of Pediatric Nursing*, vol. 31, no. 3, 2016, pp. e207–e18, doi:10.1016/j.pedn.2015.10.022.

Price, Jayne, et al. "'Managing an Unexpected Life – a Caregiver's Career': Parents' Experience of Caring for Their Child with a Non-Malignant Life-Limiting Condition." *Journal of Child Health Care*, vol. 28, no. 2, 2022, pp. 348–61, doi:10.1177/13674935221132920.

Reupert, Andrea, et al. "It Takes a Village to Raise a Child: Understanding and Expanding the Concept of the 'Village.'" *Frontiers in Public Health*, vol. 10, 2022, pp. 1–7, doi:10.3389/fpubh.2022.756066.

Rolland, John. "Mastering Family Challenges in Serious Illness and Disability." *Normal Family Processes: Growing Diversity and Complexity*. Edited by Froma Walsh. 4 ed., The Guilford Press, 2012, pp. 452–82.

Satherley, Rose-Marie, et al. "Integrated Health Services for Children: A Qualitative Study of Family Perspectives." *BMC Health Services Research*, vol. 21, no. 1, 2021, pp. 167–67, doi:10.1186/s12913-021-06141-9.

Skrobanski, Hanna, et al. "The Impact of Caring for an Individual with Aromatic L-Amino Acid Decarboxylase (Aadc) Deficiency: A Qualitative Study and the Development of a Conceptual Model." *Current Medical Research and Opinion*, vol. 37, no. 10, 2021, pp. 1821–28, doi:10.1080/03007995.2021.1955668.

Slattery, Peter, et al. "Research Co-Design in Health: A Rapid Overview of Reviews." *Health Research Policy and Systems*, vol. 18, no. 1, 2020, pp. 1–13, doi:10.1186/s12961-020-0528-9.

Solar, O., and A. Irwin. "A Conceptual Framework for Action on the Social Determinants of Health." *World Health Organization,* 2010, www.who.int/publications/i/item/9789241500852. Accessed 9 Apr. 2025.

Stein, Ruth E., and Catherine K. Riessman. "The Development of an Impact-on-Family Scale: Preliminary Findings." *Medical Care,* vol. 18, no. 4, 1980, pp. 465–72, doi:10.1097/00005650-198004000-00010.

Teicher, Jessica, et al. "The Experience of Parental Caregiving for Children with Medical Complexity." *Clinical Pediatrics,* vol. 62, no. 6, 2022, pp. 633–44, doi:10.1177/00099228221142102.

Teutsch, Suzy, et al. "Australian Children Living with Rare Diseases: Health Service Use and Barriers to Accessing Care." *World Journal of Pediatrics,* vol. 19, no. 7, 2023, pp. 701–09, doi:10.1007/s12519-022-00675-6.

Toly, Valerie Boebel, et al. "Caring for Technology-Dependent Children at Home: Problems and Solutions Identified by Mothers." *Applied Nursing Research,* vol. 50, 2019, pp. 1–9, doi:10.1016/j.apnr.2019.151195.

Toly, Valerie Boebel, et al. "Maternal Perspectives of Well Siblings' Adjustment to Family Life with a Technology-Dependent Child." *Journal of Family Nursing,* vol. 23, no. 3, 2017, pp. 392–417, doi:10.1177/1074840717721705.

Toly, Valerie Boebel, et al. "Families with Children Who Are Technology Dependent: Normalization and Family Functioning." *Western Journal of Nursing Research,* vol. 34, no. 1, 2012, pp. 52–71, doi:10.1177/0193945910389623.

Turchi, Renee M., et al. "Patient- and Family-Centered Care Coordination: A Framework for Integrating Care for Children and Youth across Multiple Systems." *Pediatrics,* vol. 133, no. 5, 2014, pp. e1451–e60, doi:10.1542/peds.2014-0318.

Vargas, Carmen, et al. "Co-Creation, Co-Design, Co-Production for Public Health–A Perspective on Definition and Distinctions." *Public Health Research & Practice,* vol. 32, no. 2, 2022, pp. 1–7, doi: 10.17061/phrp3222211.

Walkowiak, Dariusz, et al. "Professional Activity, Gender and Disease-Related Emotions: The Impact on Parents' Experiences in Caring for Children with Phenylketonuria." *Molecular Genetics and Metabolism Reports*, vol. 36, 2023, pp. 1–9, doi:10.1016/j.ymgmr.2023.100992.

Walsh, Froma. *Normal Family Processes: Growing Diversity and Complexity*. 4th ed., Guilford Publications, 2011.

Weinstein, James N., et al. *Communities in Action : Pathways to Health Equity*. The National Academies Press, 2017.

Werner, Kelly M. "The Gender Gap in Caring for Children with Medical Complexity." *Journal of Perinatology*, vol. 43, no. 7, 2023, pp. 835–36, doi:10.1038/s41372-023-01652-1.

Wolfe, Ingrid, et al. "Integrated Care Models and Child Health: A Meta-Analysis." *Pediatrics*, vol. 145, no. 1, 2020, pp. 1–12, doi:10.1542/peds.2018-3747.

Wolfe, Ingrid, et al. "Integrated Care: A Solution for Improving Children's Health?" *Archives of disease in childhood*, vol. 101, no. 11, 2016, pp. 992–97, doi:10.1136/archdischild-2013-304442.

Woodgate, Roberta L., et al. "Siblings of Children with Complex Care Needs: Their Perspectives and Experiences of Participating in Everyday Life." *Child: Care, Health & Development*, vol. 42, no. 4, 2016, pp. 504–12, doi:10.1111/cch.12345.

Woodgate, Roberta L., et al. "Intense Parenting: A Qualitative Study Detailing the Experiences of Parenting Children with Complex Care Needs." *BMC Pediatrics*, vol. 15, 2015, pp. 1–15, doi:10.1186/s12887-015-0514-5.

Woodgate, Roberta L., et al. "Exploring Fathers' Experiences of Caring for a Child with Complex Care Needs through Ethnography and Arts-Based Methodologies." *BMC Pediatrics*, vol. 24, no. 1, 2024, https://bmcpediatr.biomedcentral.com/articles/10.1186/s12887-024-04567-8. Accessed 16 Apr. 2025.

World Health Assembly. "Framework on Integrated, People-Centred Health Services." *World Health Organisation*, 2016, https://iris.who.int/handle/10665/252698. Accessed 9 Apr. 2025.

Yantzi, Nicole, et al. "The Impacts of Distance to Hospital on Families with a Child with a Chronic Condition." *Social Science & Medicine*, vol. 52, no. 12, 2001, pp. 1777–91, doi:10.1016/S0277-9536(00)00297-5.

Zurynski, Yvonne, et al. "Australian Children Living with Rare Diseases: Experiences of Diagnosis and Perceived Consequences of Diagnostic Delays." *Orphanet Journal of Rare Diseases*, vol. 12, no. 1, 2017, pp. 1–9, doi: 10.1186/s13023-017-0622-4.

13.

Raising Rural: Rethinking Raising and Caring for Children with Medical Complexity Living in Rural Communities

Ngoc Huynh

Occurring relatively recently, the transition of care from institutions to the home for children[1] with medical complexity has been multifaceted, embedded in a complex interplay of personal, social, political, historical, cultural, and economic factors. Although it has become the norm and expectation to raise medically complex children[2] in family homes, the understanding of their everyday lives is limited. To date, much of the literature and processes of care for medically complex children are separated into different issues, such as healthcare, social and educational inclusion, accessibility, and lack of resources (Green et al. 160–63; Ray 286–94). This has resulted in health, social, and political systems that have not adjusted to support raising medically complex children at home (Algood et al. 130–33; Allshouse et al. S196–199; Carnevale et al., "Daily Living" e53–56; Carnevale et al., "A Relational Ethics" 270–76; Coad et al., 49–51; Mandic et al. 445–47; McKeever and Miller 1177–79; Ray 293–97). Living at home means medically complex children are engaged in the experiences and processes of childhood, not merely the processes of medical care and management, such as school,[3] social excursions, playtime, recreational activities, and social relationships (Carnevale et al., 2006 e54-57; Davey et al. 2266-69; Green 154-57; Green et al. 160-63; McKeever and Miller 1184-87; Woodgate et al., "How Families").

Examples in the literature speak to the negotiations and work families with children who have medical complexity engage in to be part of their communities (Woodgate et al., "How Families" 1916-18; Woodgate et al., "Intense Parenting" 4-10; Woodgate et al., "The Embodied Spaces" 10-11). However, there is little research on the influence of rurality on these processes. Furthermore, there needs to be consideration of the gendered influence of raising a medically complex child or any disabled child (Currie and Szabo 1252; Green 152; Green et al. 154-56; McCann et al.; McKeever and Miller 1177-81). The space and place at the intersection of childhood, disability, mothering, and rurality have not been well explored.

This chapter presents a foray into exploring raising children with medical complexity in rural communities, moving away from focusing on caring for medically complex children and emphasizing healthcare challenges rather than raising a child. To set the chapter, I present a brief literature review illustrating the complexities of raising children with medical complexities in their rural home communities. Following the setting of the background is a summary of the methodology I used to explore the experiences of families raising medically complex children in rural communities. Next, I share the experiences of these families to emphasize the creation of liminal spaces. For this work, I used an underlying theoretical framework scaffolded on relational autonomy and disabled children's childhood studies to recognize the complexity and multiplicity of sociopolitical, socioeconomic, and sociocultural influences of normativity on raising disabled children, sitting in a liminal space of mothering, childhood, and disability (Bell 70; Curran and Runswick-Cole 21-195; Mackenzie 147-49; Mackenzie and Stoljar 211-300; Sherwin and Network 5-250; Tisdall 185-88; Tisdall and Punch 253-60).

Setting the Background: Some Facts (with a Dash of Opinion Thrown In)

Children with medical complexity are the most complex children with special healthcare needs and are defined as children with complex chronic conditions that require specialized care; they have functional limitations with substantial caregiving needs and high health resources use (Cohen et al. 530–31; Dewan and Cohen 518). Although there are several variations of this definition, most agree on these four components. Children with medical complexity are a growing population because of continuing advances in neonatal and paediatric care, medical technology, and medical equipment. The advances in care and technology have contributed to increasing survivor rates for nearly every life-threatening condition of childhood, such as complex congenital heart disease, multisystem rare diseases, and extreme prematurity (Cohen and Patel 1199–1200). A recent pan-Canadian study by the Canadian Institute for Health Information (CIHI) identified 97, 600 children with medical complexity who were differentiated into four groups: neurological impairment (8 per cent), single condition (68 per cent), multiple conditions (16 per cent), and neurological impairment with other conditions (8 per cent) (6–8). Neurological impairment is defined as a diverse group of constant and progressive health conditions that involve the central and peripheral nervous systems and result in functional and/or intellectual impairment. A single condition is clarified as a complex chronic condition that affects only a single body system severely enough to require specialty care, and frequently time in hospital (CIHI 8).

Increased survivorship and lifespan of children with medical complexity, some into adulthood, require thoughtful processes to transition these children home with their intense medical and care needs. The movement for raising children with medical complexities at home can find historical impetus from the Disability Rights Movement. Public and health policies across Canada and much of the Global North have altered to support the raising of children with medical complexities in the family home, moving away from institutional settings. Families have become responsible for providing care in their homes that in the past only occurred in hospital settings in addition to other family responsibilities and roles (Carnevale et al., "Daily Living" e49–e50; Page et al. 1146–49; Wilkinson et al. 165–68). Complicated health and social systems require parents and other caregivers to learn an incredible variety of skills, many within the specialized scopes of healthcare professionals (Nygård and Clancy 3187–90; Page et al. 1146–49; Wilkinson et al. 165–67).

Based on the reported challenges and barriers, three interlinked components should be considered to support raising a child with medical complexities at home. First, providing access to excellent community-based care is a necessity for children with medical complexity (Cohen et al. 532–34; Cohen and Patel 1199–1200; Dewan and Cohen 520). Children with medical complexity have distinctive needs requiring ongoing medical support to monitor and maintain their health leading to higher use of primary care services and hospital and emergency services (CIHI 11–14). These children see many different care providers in multiple different care settings, a situation made more challenging when living in rural communities, away from urban-centred complex care services (CIHI 11–17; Skinner and Slifkin 150–51). Compared to their counterparts without complex medical issues, children with medical complexities have double the number of primary healthcare visits. Children with multiple conditions have on average four times as many visits to specialty clinics compared to children with a single complex chronic condition. In a two-year period two-thirds of children with medical complexities had an emergency department (ED) visit, and one-third had at least one hospital stay. Children with medical technology assistance have more frequent ED visits and hospital stays than medically complex children without medical assistive technology (McKenzie et al. 10–11).

Despite multiple governments and government agencies expressing the values of home and community care, the accessibility and availability of services vary widely across Canada (Canadian Home Care Association [CHCA] vi–xix; Cohen and Patel 1199–1200). Changes to primary healthcare across most of Canada, such as multidisciplinary team approaches, have not considered the unique developmental and social needs of children with medical complexity (Cohen and Patel 1199–1200; Lin et al. 113–18), which affects hospital and emergency room use. For example, the lack of after-hours care options leaves visits to the ED as the only choice. For these visits, staff may not be familiar with the child's medical history or have the experience to safely treat their conditions and provide optimal care (CIHI 12; Skinner and Slifkin 152–53).

Second, children with medical complexity require supportive systems to engage in all other aspects and rights of being a child, such as educational and recreational activities and safe accessible housing (Carnevale et al. "A Relational Ethics" 274–77; Esser et al. 905–08; Hounsell et al. 2–6; Perkins and Agrawal S247–48; Rosenbaum and Gorter 460–61; Watkinson et al. 4–12). Although the data on home care services and school services for children with medical complexity is limited, concerning general patterns have emerged (BCEDAccess; CHCA vi–xix; CIHI 19–22).

Families have reported that they rely heavily on unpaid and informal caregiving by family members (BCEDAccess; Children's Healthcare Canada [CHC], "Inventory of Gaps" 4; CIHI 19–21). Many report the difficulty of having their children included in school (BCEDAccess; CHC, "Inventory of Gaps" 3). Even when families may receive funding for respite care, daycare, home support, and school support, care/support staff are not always available (BCEDAccess; CIHI 19–21). Lack of qualified support staff is a prevalent issue for families with medically complex children, with much of the shortfall addressed by mothers (BCEDAccess; Bristow et al. 2563–2565; CIHI 19–21; Lewis et al. 1041–50; Werner 35, 36). Additionally, children with medical complexity face unique challenges with housing due to their specific medical and support needs. There are space and layout considerations, medical technology considerations, financial considerations, and location considerations. Families must often consider tradeoffs and compromises for housing and frequently experience financial stress (CHC, "Inventory of Gaps" 2, 4; Esser et al. 905–08; Hounsell et al. 2–6; Seltzer et al. 1–2).

Supportive systems also include mental health support systems for families and individual members of the family. A 2018 report by Children's Healthcare Canada details the many areas in which families require supportive systems to raise their children with medical complexity, such as financial, social inclusion, paid care, school, housing, and personal health. All areas harmed mental health. A growing body of literature is demonstrating the need to support the mental health of family members, which is deeply embedded in all aspects of raising a child with medical complexity (Allshouse et al. S198–200; Bayer et al. 5–7; Incledon et al. 184–90; Jaaniste et al. 271–74; Scheid and Sahai e94–96; Thomson et al. 190–92). Furthermore, an underlying component in much of the literature is the amount of work and advocacy that mothers, in particular, engage in to ensure the rights of their children with disabilities (Allshouse et al. S197–200; Ferrant et al. 2–6; Green et al. 154–56; Green 154–61; Leiter; Runswick-Cole 105–09; Witt et al. 9–12; Woodgate et al., "Intense Parenting" 8–10). Supportive systems are not simply to manage the medical care of medically complex children but a broad range of services to support raising a child with medical complexity.

Fragmented funding between multiple ministries for services, such as necessary aids and devices, therapies, homecare, respite care, and inclusive education and recreation further contributes to poor coordination of and access to the necessary care supports (CHCA vi–xix; Mirenda 13–19; Peter et al. 1625–26). Compounding the issue of funding are various legislative acts, stringent eligibility criteria, and long waitlists affecting the provision and accessibility of healthcare, home and community care, and community services (CHCA vi–xix; CIHI 14–22; Peter et al. 1625–26). The disjointed coordination of care and services across multiple government programs and services leads to gaps that increase the caregiving burden on families in addition to burdensome and complicated navigation of funding and services (CIHI 14–22; Mirenda 5–15; Peter et al. 1628–33). The multiple disconnects can contribute negatively to the health of the child with medical complexity and family (CHC, "Beyond Bandaids" 2–4). The burden of complicated care coordination, fragmented funding, and insufficient supports negatively affects the capacity of families to raise their children with medical complexity (Allshouse et al. S197–200; Currie and Szabo 1254–57; Dewan and Cohen 519–21; Lewis et al. 1031–35; Page et al. 1149–51).

Third, financial support for caregivers as the intensity and time requirements of care frequently requires caregivers to give up paid employment, further affecting the financial security of families with children who have medical complexity (Chua et al. 591–95; Foster et al. 5–8; Kish et al. 346–51; Ray 293–97; Uppal 2–5). The subjective burden of emotional stress and objective material burdens contribute to the mental, physical, social, economic, and emotional pressures that families of children with medical complexities experience (Allshouse et al. S196–199; CHC, "Major Challenges" 1–5; Krantz et al. 25–28; Green et al. 156–63; Green 154–59; Thomson et al. 190–92). Many families report paying out of pocket for therapies, drugs, and homecare. Frequently, one parent is out of the workforce to provide care for their medically complex child (CIHI 21; Kish et al. 346–51). Financial support should also be directed towards affordable, safe, and accessible housing. Again, the gendered aspect of where care work and employed work are placed needs to be made more explicit in the literature and opportunities and barriers need to be considered (Bristow et al. 2562–63; Lewis et al. 1048–50; Scott, "I Feel as If I Am" 672–76; Scott, "Mother-Ready Jobs" 2660–64; Werner 35–36).

Entangled within the roots of the issues are assumptions of normalcy and sexism. A large body of social science literature has detailed how cultural and normative markers can interact with demographic indicators to create hierarchical patterns of social inequity by influencing perceptions of society and policymakers. Children with medical complexity are compared to the hegemonic norms of typical childhood milestones rather than seen on an individual level of what they develop and gain. Continued institutional mentality emphasizing the deficit perspective of disability, viewing children with medical complexities as 'something' that needs to be fixed, rather than as children that need to be raised. Also not explicitly expressed are the underlying societal assumptions and devaluation of caring as unskilled labour enacted by women alongside the accepted norm that it is women who should provide care simply because they are women, and it is the expected role (Few-Demo and Allen 330–33; Ferrant et al. 7–8; Home; Landsman, *Reconstructing*; McKeever and Miller 1177–81; Ray 294–97; Scott, "I Feel as If I Am" 678–84; Scott, "Mother-Ready Jobs" 2666–68). An external power does not impose these socially and culturally assumed norms; instead, they are reified on multiple levels by individuals, groups, institutions, structures, and systems (Campbell 4–14; Foucault; Garland-Thomson, *Extraordinary Bodies*; Garland Thomson, "Feminist Disability Studies" 1560–68; Goodley, *Dis/Ability Studies*; Keller 72–77; Titchkosky, *Reading and Writing*; Tremain 13–17).

Living at home means children with medical complexity are engaged in the social and family fabric of life, essentially childhood experiences, such as school and social relationships, recreational activities, and family activities. The funding models reflect the focus on disability and diagnosis rather than the needs of medically complex children and their families, resulting in underfunding to address the multiple components of raising a child with medical complexity (CHCA vi–xix; CIHI 10–22; Representative for Children and Youth [RCY] 6–13; Thomson et al. 190–92). Underlying assumptions about the agency and value of children with disabilities and women have an unacknowledged influence on public and health policies (Hankivsky et al., "Expanding Economic Costing" 259–61; Hankivsky et al., "An Intersectionality-Based Policy Analysis" 5–9; Hutcheon and Lashewicz 1388–91; McGibbon, *Oppression*; Ray 297–300; RCY 13–32). Policies and practices, alongside social systems and structures, have a perpetual influence on how families raise their children with medical complexity, creating opportunities and barriers.

For families living in rural communities, the situation becomes more complex. It is well known that rural communities experience challenges in resources, accessibility, and availability of services due to geographic remoteness and low population densities (Murphy et al. 500–02; RCY 29–32; Skinner and Slifkin 150–51). Rurality is not the only issue; societal and structural processes also influence socioeconomic disadvantage, service availability, and resource availability for rural communities (Smith et al. 56–60; Vilches et al. 380–84). Families with medically complex children living in rural communities face an intersectional component of societal and structural processes around rurality and children with medical complexity (Allshouse et al. S196–198; Coad et al. 49–52; Flasch 212–16; Halfacree 26–34; Murphy et al. 500–02; RCY 29–32; Skinner and Slifkin 150–51; Smith et al. 57–60; Vilches et al. 380–84). The challenges families of children who have medical complexity face in rural communities, in addition to the issues experienced by families with medically complex children in general, are long travel times and distances for specialized care, services, and medications; limited or no access to specific drugs in local pharmacies; limited access to qualified health professionals, educators, and support staff; extra costs for travel, accommodations, and childcare; and social isolation (Bristow et al. 2562–66; CIHI 10–22; Murphy et al. 500–02; Skinner and Slifkin 152–55).

Approach to Exploring Families' Experiences

With the multiple challenges faced by families with children who have medical complexities living in rural communities, what are their experiences? What is it like to raise a child with medical complexities in a rural community? This question is particularly significant when considering the three general interlinked components needed to support raising a child with medical complexities at home: access to excellent community-based care, supportive systems, and financial support for caregivers. Stories may provide some answers. In my work exploring these questions, I drew on the philosophical underpinnings of constructivism and how our understanding of the world and our interactions within it are cocreated. The co-creation of knowledge and understanding lends itself to societal norms and expectations in beliefs, roles, responsibilities, behaviours, and thoughts. Based on this conceptualization of constructivism, I chose Relational Autonomy[4] as an appropriate approach, reflecting positioning and choice within society, while recognizing that choice is inextricably influenced by multiple factors. Theoretically scaffolded with relational autonomy is Disabled Children's Childhood Studies, which focusses on interpretation and understanding from an integrated child and disability perspective.

After receiving ethics approval, I used longitudinal case study approaches to support the study's inductive exploratory nature. Because the study's purpose was to explore a specific phenomenon within a specific population, I invited only families with medically complex children living in rural communities to participate, following selective sampling strategies. The experiences of families were shared through semi-structured interviews and monthly diaries. I analyzed their stories using iterative thematic analysis over time and across cases. As with many other studies with families with children with medical complexity, the mothers shared their experiences.

The Stories

The following stories have been drawn from the experiences that families have about living and raising their children with medical complexity in rural communities. The stories have been abbreviated and, in some cases, combined when the experiences were similar, with specific details altered to protect anonymity. The formatting of the stories is intentionally different from the literature review to stress the space between the facts in the literature review and the families' experiences.

Rural Living

Beth's Story

Our house is little, but we've managed to renovate it so it is accessible for Charlie. We can get his wheelchair in and out and move around our house. I'm not sure we could have done that if it wasn't for how affordable it is here. We could afford a house and make renos. I think it would be different if we lived in a city. For one, we would be renting, and you can't make a rented place accessible. It's almost impossible to find a place that's accessible. Living in a rural community with lower costs of living lets us afford a better quality of life.

Quiet mornings are the best. Charlie doesn't have great sleeps, so when he is still asleep in the morning, we make coffee and come back to bed. We have this huge window in front of our bed and looking out we see beautiful mountains and sparkling water. It's amazing that this is out in our backyard. We have quiet and beauty.

When we hear Charlie stirring on the monitor, one of us will get him and bring him back to our bed. We snuggle him in and enjoy the moment when Charlie is not frustrated or aggressive. He enjoys looking out our big window, watching the birds fly by or watching the rain drip down. The sense of peace that we have at that moment enjoying the beauty of our home is invaluable.

From this window, we can see down the little hill from our house to the estuary. The number of times we have sat and watched bears come ambling down to look for something to eat or just get into the water. It's awesome.

Jill's Story

The cost of living gives us so many more opportunities that we wouldn't have if we had a big mortgage living in a city. Especially with inflation. We bought our house seven years ago. We have a huge backyard that the kids can run around in. There's space for a trampoline and pool. Evie can't really jump like other kids do on the trampoline, but she loves rolling around on it and getting gently bounced by her big sister. When it's hot in the summer, and Evie is feeling up to it, we jump in the pool where she loves the feeling of water over her body as she floats.

We couldn't have this if we lived in a big city. Plus, the air is clean and pure; there's no pollution. It's hard to get some of the therapies that Evie needs, but we've turned a room in our house into her therapy room. Again, we couldn't have done that if it weren't for how affordable houses are here and how our community supports us and Evie. Her support worker and I do online physiotherapy for Evie and speech-language therapy with the therapists from the Children's Development Centre (CDC). It's just become a way of life.

It does get hard to manage all the roles, but at least we can get some therapy, even though it's online. Without the internet, I'm not sure Evie would get any therapy. We're lucky that right now a physiotherapist (PT) travels twice a month here to provide hands-on therapy. But they don't always have someone in that role. We have options, though, and we are set up with Evie's therapy room. That's the other thing: There's a lot that isn't covered, and we can pay for these things because our mortgage doesn't take up all our income. It means that when we have to travel for appointments, we can, and it doesn't put too much pressure on us. I can imagine that it's much harder for other families in big cities, where you have to pay more just for somewhere to live.

Accessibility of the Outdoors

Beth's Story

Being outdoors is important to us. We have access to all these trails. Right behind our house, there are dirt trails we go on and, in the winter, they are so beautiful with the trees covered in snow. We also have paved trails that are easily accessible. The dirt trails are wide and relatively flat, and Charlie's wheelchair can go on them. It's harder in winter for sure because of the snow and slush. But we don't have to pack up all the stuff like a wheelchair, stroller, emergency bag, blankets, supplies, and everything else that we need just to go somewhere to be outside. Being able to putter in our garden, go down to the estuary, walk in the forest, walk into town. Everything is walkable. We don't need to drive to be able to get out.

Donna's Story

It's beautiful where we live. We have mountains, lakes, fresh air, and trails. Hunter gets to go horse riding regularly. We have to get outdoors. I think it's so healing for Hunter. When we see his specialists, they are always surprised by how well he is doing. I really think it's because he can be outside. We just go down the road for his horse riding. The ski trails are also down the road. We go past our backyard to go snowmobiling. Going out to hike or cross-country skiing helps with my mental health. It's time to decompress. Of course, that's really only possible if I have someone I can leave Hunter with. That can be hard when we don't always have someone to do the respite hours. Lots of times, we go as a family, but sometimes, I just need that space and time to myself. There's so much I am responsible for as a mom, life stuff and then all of Hunter's stuff on top. Not just the care, but all the coordinating and fighting for him to be included and have access, too. When I am outside, I am just enjoying the air, the space, the quiet. I need that. Living here gives me that. My husband needs that, too. He grew up hunting, fishing, skiing, and snowmobiling. I know being outside also resets him.

Community Support

Emma's Story

It can be scary when we are adjusting or trialling new medications for Rae because her specialist isn't here. We have a family doctor now, but we didn't for a while. When things aren't going right, and we have to take Rae into the ER, they don't have an EEG machine. They don't have an MRI machine. They don't have someone who is experienced with complex kids and so many other things. But they talk to us, they listen and say you are the expert with your child. We are the experts in hospital stuff and how can we work together to help Rae. They are so good at connecting with the children's hospital and pushing to get us accepted there when we don't know what is going on and need more help. Whereas when we're at the pediatric hospital, we have to fight to be heard because they are the experts. We don't have all the tools or resources here, but we have good people who want the best for us, and that means something. They actually care about us.

Jill's Story

The community here is amazing. They all know Evie. When we go grocery shopping, the store has toys there specifically for her to play with. All the workers will come to say hi to Evie. She loves being the center of attention. Our daycare is wonderful. Her caregiver there knows Evie like the back of her hand. It means I can trust her to know when Evie is having an episode and to manage Evie with love. It's going to be hard to move Evie into the school system. We don't know who we will have as her education assistant (EA). From another family we heard that they miss several days because the EA is not there or has been pulled and their kid can't go to school. We should be funded for a full-time EA for school, but that doesn't mean there will be someone to pay for. Our daycare lady has offered to see about taking care of Evie if that happens when she goes to school next year. I'm not sure if we would have that support if Evie wasn't in a home daycare with someone who really cares about her.

Beth's Story

Our support system here is amazing. We feel cared for. When I am sitting in the ER with Charlie, someone will come and bring me coffee or see if I need anything. They will make sure my partner is okay with the baby because he still needs to work too. Our neighbour will let the dog out or bring him back in if we aren't there. When we came back from the children's hospital, our friends brought meals for us. They knew we needed support, and we didn't have to ask. They don't really understand what we are going through, but they were just there.

It's the same with our healthcare team. They go above and beyond. Our doctor will make home visits. For respite, it's supposed to be only direct support, but our respite workers will help with all the prep stuff for Charlie, like cleaning his feeding tubes so I can spend time being with him. Because we got new autism funding, they are trying to take away some of our respite funding. The funding really helps with paying for therapies and respite support, it just doesn't make sense when they try to take some away. He's still the same kid with the same issues, just a new diagnosis. Our social worker is always trying to find ways to help us keep funding and stretch it further. We really feel cared for and supported by our community. Our friends have become our family here.

We don't have family here, but we stay connected through facetime. When they are here, they are really engaged with Charlie, and he is engaged with them. It's great to be able to have that connection even though they aren't here physically. To know that he can have that connection with people other than us is amazing.

Donna's Story

Everyone knows Hunter. When I take him to the playground, even though it's not fully accessible, all the kids come up and say, "Hi." They're happy to see him. Some of them will see if he wants to get pushed around. When we wanted Hunter to play tee-ball, we knew who to talk to, and everyone was supportive in ensuring Hunter was included. It wasn't a "No, you can't," but a "How can we make this work for everyone?" The playground that's not fully accessible, the school applied for a grant to fix the playground when I pointed out that Hunter is excluded because it isn't accessible. Everyone knows everyone.

Family is hugely important to us. Hunter's grandparents are so close that he gets to see them almost every day, both sets. My mom is a rock, she will help on days when we need an extra hand because respite hasn't been able to show up or if Hunter can't go to school because his support person is away or if he is sick.

Being a Mom

Jill's Story

It just falls on you as the mom. The care and coordination fall on you to do because your partner still needs to work. It's also a personality thing. I am really into details, and you need that to manage and stay on top of everything Evie has going on. I need to know everything that is going on with Evie, and I don't share all of that with my husband because he needs to know everything going on with his work. It's exhausting though. I do not get enough sleep and that affects me too. I always worry about Evie. What if I miss something? I could have an outside job, but then that would require us to rejig our finances and see if we could afford a nanny. And I would still be responsible for all of Evie's appointments, medications, and behaviour. An outside job wouldn't work for me, but I am grateful that right now we don't need that income.

Beth's Story

Charlie is amazing and has helped me to open my mind. When he was first diagnosed, I thought this was the worst thing, and then we had no more time to think about it because of the intensity of the situation, which hasn't really let up. There's no time to really process as a mom because you have to learn to be a mom and learn to be a caregiver. It does just become a part of normal life. Charlie eats through a G-tube, and that's normal for us. It's become no big deal, whereas in the beginning I was so scared. I was so scared I would do something wrong. You carry that worry and guilt as a mother if something does go wrong. You wonder, what did I miss? What did I do wrong?

The worry is not as much on my partner because I am the one who does most of the care and coordinates everything, and Charlie is a busy boy. Charlie is a delight; it's the other stuff that pushes us to our capacity. I wish we were told as pregnant women, "Hey, there's this chance of your baby having health problems. Here are some tips. Find an online community. Find families that have a similar journey. Here's where you look for resources." Just practical stuff. I think I would have appreciated that information when I was pregnant with Charlie. But they don't want to scare you; moms will become too hysterical. It's harder to go in without even a clue of what to do.

As a mom in a rural community, I think I worry more because I worry about can we get out? Can we get to the children's hospital if we need to? It gets very snowy here, and we can't always fly out. Luckily, we have been able to when we have needed to. They let us go from the children's hospital when Charlie was stable and able to feed and said we would have the supports needed. We live in a rural community; those supports aren't here. It's a mix of teams and places that we have to go. For example, to manage Charlie's G-tube and feeding, we have a team in the next biggest town over, a four-hour drive. But that team does not talk to the team at the children's hospital when we had to see that team for complications with Charlies' feeds. I am the go-between to make sure everyone knows what is going on. It's layers of complications that fall on us as parents. Or rather me.

Liminal Spaces

What does this brief foray into raising children with medical complexity in rural communities tell us about the complexity and multiplicity of sociopolitical, socioeconomic, and sociocultural influences on raising disabled children at the intersection of childhood, disability, mothering, and rurality? On the surface, the challenges of caring for children with medical complexity because of their complex and multiple care needs are evident. Their care requires specialized skills, intense resource use, long-term support, and individualized care. Living in rural communities highlights how these requirements are influenced by urban and rural bias in resource access and provision. However, if we look deeper, the access and provision of resources, care, and support are linked to assumptions of normalcy underlying conceptualizations of what it is like to provide care for a medically complex child rather than focus on what is needed to raise a child with medical complexity.

Stories shared by the mothers reflect four themes about raising a child with complex medical needs rather than caring for a medically complex child, which connotates a medicalized approach. The four themes of living rural, accessibility of the outdoors, community support, and being a mom speak to the integrated components of living in a rural community enabling the creation of a liminal space where their children can be children, and they get to be moms. The stories shared by the mothers demonstrate how they push back against boundaries and create opportunities to raise their children by enacting autonomy within rural spaces.

The mothers tell us it is a choice to raise their children with medical complexity in rural communities because of their ability to create a quality of life that sustains them as individuals and as a family. Although there are limitations and challenges to accessing services, medical care, medications, and therapies, the mothers feel their families are supported and included by their communities. They feel listened to and supported in addressing barriers and creating opportunities for the inclusion of their medically complex children. In times of need, the mothers knew their communities would be there to help without needing to ask. The mothers felt their children were acknowledged and seen, not merely present. These relationships are invaluable and a source of comfort and joy. The emphasis on relationships and community support and inclusion reflects how the community can contribute to the supportive systems that are one of the three general components to support raising medically complex children at home. According to these mothers, their choice to live in rural communities is based on how space and place contributed to their families' quality of life, further demonstrating how families create supportive systems within their communities when broader health and social systems are not supportive. The mothers iterated how being and engaging with their outdoor environment supported their mental and physical health and that of their families. The ability to simply step outside with their medically complex child and enjoy being outdoors opened opportunities to connect freely with their child that were not restricted by socially or environmentally driven inaccessibility. Ease of accessibility enabled parents to give their children chances to experience the beauty of nature, breathe the fresh air, feel the wind, smell the trees, feel the bumpy trail, touch the water, and experience rain. Mothers stressed the significance of being able to be with their medically complex child and enjoy the same experiences children without complex care needs can access without the additional needs of planning for accessibility and inclusion challenges. Living in rural communities gave their children with medical complexity opportunities to have experiences that may not have been possible in urban settings.

The mothers shared that by living in rural communities, their families had the financial means to have space and place to adapt to their medically complex children's needs, whether this was a physical adaptation to make their home or community space more accessible, social adaptation so that their children could be included, or collaboration with healthcare professionals and support staff to meet the needs of their children with medical complexity as best they could with the resources available. Having space and place enabled families, particularly mothers, to develop workarounds for some of the inequalities in resources, support, and healthcare access and provision for people with disabilities living in rural communities, creating opportunities to raise their children with medical complexity. The approaches described by the mothers touch upon the three interlinked components needed to support raising children with medical complexity at home: access to excellent community-based care, supportive systems, and financial support.

The mothers experienced the challenges and barriers found in much of the literature on children with medical complexity. However, the choice to live in rural communities has also given families of children with medical complexity opportunities to create a liminal space between disability and childhood where their medically complex children can share in the experiences of childhood. Entwined in the liminal space is mothering, where living in a rural community enabled mothers of medically complex children to mother their children rather than staying in the role of advocate, caregiver, navigator, and multiple other roles. Within this liminal space, the persistent concerns and energy towards addressing barriers and challenges are not at the forefront; mothering their children is.

Despite multiple challenges, families choose to live in rural communities because of the quality of life that space and place enable them to achieve and maintain. Their stories highlight how many of the challenges to raising children with medical complexity are the results of systems and structures with inherent biases that place complicated components of care external to that of raising a child on the shoulders of families, mainly mothers, without sufficient support systems and services. Raising children with medical complexity in rural settings is about quality of life, relationships, and support; it is about opportunities and inclusion and about space and place—that is, a liminal space to be a child and to be a mom.

Endnotes

1. For the purposes of this chapter, "children" will refer to any child between birth and eighteen years of age.

2. The terms "children with medical complexity" and "medically complex children" will be used interchangeably to recognize that some individuals prefer person-first language and others prefer identity-first language.
3. The term "school" is used to reflect the multiple sociodevelopmental aspects of being in school (Woodgate et al., "Intense Parenting" 4–14; Woodgate et al., "The Embodied Spaces" 8–11).
4. For more material on relational autonomy, see Bell, *Relational Autonomy*; Mackenzie and Stoljar, *Relational Autonomy*.

Works Cited

Algood, Carl L., Cynthia Harris, and Jun S. Hong. "Parenting Success and Challenges for Families of Children with Disabilities: An Ecological Systems Analysis." *Journal of Human Behavior in the Social Environment*, vol. 23, no. 2, 2013, pp. 126–136.

Allshouse, Carolyn, et al. "Families of Children with Medical Complexity: A View from the Front Lines." *Pediatrics (Evanston)*, vol. 141, no. Suppl 3, 2018, pp. S195–S201, doi:10.1542/peds.2017-1284D.

Bayer, N. D., et al. "A National Mental Health Profile of Parents of Children with Medical Complexity." *Pediatrics*, vol. 148, no. 2, 2021, pp. 1–10, doi:10.1542/peds.2020-023358.

BCEDAccess Society. "Exclusion Tracker Report 2022–23." 2023, https://bcedaccess.com/wp-content/uploads/2024/04/d3882-exclusion-tracker-2022-23-5.pdf. Accessed 10 Apr. 2025.

Bell, Jennifer. "Relational Autonomy as a Theoretical Lens for Qualitative Health Research." *International Journal of Feminist Approaches to Bioethics*, vol. 13, no. 2, 2020, pp. 69–92, doi:10.3138/ijfab.13.2.09.

Bristow, Sally, et al. "The Rural Mother's Experience of Caring for a Child with a Chronic Health Condition: An Integrative Review." *Journal of Clinical Nursing*, vol. 27, no. 13–14, 2018, pp. 2558–68, doi:10.1111/jocn.14360.

Campbell, Fiona Kumari. *Contours of Ableism: The Production of Disability and Abledness*. Palgrave Macmillan, 2009.

Canadian Home Care Association (CHCA). "Home and Community-Based Services and Supports: Children with Complex Care Needs."

CHCA, 2016, https://cdnhomecare.ca/wp-content/uploads/2020/02/CHCA-Children-with- Complex-Care-Needs.pdf. Accessed 10 Apr. 2025.

Canadian Institute for Health Information (CIHI). *Children and Youth with Medical Complexity in Canada*. CIHI, 2020, https://www.cihi.ca/sites/default/files/document/children-youth-with-medical-complexity-report-en.pdf. Accessed 10 Apr. 2025.

Carnevale, Franco A. et al. "Daily Living with Distress and Enrichment: The Moral Experience of Families with Ventilator-Assisted Children at Home." *Pediatrics (Evanston)*, vol. 117, no. 1, 2006, pp. e48–e60, doi:10.1542/peds.2005-0789.

Carnevale, Franco A., et al. "A Relational Ethics Framework for Advancing Practice with Children with Complex Health Care Needs and Their Parents." *Comprehensive Child and Adolescent Nursing*, vol. 40, no. 4, 2017, pp. 268–84, doi:10.1080/24694193.2017.1373162.

Children's Healthcare Canada (CHC). *Inventory of Gaps and Barriers*. CHC, 2018. https://www.childrenshealthcarecanada.ca/en/networks-and-hubs/Changing-Your- Lens/Inventory-of-Gaps-and-Barriers---Final-Feb-2-2018-(1).pdf. Accessed 10 Apr. 2025.

Children's Healthcare Canada (CHC). "Beyond Bandaids: Delivering Healthcare Fit for Kids." *CHC*, May 2024. https://www.childrenshealthcarecanada.ca/en/child-health-advocacy/Right-Sizing/Beyond-Bandaids-Report.pdf. Accessed 10 Apr. 2025.

Chua, Clara, et al. "Income Support for Parents of Children with Chronic Conditions and Disability: Where Do We Draw the Line? A Policy Review." *Archives of Disease in Childhood*, vol. 107, no. 6, 2022, pp. 591–95, doi:10.1136/archdischild-2021-322663.

Coad, Jane, et al. "Exploring the Perceived Met and Unmet Need of Life-Limited Children, Young People and Families." *Journal of Pediatric Nursing*, vol. 30, no. 1, 2015, pp. 45–53, doi:10.1016/j.pedn.2014.09.007.

Cohen, Eyal, et al. "Children with Medical Complexity: An Emerging Population for Clinical and Research Initiatives." *Pediatrics (Evanston)*, vol. 127, no. 3, 2011, pp. 529–38, doi:10.1542/peds.2010-0910.

Cohen, Eyal, and Hema Patel. "Responding to the Rising Number of Children Living with Complex Chronic Conditions." *Canadian Medical Association Journal*, vol. 186, no. 16, 2014, pp. 1199–1200, doi:10.1503/cmaj.141036.

Curran, Tillie, and Katherine Runswick-Cole. *Disabled Children's Childhood Studies: Critical Approaches in a Global Context.* Palgrave Macmillan, 2013.

Currie, Genevieve, and Joanna Szabo. "'It Would Be Much Easier If We Were Just Quiet and Disappeared': Parents Silenced in the Experience of Caring for Children with Rare Diseases." *Health Expectations: An International Journal of Public Participation in Health Care and Health Policy*, vol. 22, no. 6, 2019, pp. 1251–1259, doi:10.1111/hex.12958.

Davey, Heather, et al. "'Our Child's Significant Disability Shapes Our Lives': Experiences of Family Social Participation." *Disability and Rehabilitation*, vol. 37, no. 24, 2015, pp. 2264–71.

Dewan, Tammie, and Eyal Cohen. "Children with Medical Complexity in Canada." *Paediatrics & Child Health*, vol. 18, no. 10, 2013, pp. 518–22, doi:10.1093/pch/18.10.518.

Esser, Kayla, et al. "Housing Need among Children with Medical Complexity: A Cross-Sectional Descriptive Study of Three Populations." *Academic Pediatrics*, vol. 22, no. 6, 2022, pp. 900–09, doi:10.1016/j.acap.2021.09.018.

Ferrant, Gaëlle, et al. *Unpaid Care Work: The missing link in the analysis of gender gaps in labor outcomes.* OECD Development Centre, 2014, https://www.oecd.org/en/publications/unpaid-care-work-the-missing-link-in-the-analysis-of-gender-gaps-in-labour-outcomes_1f3fd03f-en.html. Accessed 10 Apr. 2025.

Few-Demo, April L., and Katherine R. Allen. "Gender, Feminist, and Intersectional Perspectives On families: A Decade in Review." *Journal of Marriage and Family*, vol. 82, no. 1, 2020, pp. 326–45, doi:10.1111/jomf.12638.

Flasch, Elizabeth A. "Health Equity and Children with Medical Complexity/Children and Youth with Special Health Care Needs: A Scoping Review." *Journal of Pediatric Health Care*, vol. 38, no. 2, 2024, pp. 210–18, doi:https://doi.org/10.1016/j.pedhc.2023.07.007. Accessed 10 Apr. 2025.

Foster, Carolyn C., et al. "Children with Special Health Care Needs and Forgone Family Employment." *Pediatrics*, vol. 148, no. 3, 2021, pp. 1–18, doi:10.1542/peds.2020-035378.

Foucault, Michel. *Archaeology of Knowledge*. Translated by Sheridan Smith. Taylor and Francis, 2013.

Foucault, Michel. *The Birth of the Clinic*. Routledge, 1977.

Garland-Thomson, Rosemarie, *Extraordinary Bodies: Figuring Physical Disability in American Culture and Literature*. Columbia University Press, 1997.

Garland-Thomson, Rosemarie. "Feminist Disability Studies." *Signs: Journal of Women in Culture and Society*, vol. 30, no. 2, 2005, pp. 1557–87, doi:10.1086/423352.

Goodley, Dan. *Dis/Ability Studies: Theorising Disablism and Ableism*. Routledge, Taylor & Francis Group, 2014.

Green, Sara E., et al. "Has the Parent Experience Changed over Time? A Meta-Analysis of Qualitative Studies of Parents of Children with Disabilities from 1960 to 2012." *Disability and Intersecting Statuses*, vol. 7, 2013, pp. 97–168, https://go.exlibris.link/t0QjJcPW.

Green, Sara Eleanor. "'We're Tired, Not Sad': Benefits and Burdens of Mothering a Child with a Disability." *Social Science & Medicine (1982)*, vol. 64, no. 1, 2007, pp. 150–63, doi:10.1016/j.socscimed.2006.08.025.

Halfacree, Keith. "Locality and Social Representation: Space, Discourse and Alternative Definitions of the Rural." *Journal of Rural Studies*, vol. 9, no. 1, 1993, pp. 23–37, doi:10.1016/0743-0167(93)90003-3.

Hankivsky, Olena, et al. "Expanding Economic Costing in Health Care: Values, Gender and Diversity." *Canadian Public Policy/Analyse de Politiques*, vol. 30, no. 3, 2004, pp. 257–82, doi:10.2307/3552302.

Hankivsky, Olena et al. "An Intersectionality-Based Policy Analysis Framework: Critical Reflections on a Methodology for Advancing Equity." *International Journal for Equity in Health*, vol. 13, no. 1, 2014, p. 119, doi:10.1186/s12939-014-0119-x.

Home, Alice. "Challenging Hidden Oppression: Mothers Caring for Children with Disabilities." *Critical Social Work*, vol. 3, no. 1, 2018, https://go.exlibris.link/cylB0lS0.

Hounsell, Kara Grace, et al. "The Experience of Housing Needs among Families Caring for Children with Medical Complexity." *Pediatrics*, vol. 148, no. 1, 2021, pp. 1–9, doi:10.1542/peds.2020-018937.

Hutcheon, Emily, and Bonnie Lashewicz. "Theorizing Resilience: Critiquing and Unbounding a Marginalizing Concept." *Disability &*

Society, vol. 29, no. 9, 2014, pp. 1383–97, doi:10.1080/09687599.2014.934954.

Incledon, Emily, et al. "A Review of Factors Associated with Mental Health in Siblings of Children with Chronic Illness." *Journal of Child Health Care*, vol. 19, no. 2, 2015, pp. 182–94, doi:10.1177/1367493513503584.

Jaaniste, Tiina, et al. "Living with a Child Who Has a Life-Limiting Condition: The Functioning of Well-Siblings and Parents." *Child: Care, Health and Development*, vol. 48, no. 2, 2022, pp. 269–76, doi:https://doi.org/10.1111/cch.12927.

Keller, Reiner. "Michel Foucault: Discourse, Power/Knowledge and the Modern Subject." *The Routledge Handbook of Language and Politics*. Edited by Bernhard Forchtner, vol. 1, Routledge, 2018, pp. 67–81. https://go.exlibris.link/ys4x3cCN.

Kish, Antonia M., et al. "Working and Caring for a Child with Chronic Illness: A Review of Current Literature." *Child: Care, Health & Development*, vol. 44, no. 3, 2018, pp. 343–54, doi:10.1111/cch.12546.

Krantz, Chantal, et al. "The Price of Love: Understanding the Financial and Psychosocial Costs of Caring for Children with Medical Complexities." *Healthcare Quarterly*, vol. 26, no. 4, 2024, pp. 24–30.

Landsman, Gail. *Reconstructing Motherhood and Disability in the Age of "Perfect" Babies*. Routledge, 2009.

Leiter, Valerie. "Parental Activism, Professional Dominance, and Early Childhood Disability." *Disability Studies Quarterly*, vol. 24, no. 2, 2004, doi:10.18061/dsq.v24i2.483.

Lewis, Suzan, et al. "Dual-Earner Parents with Disabled Children: Family Patterns for Working and Caring." *Journal of Family Issues*, vol. 21, no. 8, 2000, pp. 1031–60, doi:10.1177/019251300021008005.

Lin, Jia Lu Lilian, et al. "Process Evaluation of a Hub-and-Spoke Model to Deliver Coordinated Care for Children with Medical Complexity across Ontario: Facilitators, Barriers and Lessons Learned." *Healthcare Policy*, vol. 17, no. 1, 2021, pp. 104–122, doi:10.12927/hcpol.2021.26574.

Mackenzie, Catriona. "Feminist Innovation in Philosophy: Relational Autonomy and Social Justice." *Women's Studies International Forum*, vol. 72, 2019, pp. 144–51, doi:10.1016/j.wsif.2018.05.003.

Mackenzie, Catriona, and Natalie Stoljar. *Relational Autonomy: Feminist Perspectives on Automony, Agency, and the Social Self.* Oxford University Press, 2000.

Mandic, Carmen Gomez, et al. "Impact of Caring for Children with Medical Complexity on Parents' Employment and Time." *Community, Work & Family*, vol. 20, no. 4, 2017, pp. 444–58, doi:10.1080/13668 803.2016.1202195.

McGibbon, Elizabeth Anne. *Oppression: A Social Determinant of Health.* Fernwood, 2012.

McKeever, Patricia, and Karen-Lee Miller. "Mothering Children Who Have Disabilities: A Bourdieusian Interpretation of Maternal Practices." *Social Science & Medicine (1982)*, vol. 59, no. 6, 2004, pp. 1177–91, doi:10.1016/j.socscimed.2003.12.023.

McKenzie, Katherine, et al. "How Children and Youth with Medical Complexity Use Hospital and Emergency Department Care across Canada." *Healthcare Quarterly*, vol. 24, no. 1, 2021, pp. 10–13.

Mirenda, Pat. *Key Components of Effective Service Delivery for Children and Youth with Support Needs and Their Families: A Research Review and Analysis. Representative for Children and Youth*, 2023, https://rcybc.ca/reports-and-publications/reports/key-components/. Accessed 10 Apr. 2025.

Murphy, Kelly L., et al. "Rural and Nonrural Differences in Providing Care for Children with Complex Chronic Conditions." *Clinical Pediatrics*, vol. 51, no. 5, 2012, pp. 498–503, doi:10.1177/000992281 2436884.

Nygård, Carina, and Anne Clancy. "Unsung Heroes, Flying Blind—a Metasynthesis of Parents' Experiences of Caring for Children with Special Health Care Needs at Home." *Journal of Clinical Nursing*, vol. 27, no. 15–16, 2018, pp. 3179–96, doi:10.1111/jocn.14512.

Page, Bethan F., et al. "The Challenges of Caring for Children Who Require Complex Medical Care at Home: 'The Go-Between for Everyone Is the Parent and as the Parent That's an Awful Lot of Responsibility.'" *Health Expectations: An International Journal of Public Participation in Health Care and Health Policy*, vol. 23, no. 5, 2020, pp. 1144–54, doi:10.1111/hex.13092.

Perkins, Jane, and Rishi Agrawal. "Protecting Rights of Children with Medical Complexity in an Era of Spending Reduction." *Pediatrics (Evanston)*, vol. 141, no. Suppl 3, 2018, pp. S242–S49, doi:10.1542/peds.2017-1284I.

Peter, Elizabeth, et al. "Neither Seen nor Heard: Children and Homecare Policy in Canada." *Social Science & Medicine (1982)*, vol. 64, no. 8, 2007, pp. 1624–35, doi:10.1016/j.socscimed.2006.12.002.

Ray, Lynne D. "The Social and Political Conditions That Shape Special-Needs Parenting." *Journal of Family Nursing*, vol. 9, no. 3, 2003, pp. 281–304, doi:10.1177/1074840703255436.

Representatative for Children and Youth (RCY). *Still Left Out: Children and Youth with Disabilities in B.C. Representative for Children and Youth*, 2023, https://rcybc.ca/wp-content/uploads/2023/11/RCY_Still-Left-Out_Nov2023_Final_10-Nov-2023.pdf. Accessed 10 Apr. 2025.

Rosenbaum, Peter, and Jan W. Gorter. "The 'F-Words' in Childhood Disability: I Swear This Is How We Should Think." *Child : Care, Health & Development*, vol. 38, no. 4, 2012, pp. 457–63, doi:10.1111/j.1365-2214.2011.01338.x.

Runswick-Cole, Katherine. "'Wearing It All with a Smile': Emotional Labour in the Lives of Mothers and Disabled Children." *Disabled Children's Childhood Studies*. Edited by Tillie Curran and Katherine Runswick-Cole. Palgrave Macmillan UK, 2016, pp. 105–18.

Scheid, Andrea, and Shashi Sahai. "Psychological Care of the Family of Children with Medical Complexities." *Pediatric Annals*, vol. 53, no. 3, 2024, pp. e93–e98, doi:10.3928/19382359-20240109-03.

Scott, Ellen K. "'Feel as If I Am the One Who Is Disabled': The Emotional Impact of Changed Employment Trajectories of Mothers Caring for Children with Disabilities." *Gender & Society*, vol. 24, no. 5, 2010, pp. 672–96, doi:10.1177/0891243210382531.

Scott, Ellen K. "Mother-Ready Jobs: Employment That Works for Mothers of Children with Disabilities." *Journal of Family Issues*, vol. 39, no. 9, 2018, pp. 2659–84, doi:10.1177/0192513X18756927.

Seltzer, Rebecca R., et al. "The Daunting Problem of Medical Complexity and Housing Instability." *Pediatrics*, vol. 146, no. 1, 2020, pp. 1–3, doi:10.1542/peds.2019-3284.

Sherwin, Susan, and Feminist Health Care Ethics Research Network. *The Politics of Women's Health: Exploring Agency and Autonomy*. Temple University Press, 1998.

Skinner, Asheley Cockrell, and Rebecca T. Slifkin. "Rural/Urban Differences in Barriers to and Burden of Care for Children with Special Health Care Needs." *The Journal of Rural Health*, vol. 23, no. 2, 2007, pp. 150–57, doi:10.1111/j.1748-0361.2007.00082.x.

Smith, Karly B., et al. "Addressing the Health Disadvantage of Rural Populations: How Does Epidemiological Evidence Inform Rural Health Policies and Research?" *The Australian Journal of Rural Health*, vol. 16, no. 2, 2008, pp. 56-66, doi:10.1111/j.1440-1584.2008.00953.x.

Thomson, Joanna, et al. "Financial and Social Hardships in Families of Children with Medical Complexity." *The Journal of Pediatrics*, vol. 172, 2016, pp. 187–93, doi:10.1016/j.jpeds.2016.01.049.

Tisdall, E. Kay M. "The Challenge and Challenging of Childhood Studies? Learning from Disability Studies and Research with Disabled Children." *Children & Society*, vol. 26, no. 3, 2012, pp. 181–91, doi:10.1111/j.1099-0860.2012.00431.x.

Tisdall, Kay E., and Samantha Punch. "Not so 'New'? Looking Critically at Childhood Studies." *Children's Geographies*, vol. 10, no. 3, 2012, pp. 249–64, https://doi.org/10.1080/14733285.2012.693376.

Titchkosky, Tanya. *Reading and Writing Disability Differently: The Textured Life of Embodiment*. University of Toronto Press, 2007.

Tremain, Shelley. "Foucault, Governmentality, and Critical Disability Theory Today: A Genealogy of the Archive." *Foucault and the Government of Disability*. Edited by Tremain Shelley. University of Michigan Press, 2015, pp. 9–23.

Uppal, Sharanjit. *Employment Patterns of Families with Children*. Statistics Canada, 2015, https://publications.gc.ca/collections/collection_2015/statcan/75-006-x/75-006-2015001-6-eng.pdf. Accessed 10 Apr. 2015.

Vilches, Silvia L., et al. "Documenting the Urbanistic Policy Bias in Rural Early Childhood Services: Toward a Functional Definition of Rurality: Urbanistic Policy Bias." *The Canadian Geographer*, vol. 61, no. 3, 2017, pp. 375–388, doi:10.1111/cag.12359.

Watkinson, Michelle D., et al. "Interventions in the Home and Community for Medically Complex Children: A Systematic Review." *Pediatrics*, vol. 151, no. 5, 2023, doi:10.1542/peds.2022-058352.

Werner, Kelly M. "The Gender Gap in Caring for Children with Medical Complexity." *Journal of Perinatology*, vol. 43, no. 7, 2023, pp. 835–36, doi:10.1038/s41372-023-01652-1.

Wilkinson, Catherine, et al. "Not a Nurse but More Than a Mother: The Everyday Geographies of Mothering Children with Complex Heath Care Needs." *Children's Geographies*, vol. 19, no. 2, 2021, pp. 158–71, doi:10.1080/14733285.2020.1755420.

Witt, Stefanie, et al. "Living with a Rare Disease – Experiences and Needs in Pediatric Patients and Their Parents." *Orphanet Journal of Rare Diseases*, vol. 18, no. 1, 2023, p. 242, doi:10.1186/s13023-023-02837-9.

Woodgate, Roberta L., et al. "Intense Parenting: A Qualitative Study Detailing the Experiences of Parenting Children with Complex Care Needs." *BMC Pediatrics*, vol. 15, no. 1, 2015, p. 197, doi:10.1186/s12887-015-0514-5.

Woodgate, Roberta L., et al. "The Embodied Spaces of Children with Complex Care Needs: Effects on the Social Realities and Power Negotiations of Families." *Health & Place*, vol. 46, 2017, pp. 6–12, doi:https://doi.org/10.1016/j.healthplace.2017.04.001.

Woodgate, Roberta Lynn, et al. "How Families of Children with Complex Care Needs Participate in Everyday Life." *Social Science and Medicine*, vol. 75, no. 10, 2012, pp. 1912–20, doi:10.1016/j.socscimed.2012.07.037.

Afterword

Fierce Advocacy, Fierce Love

Eva Feder Kittay

I am a mother, much like the mothers who authored or are described in these chapters. I have an adult child, a wonderful woman who is now fifty-six years old. She, like the multiply disabled and medically complex children discussed in this rich volume, has enhanced my life so far beyond anything I could have imagined—and certainly more than the cold impersonal words we received in 1970: "She is severely to profoundly retarded [a term still in use at the time that was as cutting then as it is now] and will always be. She won't be able to talk—beyond a few words at best—or walk." These words were uttered by a physician who then promptly left the room. Some chapters speak of that moment's devastation and the hardships that followed. Yet the mothers invariably recount how their children have brought joy and richness into the lives of their families and often into the lives of others, such as caregivers, neighbours, therapists, and friends. They recount that although these children have placed certain bounds on their lives, they have also expanded what they had previously thought possible for themselves and their children. Mothering these atypical children, and facing the world's stigma, incomprehension and cruelties, has made them more fierce, more determined, and more innovative in their thinking. These changes were propelled by a love that was equally fierce and enriching.

The volume contains autoethnographic accounts—that is, engaging stories by the mothers about their own experiences. Such stories need to be told and in the first person. They add depth to the more formal presentations of data and research found herein. I have found in my work the need to speak about my daughter and my experiences parenting her because the general knowledge about our children and our lives is so impoverished that otherwise putting forward generalizations in theoretical or empirical terms does not bring the message home.

The stories and research reported in this volume comprise a kaleidoscope for the reader. We hear stories from rarely heard voices and watch the stories shift as writers speak from their different perspectives, yet the voices interweave with common themes. We hear from mothers with medically complex children, others who cannot speak and are fully dependent, and still others who seek supported employment, want more independent lives, or hope to fulfill dreams shaped before a chronic illness. Whether the women are privileged and have economic resources or are struggling with the extra financial costs of raising their unique children, all speak of finding a trail they must blaze for themselves with few guideposts and little support. Most importantly, we hear of their fierce advocacy born from their unbounded and intense love.

We hear the voice of a Black mother, Yvette C. Latunde, who struggles to help her talented athletic daughter, who developed a chronic medical condition, navigate the difficult straits through medical and educational institutions, hoping to realize her daughter's dreams of becoming an elite athlete. Like so many others in the volume, this chapter is a methodological blend of autoethnographic and empirical research. Using the theoretical framework of intersectionality, Latunde highlights the problems Black mothers encounter given the intersectionality of race, gender, and disability.

We hear the experiences of rural women who appreciate the beauty and freedom that rural life can provide. Yet they are also forced to seek resources that their rural environment does not provide. It is a balance I understand all too well, living as our family does in a beautiful setting where we can bring our daughter to a restaurant and know she will be welcomed. Yet we have to deal with her medical complexities in a region with poor medical facilities, scarce outside help, and few therapies to supplement those she receives in her program.

Two chapters by siblings provide a perspective so often missing in caregiving discussions. As mothers of a multiply disabled child who needs so much more attention and care than the typical child, we try to find ways not to deprive siblings of a good childhood and to avoid burdening their futures by the prospect of having to be responsible for their sibling.

But as mothers, we often fail to see how much the sibling yearns to be part of the process and plan of caregiving. At the same time, there is hurt and pain that we blind ourselves to. I found these two chapters particularly moving and often wiped away tears while reading them, thinking of how my son had lived with the situation and how I could have done better.

A striking chapter by Gretchen Good, a woman who is herself disabled and who adopted two disabled children, speaks of the almost impossible task of managing such complex caregiving. Yet readers are left less with the hardship and more with the joy and delight she and her husband take in two rambunctious, wonderful children—individuals the world has much difficulty accommodating. What also emerges from her story is a theme echoed often in the other chapters. Much of the hardship in raising our non-normative children comes from dealing with the outside world—the schools, the doctors, unaccommodating surroundings, uncomprehending strangers, and pervasive ableism—and an ableism that also leads us to presume that the carer cannot be disabled.

In some chapters, we hear the pain more loudly. In others, we hear the articulations of what is needed to make the mothers' and caregivers' children's lives the best that they can be. The volume provides helpful suggestions, such as including siblings more deeply in the knowledge of medical issues and decision-making. Models of caregiving are also provided by mothers who decided they are tired of bucking the system and instead are undertaking homeschooling, as Anne Borden King recounts. But she also finds, as do so many of us, that our children want to be with peers as they grow and mature. For my daughter, who lived at home with us for thirty-two years, this meant finding a residential facility that I felt I could trust and in which she could thrive. When my husband and I (tearfully) left her at her new residence, her attitude (expressed silently as she cannot speak) was "Bye, Mom," and she turned to her new friends. For others, this means finding an integrated setting with the necessary accommodations that will allow them to be included in society. Still another innovative suggestion is the integrated care model discussed by Anneliese de Groot and colleagues. They call it an "integrated village approach," an idea we can learn more about through the thoroughly documented references cited in that chapter.

In most of the chapters, we hear the mothers' concern about their children's future, one in which they may no longer be able to be their fierce advocates. Having learned of an organization founded by parents to answer the question "Who will care for and about my child with disabilities after I die?", Donna Thompson speaks inspiringly of how this discovery made her decide to set aside her worries of whether her son would survive and instead create an affiliate to the organization. She writes that this moved her from advocacy for her son to "crusadership," using the terminology of Roselyn Darling. It was in the process of imagining and attempting to create what would be a good life for her multiply disabled and medically complex son that she was led, together with two other parent-advocates, to create The Family Engagement in Research Program, an online course at McMaster University.

Such crusadership is mirrored in other autoethnographies and other research discussed in the book. Ann Borden King, for instance, tells us that she cofounded autistic self-advocacy organizations in Canada to educate health providers on how to communicate with autistic patients. Other parents changed the focus of their professional careers to organize institutions, teach, and contribute to the research and the literature in the area. They used whatever talents and skills they possessed to help other parents navigate through the uncharted territory of mothering disabled children. Such crusadership shows how caring, especially the intensive kind, does not have to isolate us in the long term but can expand our circle of care to help others meet the task more easily.

I have scarcely touched on all the riches in this book. It has offered me insights from perspectives I have not often seen in print, conveyed directions and innovations that need to be pursued, and given me a sense of comradeship with so many thoughtful people working in an area that has come to define me and my family.

I, and I am sure others, will be grateful for its publication.

Notes on Contributors

Samantha Bellefeuille is a sibling partner who has a younger brother with CDKL5. She is the executive director and founder of a day program for adults with exceptionalities called Fostering Forever Friendships, in Ottawa, Ontario.

Genevieve Currie is a parent of two children; both have neurodevelopmental disorders, and one has a rare medically complex disease. She is a parent advocate, registered nurse, and researcher. She completed her PhD in nursing at the University of Calgary and is an associate professor in the School of Nursing and Midwifery at Mount Royal University, Calgary, Alberta, Canada. Her current research and expertise interests are focussed on family-centred care, family engagement in healthcare and research, and peadiatric medical complexity and rare diseases.

Hanae Davis is a sibling partner who has a younger brother with cerebral palsy. She completed her PhD in experimental psychology and worked as a postdoctoral fellow at CanChild Centre for Childhood Disability Research at McMaster University. She currently works in program management at the University Health Network in Toronto, Ontario.

Anneliese de Groot is from a large family in rural Tasmania. Practicing in Allied Health settings as a Remedial Massage Therapist, she focused on family-based and perinatal support. A Master of Public Health, majoring in health promotion, Anneliese has conducted qualitative research with Menzies School of Health Research and University of Queensland. Anneliese is a PhD candidate with the Australian Institute of Health Innovation, exploring experiences of rural families caring for children with medical complexity.

Sharon Desormeau is a registered social worker in rural Ontario. During her undergraduate social work degree, she worked as a research assistant on the research project "The View from Here: Impact of COVID-19 on the Everyday Life and Care of Adults with Intellectual and Developmental Disabilities Living in Rural Ontario."

Sarah Ederer is a Bachelor of Social Work student at Nipissing University. Sarah is interested in inclusive research with persons with intellectual disabilities and issues central to rural living.

Jeffrey Fletcher is an experienced paediatric physician consultant in paediatric nephrology, general, and behavioural needs. Jeff has worked in public and private healthcare for twenty years in rural, remote, regional, and tertiary hospitals. Jeff's passion is to ensure all kids receive care as close to home as possible with care coordinated to support kids and families accessing medical care, education, and additional support to strive and reach their goals socially, academically, and personally.

Gretchen Good, PhD, is a proud mum to two children with Down syndrome. She is an American living in New Zealand, an academic, a disability advocate, and an activist. She identifies as disabled. Her research, teaching, and service work focus on disability across the lifespan, disaster and disability, adoption, and disability and mothering.

Amy Hickman is a senior lecturer in public health at Flinders University College of Medicine and Public Health. She is the course coordinator for the Master of Public Health Program, leads the Work Integrated Learning Program in public health, and teaches health promotion. Amy's research centres around qualitative and community-based methodologies specializing in participatory action research. As a teaching specialist, Amy has developed a research program in reflexivity in learning and teaching.

Karen Hutchinson is a clinician-researcher with the Centre for Healthcare Resilience and Implementation Science at the Australian Institute of Health Innovation, Macquarie University, and an honorary conjoint scholar with the Central Coast Local Health District. Her clinical and research interests focus on implementation science and practice, and the codesign and evaluation of integrated models of care specific to individuals and families living with chronic and complex conditions.

Ngoc Huynh is a nurse educator who is privileged to work and raise her family on the unceded, ancestral, and traditional territory of the Lheidli T'enneh. Her academic work focuses on sociocultural, sociopolitical, and socioeconomic influences around equity, accessibility, social justice, and power and oppression. She is committed to reflecting on and questioning the socially constructed narratives of under-represented communities and individuals.

Anne Borden King is a Toronto-based podcaster, print journalist, and human rights advocate. Her writing has appeared in *The New York Times, Healthy Debate, FactKeepers,* and the *Thinking Person's Guide to Autism*, among other publications. She is the host of *Noncompliant*, a popular podcast about neurodiversity. A cofounder of Autistics for Autistics, the Canadian autistic self-advocacy organization, she has presented before the Canadian Senate and is director of the Autistic Health Access Project.

Eva Feder Kittay is Distinguished Professor of Philosophy Emerita at Stony Brook University. Her work has profoundly influenced feminist philosophy, ethics of care, and disability studies. Kittay's scholarship centres on the moral and political significance of human dependency and caregiving, challenging traditional notions of autonomy and justice. Her most recent book is *Learning from My Daughter: The Value and Care of Disabled Minds.* She is the mother of an adult son, a daughter with multiple disabilities and medical complexities, and a grandmother. She has authored and edited numerous books and articles on the ethics of care, mothering, disability, and the philosophy of language.

Yvette C. Latunde, Yvette C. Latunde, EdD, former director of a Center for Educational Equity and Intercultural Research (CEEIR) and professor at the University of San Diego, boasts over two decades of educational expertise. An advocate for students worldwide, she emphasizes leveraging strengths within communities. Dr. Latunde cofounded African American Advisory Councils in California and authored influential works like "Equitable by Design" and "Research in Parental Involvement." Her research focusses on Black family engagement and Black women thriving. Through her framework for hospitality, she promotes safe spaces and trust in organizations, affecting education at all levels.

Raghu Lingam is a senior clinical academic with expertise in maternal and child health services research. He is a professor in paediatric population and health services research at the University of New South

Wales, an honourary professor of population child health at King's College London, and the Black Dog Institute (NSW), and a consultant paediatrician within the Sydney Children's Hospital Network. He leads the Population Child Health and Health Services Research Group, UNSW Sydney.

Linda Nguyen is an Azrieli Accelerator assistant professor in youth, sibling, and community-engaged research, Faculty of Social Work, University of Calgary, Canada, and established a Sibling Youth Advisory Council (SibYAC) in 2018 as a part of her doctoral studies. Her doctoral studies focussed on understanding the experiences of siblings who are youth and young adults and have a sibling with a disability, as well as synthesizing resources to support siblings. In her current work, she continues to partner with SibYAC to cocreate resources to support siblings.

Kinga Pozniak is a sociocultural anthropologist and is currently a postdoctoral researcher at CanChild Centre for Childhood Disability Research at McMaster University, Canada. Her research focusses on the experiences of disabled children and their families. She is also a mother of two boys, one of whom lives with a disability.

Anna Przednowek is an assistant professor at the School of Social Work at Nipissing University. Before entering academia, Anna was a frontline clinician supporting children, youth, and adults with intellectual and developmental disabilities and their families in rural and urban Ontario.

Ana Carolina Rodriguez is a lecturer at the College of Education and Human Development, University of Minnesota. Her research interests revolve around the relationship between paid work and other aspects of our lives, such as caregiving and self-care. In particular, she focusses on diversity, inclusion, and belonging, as well as the adoption of ethics of care as a moral framework for human resource development. She worked for over twenty years as a practitioner in organizations.

Mary Sword is currently a PhD student at York University in critical disability studies. Her research interests focus on disability theatre with a particular interest in the portrayal of high-needs and multiple disabilities on the theatrical stage. She graduated in 2020 with a Master of Arts in theatre and performance studies from York University and received her Bachelor of Arts (Honours) in English literature from Carleton University in 2019.

Joanna Szabo, RN, PhD, is an associate professor at Mount Royal University with a professional background in critical care and paediatric nursing. Arts-based qualitative methods have been her predominant approach to inquiry throughout her graduate education and academic work.

Joy Seguin is a mother of an adult son with a profound developmental disability and autism. Joy's life, as she knew IT, led her into a journey of new métiers, advocacy, trials, and tribulations. Joy published a book titled *Is Advocating a Crime? Trust Everyone Trust No One*. Her book is based on real-life experiences navigating obstacles within a failed social healthcare system designed to deflate and defeat caregivers. Joy has joined the expected yet unexpected new "sandwich generation." Her advocacy struggling with providing her disabled son with a quality of life would be beneficial in caring and speaking up for numerous senior family members.

Donna Thomson is the mother of two grown children, one who has cerebral palsy. She is the coauthor of *The Unexpected Journey of Caring* (Rowman & Littlefield, 2019) and the author of *The Four Walls of My Freedom* (The House of Anansi Press, 2014). Donna is a codesigner and codirector of the CanChild Family Engagement in Research Program, and she facilitates the Caregiving Essentials Course, both at McMaster University. When not writing or teaching, Donna partners on research projects that relate to complex care parenting and social support networks.

Yvonne Zurynski is a professor of health system sustainability at the Australian Institute of Health Innovation, Macquarie University. Her research focusses on rare diseases, health services, health systems, new models of integrated care, learning health systems, and the health workforce. As a mixed methods researcher, implementation scientist, and policy analyst, she collaborates with consumers, clinicians, and policymakers to create transdisciplinary and translational research to improve healthcare for children and families.

Deepest appreciation to
Demeter's monthly Donors

Daughters
Khin May Kyawt
Debbie Byrd
Tanya Cassidy
Myrel Chernick
Marcella Gemelli
Donna Lee, In Memory of Dee Stark, RN, LNHA,
Trailblazer for Women, Women's Rights Advocate
Catherine Cheleen-Mosqueda

Sisters
Fiona Green
Paul Chu
Amber Kinser
Nicole Willey

Mother
Mildred Bennett Walker (Trainor)

Grandmother
Tina Powell